CULTIVATION
ANALYSIS

SOME OTHER VOLUMES IN THE
SAGE FOCUS EDITIONS

CULTIVATION ANALYSIS

New Directions in Media Effects Research

Edited by
Nancy Signorielli
and Michael Morgan

SAGE PUBLICATIONS
The Publishers of Professional Social Science
Newbury Park   London   New Delhi

For information address:

SAGE Publications, Inc.
2111 West Hillcrest Drive
Newbury Park, California 91320

SAGE Publications Ltd.
28 Banner Street
London EC1Y 8QE
England

SAGE Publications India Pvt. Ltd.
M-32 Market
Greater Kailash I
New Delhi 110 048 India

Printed in the United States of America

Library of Congress Cataloging-in-Publication Data

Main entry under title:

Cultivation analysis : new directions in media effects research /
    edited by Nancy Signorielli, Michael Morgan.
        p.   cm. — (Sage focus editions ; 108)
    Includes bibliographical references.
        Contents: Cultivation analysis : conceptualization and methodology
/ by Michael Morgan and Nancy Signorielli — Divergent psychological
processes in constructing social reality from mass media content /
by Robert P. Hawkins and Suzanne Pingree — Cultivation and
involvement with local television news / by Elizabeth M. Perse —
Patterns of viewing and VCR use / by Julia R. Dobrow — Television's
mean and dangerous world / by Nancy Signorielli — Pornography and
the construction of gender / by Elizabeth Hall Preston —
Television, religion, and religious television / by Stewart M.
Hoover — Mennonites and television / by Diane Zimmerman Umble —
The role of cultural diversity in cultivation research / by Ron
Tamborini and Jeonghwa Choi — Cultivated viewers and readers / by
Bo Reimer and Karl Erik Rosengren — Does television cultivate the
British? / by J. Mallory Wober — International cultivation analysis
/ by Michael Morgan.
        ISBN 0-8039-3295-2. — ISBN 0-8039-3296-0 (pbk.)
        1. Mass media — Audiences.   2. Mass media — Psychological aspects.
    3. Reality.   I. Signorielli, Nancy.   II. Morgan, Michael.
    P96.A83C85   1989
        302.23 — dc20   89-37645
                                                                                            CIP

FIRST PRINTING, 1990

Contents

To
Amelia, David, Fanny, Kevin, Laura Jane, and Robert,
For what they cultivate in us

Acknowledgments

Our work on this book reflects many years of collaboration and friendship with George Gerbner and Larry Gross. Without their ideas, insights, and inspirations, there would be no cultivation analysis upon which to advance. We gratefully extend to them our deepest appreciation, and look forward to the next 20 years.

We also collectively thank all our colleagues and students who have challenged, sharpened, and developed our thinking about cultivation analysis. We also would like to thank Ann West at Sage Publications and Myrna Hofmann at the University of Delaware for all their assistance. Finally, we thank all of the contributors to this volume, who (mostly) met our deadlines and did not complain (at least to us) when we asked for revisions.

Preface

The Cultural Indicators research project, devised and developed by George Gerbner, has now been in progress for over 20 years. The project represents a historically driven, theoretically guided, and empirically supported attempt to understand the consequences of living in a mass-produced symbolic and cultural environment dominated by television. Cultural Indicators research asks three interrelated questions:

1. What are the processes, pressures, and constraints that influence and underlie the production of mass media content?
2. What are the dominant, aggregate patterns of images, messages, facts, values, and lessons expressed in media messages?
3. What is the independent contribution of these messages to audiences' conceptions of social reality?

This book focuses on some recent developments in the third part of this research, called cultivation analysis. In its simplest form, cultivation analysis attempts to determine the extent to which people who watch greater amounts of television (generally referred to as *heavy viewers*) hold different conceptions of social reality from those who watch less, other factors held constant. The basic hypothesis is that

9

heavy viewers will be more likely to perceive the real world in ways that reflect the most stable and recurrent patterns of portrayals in the television world.

Yet, what might appear to be a relatively simple, straightforward, and unassuming hypothesis has turned out to be anything but. Cultivation analysis has not been a static research approach, and has evolved and developed in numerous ways, making it more complex and intricate but also more dynamic and intriguing. A number of theoretical, methodological, and epistemological critiques have produced lively (and sometimes bitter) debates that have in turn led to refinements and enhancements in the theory and the methodology of cultivation analysis.

In recent years, more independent researchers have undertaken cultivation research. Some have examined intervening variables and processes (such as perceived reality, active vs. passive viewing, the psychological mechanisms underlying cultivation, cultivation and interpersonal influences, and so on); some have explored new substantive areas, technologies, and subgroups, and others have attempted to apply cultivation analysis outside the United States. At the present time a worldwide team of investigators has come together to conduct global-level, cross-cultural studies using the Cultural Indicators paradigm in more than 25 countries in North, South, and Central America, Africa, the Middle East, eastern and western Europe, the Soviet Union, and Asia.

As a broad-based research agenda with a challenging set of theoretical and methodological procedures, cultivation analysis stands out as one of the dominant contemporary approaches to studying the impacts and functions of mass communication. This book brings together some of the most recent developments in the conceptual, methodological, and substantive aspects of cultivation analysis, and includes chapters by the original investigators and by independent researchers who have taken up the questions and challenges the approach raises. The research presented here examines cultivation in the United States as well as in other countries, for adults, children, and adolescents, and in relation to some specific ethnic subgroups. The chapters cover a wide variety of topics with contributions by some of those who originally developed cultivation analysis, by those who have worked with or have been associated with the original research team, and by those who have independently explored cultivation.

Organization of the Book

Cultivation Analysis begins with an introductory chapter in which we explain the conceptualization, theoretical framework, and methodology of cultivation analysis. This chapter describes some of the methodological and conceptual critiques — often revolving around issues of definition and questions of spuriousness and controls — that have been the focus of a number of colloquies. It also lays out some of the current issues and questions relating to cultivation. In short, this chapter sets the stage for the subsequent chapters by describing how the theory of cultivation is an attempt to understand and explain the dynamics of television as a distinctive feature of our age.

Chapter 2 discusses how cultivation occurs. Robert Hawkins and Suzanne Pingree delve into the complex and challenging questions relating to uncovering the psychological processes and cognitive mechanisms that best explain the ways in which heavy viewers incorporate television content into their conceptions of social reality. This line of work and questioning is further explored in Chapter 3, where Elizabeth Perse examines how viewers' involvement with a specific television genre (local news) may be related to cultivation. Chapter 4 moves away from the processes that may be involved in cultivation to examine changes in the delivery of mass mediated messages may affect cultivation theory. In this chapter, Julia Dobrow examines the implications of a new technology — the videocassette recorder (VCR) — which changes the way people watch television, for cultivation theory.

Chapters 5 through 8 update and extend the more traditional and empirical uses of cultivation theory and analysis to explore the enduring and common consequences of growing up and living with television. In Chapter 5, Nancy Signorielli presents the most current data and analyses relating to the area of investigation most often associated with cultivation analysis: fear and the mean world syndrome. In Chapter 6, Elizabeth Preston explores how the shift from a basic stimulus-response model to the cultivation model permits new insights into the broad role pornography may play in the maintenance of social structures built on sex-based inequalities. In Chapter 7, Stewart Hoover uses cultivation theory and analysis to explore relationships among religion, religious values, religiosity, and the viewing of religious and conventional programming. This portion of the book ends with Diane Umble's application of cultivation analysis to study a distinct religious subculture, the Mennonites (Chapter 8).

The next several chapters focus on the application of cultivation theory and analysis in international and intercultural contexts. In Chapter 9, Ron Tamborini and Jeonghwa Choi examine the role of cultural diversity in cultivation research using findings from a number of studies conducted on samples of foreign-born respondents in the United States and members of other cultures. Then, Bo Reimer and Karl Erik Rosengren (Chapter 10) examine cultivation from a Swedish perspective, applying a life-style framework to study cultivation and human values. In Chapter 11, Mallory Wober discusses a number of different studies that attempt to apply aspects of cultivation theory and analysis in Great Britain. In a similar vein, Michael Morgan (Chapter 12) explores cultivation analysis in the international setting, using findings from samples of respondents from Argentina, the People's Republic of China, and South Korea.

Finally, George Gerbner, the "founding father" of cultivation theory, presents an epilogue in which he reflects on some of the advances described in the book and develops what he sees as the most appropriate agenda for cultivation analysts to pursue.

Overall, this collection provides a broad glimpse into the ways cultivation analysis has evolved on both micro and macro levels. We hope the book advances the important role that the theory, methods, and findings of cultivation analysis have played and will continue to play in communication research.

1

Cultivation Analysis:

Conceptualization and Methodology

MICHAEL MORGAN
and
NANCY SIGNORIELLI

We are a mass mediated society. The mass media, especially television, play important, if often invisible and taken-for-granted, roles in our daily lives. Television sets are usually placed in prominent positions in our homes, whether in the family room, the living room, the kitchen, the bedroom, or all of the above. Few can remember, or care to remember, what life was like before television.

Each day, in the average American household, a television set is turned on for over 7 hours. Individual family members watch it for about 3 hours. Children and older people watch the most; adolescents watch the least, but even they view an average of 20 or more hours each week. Although most Americans report that they read a daily newspaper, television is often cited as their major source of news and information.

Television has become our nation's (and increasingly the world's) most common and constant learning environment. It both (selectively) mirrors and leads society. Television is first and foremost, however, a storyteller — it tells most of the stories to most of the people most of the time. As such, television is the wholesale distributor of images and forms the mainstream of our popular culture. Our children are born into homes in which, for the first time in human history, a centralized commercial institution rather than parents, the church, or the school tells most of the stories. The world of television shows and tells us about life: people, places, striving, power, and fate. It presents both the good and bad, the happy and sad, the powerful and the weak, and lets us know who or what is successful or a failure.

As with the functions of culture in general, the substance of the consciousness cultivated by television is not so much composed of specific attitudes and opinions as it is by broad, underlying, global assumptions about the "facts" of life. Television is only one of the many things that serve to explain the world; yet television is special because its socially constructed version of reality bombards all classes, groups, and ages with the same perspectives at the same time. The views of the world embedded in television drama do not differ appreciably from images presented in other media, and its rules of the social hierarchy are not easily distinguishable from those imparted by other powerful agents of socialization. What makes television unique, however, is its ability to standardize, streamline, amplify, and share common cultural norms with virtually all members of society.

Although television has a great deal in common with other media, it is different in some important ways. For one thing, people spend far more time with television than with other media; more time is spent watching television than doing anything else besides working and sleeping. Most people under 35 have been watching television since before they could read or probably even speak. Unlike print media, television does not require literacy; unlike theatrical movies, television runs almost continuously, and can be watched without leaving one's home; unlike radio, television can show as well as tell. Each of these characteristics is significant; their combined force is unprecedented and overwhelming.

Almost since the first television show was broadcast people have been concerned about the effects of this phenomenal medium. The popular press and the government ask, What does television do to us? Parents and teachers wonder whether television makes children more aggressive or if television helps or hinders learning. Students in both high school and college want to study the effects of the mass media but want simple, straightforward answers to questions. Yet, as numerous communication scholars have found, the questions are complex and the answers are neither simple nor straightforward.

Cultivation Analysis

Cultivation analysis is one approach to these broad questions. It represents a particular set of theoretical and methodological assumptions and procedures designed to assess the contributions of television viewing to people's conceptions of social reality. Cultivation analysis is the third component of a research paradigm called Cultural Indicators that investigates (1) the institutional processes underlying the production of media content, (2) images in media content, and (3) relationships between exposure to television's messages and audience beliefs and behaviors. Cultivation analysis is what this book is all about.

Like so many projects in the history of communications research, Cultural Indicators was launched as an independently funded enterprise in an applied context (Gerbner, 1969). The research began during the late 1960s, a time of national turmoil after the assassinations of Martin Luther King and Bobby Kennedy when the National Commission on the Causes and Prevention of Violence was set up to examine violence in society, including violence on television (see Baker & Ball, 1969). The earliest research of what was eventually to become the Cultural Indicators Project attempted to ascertain the degree of violence on television; it documented the extent to which violence predominated most dramatic television programming, described the nature of this violence, and established a baseline for long-term monitoring of the world of television (see Gerbner, 1969).

Nationwide unrest continued as did concerns about television's impact on Americans. In 1969, even before the report of the National Commission on the Causes and Prevention of Violence was released, Congress appropriated one million dollars and set up the Surgeon General's Scientific Advisory Committee on Television and Social Behavior to continue this area of investigation. All together, 23 projects, including Cultural Indicators, were funded at this time. Again, Cultural Indicators research focused primarily on the content of prime-time and weekend-daytime network dramatic programming (see Gerbner, 1972).

The cultivation analysis phase of the Cultural Indicators research paradigm was fully implemented with the first national probability survey of adults during the early 1970s in research funded by the National Institute of Mental Health (see Gerbner & Gross, 1976). The research continued in the 1970s and 1980s with funding by the National Institute of Mental Health (NIMH), the American Medical Association, the Office of Telecommunications Policy, the Administration on Aging, the National Science Foundation, the Ad Hoc Committee on Religious Television Research, and other agencies.

Although these early efforts (and many published reports) focused primarily on the nature and functions of television violence, the Cultural Indicators project was broadly based from the outset. Even violence was studied as a demonstration of the distribution of power in the world of television, with serious implications for the confirmation and perpetuation of minority status in the real world (Gerbner et al., 1979; Morgan, 1983), and the project continued to take into account a wide range of topics, issues, and concerns. The Cultural Indicators research team has investigated the extent to which television viewing contributes to audience conceptions and actions in such realms as sex roles (Gerbner & Signorielli, 1979; Morgan, 1982; Signorielli, 1989), age-role stereotypes (Gerbner et al., 1980), health (Gerbner, Morgan, & Signorielli, 1982), science (Gerbner et al., 1981d), the family (Gerbner et al., 1980c), educational achievement and aspirations (Morgan & Gross, 1982), politics (Gerbner, Gross, Morgan, & Signorielli, 1982, 1984), religion (Gerbner et al., 1984), and many other issues (see Gerbner et al., 1986).

The methods and assumptions behind cultivation analysis are different from those traditionally employed in mass communication research. Research and debate on the impact of mass communication has often focused on individual messages, programs, episodes, series, or genres and their ability to produce immediate change in audience attitudes and behaviors. Cultivation analysis is concerned with the more general and pervasive consequences of cumulative exposure to cultural media. Its underlying theoretical framework could be applied to any dominant form of communication. Most cultivation analyses, however, have focused on television because of the medium's uniquely repetitive and pervasive message characteristics and its dominance among other media in the United States.

Cultivation analysis generally begins with identifying and assessing the most recurrent and stable patterns in television content, emphasizing the consistent images, portrayals, and values that cut across most program genres. In its simplest form, cultivation analysis tries to ascertain if those who spend more time watching television are more likely to perceive the real world in ways that reflect the most common and repetitive messages and lessons of the television world, compared with people who watch less television but are otherwise comparable in important demographic characteristics.

People who regularly watch a great deal of television differ from light viewers in many ways. Although all social groups include both heavy and light viewers (relative to the group as a whole), there are overall differences between heavy and light viewers according to sex, income, education, occupation, race, time use, social isolation/integration, and a host of other demographic and social variables. But there are also differences in terms of the extent to which television dominates their sources of consciousness. Cultivation theory assumes that light viewers tend to be exposed to more varied and diverse information sources (both mediated and interpersonal), while heavy viewers, by definition, tend to rely more on television.

The goal of cultivation analysis is to determine whether differences in the attitudes, beliefs, and actions of light and heavy viewers reflect differences in their viewing patterns and habits, independent of (or in interaction with) the social, cultural, and personal factors that differentiate light and heavy viewers. Thus, cultivation analysis attempts to document and analyze the independent contributions of television viewing to viewers' conceptions of social reality. The chapters in this book vividly demonstrate that we have come a long way toward this goal; at the same time, the more work that is done, the more complex the questions (and the answers) become.

Cultivation vs. Change or Effects

The vast bulk of scientific inquiry about television's social impact can be seen as directly descended from the theoretical models and the methodological procedures of marketing and attitude change research. Large amounts of time, energy, and money have been spent in attempts to determine how to change people's attitudes or behaviors. People believe "X"; how do you get them to believe "Y"? Or, people do "X"; how do you get them to do "Y"? The Xs and Ys have covered such diverse topics as authoritarianism vs. egalitarianism, one brand of toothpaste vs. another, or one political candidate vs. another.

Sometimes a message or campaign works (and sometimes it doesn't), but there is usually little question about what the effect should look like: an explicit change of one sort or another. The effects usually sought are those that occur immediately or soon after exposure to a single, specific message, often in a relatively artificial context of exposure and for subjects (such as college students in introductory communication classes) who are usually not particularly representative of the larger population.

This scenario of classic laboratory experiments in mass communication has, we believe, influenced a great deal of popular as well as scholarly thinking about media effects. It leads to thinking about communication (and television's messages) as foreign "objects" somehow inserted or injected into us, as discrete, scattered "bullets" that either hit or miss us. In contrast, cultivation analysis looks at those messages as an environment within which people live, define themselves and others, and develop and maintain their beliefs and assumptions about social reality.

Others have, of course, suggested that mass media may involve functions and processes other than overt change. Forty years ago, Lazarsfeld and Merton (1948/1974) argued that the primary impact of exposure to mass communication was not likely to be change, but maintenance of the status quo. Similar notions have been expressed since then by Glynn (1956) and Bogart (1956).

Similarly, "cultivation" does not imply any sort of simple, linear "stimulus-response" model of the relationships between media content and audiences. Rather, it implies long-term, cumulative consequences of exposure to an essentially repetitive and stable system of messages, not immediate short-term responses or individual interpretations of content. It is concerned with continuity, stabilization, and gradual shifts rather than outright change. A slight but pervasive shift in the cultivation of common perspectives may not change much in individual outlooks and behavior but may later change the meaning of those perspectives and actions profoundly.

Thus, the use of the term *cultivation* for television's contribution to conceptions of social reality is not simply a fancier word for "effects." Most of all, it does not imply a one-way, monolithic process. Cultivation also should not be confused with "mere" reinforcement (as if reaffirmation and stability in the face of intense pressures for change were a trivial feat); nor should it suggest that television viewing is simply symptomatic of other dispositions and outlook systems. Finally, it should not be assumed that no change is involved. The "independent contribution" of television viewing, means, quite specifically, that the generation (in some) and maintenance (in others) of some sets of outlooks or beliefs can be traced to steady, cumulative exposure to the world of television.

The cultivation process is not thought of as a unidirectional flow of influence from television to audiences, but rather part of a continual, dynamic, ongoing process of interaction among messages and contexts. This holds true even though (and in a sense especially because) the hallmark of the process is either stability or slow change. Habits and styles of media exposure tend to be stable over long periods of time (Himmelweit & Swift, 1976), and cultivation analysis seeks to illuminate the consequences of the presence of television in stable styles of life and environments. It is designed to understand gradual, long-term shifts and transformations in the way generations are socialized (not short-term, dramatic changes in individuals' beliefs or behaviors). As successive generations become enculturated into the mainstream of television's version of the world, the former traditional distinctions become blurred. Cultivation thus means the steady entrenchment of mainstream orientations in most cases and the systematic but almost imperceptible modification of previous orientations in others; in other words, affirmation for the believers and indoctrination for the deviants.

Procedures Used in Cultivation Analysis

Cultivation analysis begins with content (message system) analysis: identifying and assessing the most recurrent and stable patterns of television content (the consistent images, portrayals, and values that cut across most types of programs). There are many critical discrepancies between the world and the world as portrayed on television. The shape and contours of the television world rarely match objective reality, though they often do match dominant ideologies and values.

Findings from systematic analyses of television's content are then used to formulate questions about people's conceptions of social reality. Some of the questions are semiprojective, some use a forced-error format, and other simply measure beliefs, opinions, attitudes, or behaviors.

Using standard techniques of survey methodology, the questions are posed to samples (national probability, regional, convenience) of children, adolescents, or adults. Secondary analysis of large scale national surveys (for example, the National Opinion Research Center's General Social Surveys) have often been used when they include questions that relate to identifiable aspects of the television world as well as television viewing.

Television viewing is usually assessed by asking how much time the respondent watches television on an average day. Since amount of viewing is seen as in relative terms, the determination of what constitutes light, medium, and heavy viewing is made on a sample-by-sample basis, using as close to a three-way split of hours of self-reported daily television viewing as possible. What is important is that there are basic differences in viewing levels, not the actual or specific amount of viewing.

The questions posed to respondents do not mention television, and the respondents' awareness of the source of their information is seen as irrelevant. The resulting relationships, if any, between amount of viewing and the tendency to respond to these questions in the terms of the dominant and repetitive facts, values, and ideologies of the world of television (again, other factors held constant) illuminate television's contribution to viewers' conceptions of social reality.

The observable empirical evidence of cultivation is likely to be modest in terms of its absolute size. Even light viewers may be watching up to 7 hours of television a week; a trivial, and demographically eclectic, handful say they do not watch at all. But, if we argue that the messages are stable, that the medium is virtually ubiquitous, and that it is accumulated exposure that counts, then almost everyone should be affected, regardless of how much they watch. Even light viewers may watch a substantial amount of television per week and in any case live in the same cultural environment as heavy viewers; what they do not get through television can be acquired indirectly from others who do watch more. It is clear, then, that the cards are stacked against finding evidence of cultivation. Therefore, the discovery of a systematic pattern of even small but pervasive differences between light and heavy viewers may indicate far-reaching consequences.

Accordingly, we should not dismiss what appear to be small effects, because small effects may have profound consequences. For example, a slight but pervasive (e.g., generational) shift in the cultivation of common perspectives may alter the cultural climate and upset the balance of social and political decision making without necessarily changing observable behavior. A single percentage point difference in ratings is worth many millions of dollars in advertising revenue. It takes but a few degrees' shift in the average global temperature to have an ice age. A range of 3 percent to 15 percent margins (typical of most differences between light and heavy viewers) in a large and otherwise stable field often signals a landslide, a market takeover, or an epidemic, and it certainly tips the scale of any closely balanced choice or decision.

Variations in Cultivation

We have noted that cultivation is not a unidirectional flow of influence from television to audience, but part of a continual, dynamic, ongoing process of interaction between messages and contexts. In some cases, those who watch more television (the heavy viewers) are more likely — in all or most subgroups — to give the "television answers." But, in many cases the patterns are more complex. Television viewing usually relates in different ways to different groups' life situations and world views.

Cultivation is both dependent on and a manifestation of the extent to which television's imagery dominates viewers' sources of information. For example, personal interaction makes a difference. Parental co-viewing patterns and orientations toward television can either increase (Gross & Morgan, 1985) or decrease (Rothschild & Morgan, 1987) cultivation among adolescents; also, children who are more integrated into cohesive peer or family groups are relatively immune to cultivation (Rothschild, 1984).

Direct experience also plays a role. The relationship between amount of viewing and fear of crime is strongest among those who live in high crime urban areas (a phenomenon called *resonance,* which in everyday reality and television provides a double dose of messages that "resonate" and amplify cultivation). Further, relationships between amount of viewing and the tendency to hold exaggerated perceptions of violence are more pronounced within those real-world demographic subgroups (minorities) whose fictional counterparts are more frequently victimized on television (Morgan, 1983).

Television viewing usually relates in different but consistent ways to different groups' life situations and world views. A major theoretical and analytical thrust of many recent cultivation analyses has been directed toward the determination of the conditional processes that enhance, diminish, or otherwise mediate cultivation. Many researchers are trying to figure out what types of people are most vulnerable to television's messages, in what specific substantive areas, and why. This type of research, well represented in this volume, investigates which subgroups are more or less susceptible to television on which issues, and has significantly enlarged our understanding of the more subtle and fundamental consequences of living with television.

There are a wide variety of factors and processes that produce systematic and theoretically meaningful variations in cultivation patterns. One process, however, stands out, both as an indicator of differential vulnerability and as a general, consistent pattern representing one of the most profound consequences of living with television: mainstreaming.

Mainstreaming

Our culture consists of many diverse currents, some weak, some strong. Some flow in the same general directions, some at crosscurrents. Yet there is a dominant set of cultural beliefs, values, and practices, in some ways at the core of all the other currents, and in some ways surrounding them. This dominant current is not simply the sum total of all the crosscurrents and subcurrents; rather, it is the most general and stable (though not static) mainstream, representing the broadest and most common dimensions of shared meanings and assumptions. It ultimately defines all the other crosscurrents and subcurrents. Because of television's unique role in our society, it is obvious that television can and should be seen as the primary manifestation of the mainstream of our culture.

Transcending historic barriers of literacy and mobility, television has become a primary, common source of everyday culture of an otherwise heterogeneous population. Television provides, perhaps for the first time since preindustrial religion, a strong cultural link between the elites and all other publics. It provides a shared daily ritual of highly compelling and informative content for millions of otherwise diverse people in all regions, ethnic groups, social classes, and walks of life. Television provides a relatively restricted set of choices for a virtually unrestricted variety of interests and publics; its programs eliminate boundaries of age, class, and region and are designed by commercial necessity to be watched by nearly everyone.

The mainstream can thus be thought of as a relative commonality of outlooks and values that heavy exposure to the features and dynamics of the television world tends to cultivate. *Mainstreaming* means that heavy viewing may absorb or override differences in perspectives and behavior that ordinarily stem from other factors and influences. In other words, differences found in the responses of different groups of viewers, differences that usually are associated with the varied cultural, social, and political characteristics of these groups, are diminished or even absent from the responses of heavy viewers in these same groups.

As a process, mainstreaming represents the theoretical elaboration and empirical verification of the assertion that television cultivates common perspectives. It represents a relative homogenization, an absorption of divergent views, and a convergence of disparate viewers. Former and traditional distinctions (which flourished, in part, through the diversity provided by print culture) become blurred as successive generations and groups become enculturated into television's version of the world. Through the process of mainstreaming, television has in essence become the true 20th century melting pot of the American people.

In summary, the theory of cultivation is an attempt to understand and explain the dynamics of television as a distinctive feature of our age. It is not a substitute for, but a complement to, traditional approaches to media effects research concerned with processes more applicable to other media. Designed primarily for television and focusing on its pervasive and recurrent patterns of representation and viewing, cultivation analysis concentrates on the enduring and common consequences of growing up with and living with television: the cultivation of stable, resistant, and widely shared assumptions, images, and conceptions reflecting the institutional characteristics and interests of the medium itself and the larger society. Television has become the common symbolic environment that interacts with most of the things we think and do. Therefore, understanding its dynamics can help develop and maintain a sense of alternatives and independence essential for self-direction and self-government in the television age.

The Battles

The methodology and findings of message-system analysis, particularly in the area of violence, were the focus of a number of colloquies in the 1970s. Most of these stemmed from critiques by industry researchers and involved differences over definitions (What is violence? What is a violent act? How is violence unitized? etc.). They also addressed concerns over sample size, reliability, validity, and numerous related issues (see Blank, 1977a, 1977b; Coffin & Tuchman, 1972-73a,

1972-73b; Eleey et al., 1972-73a, 1972-73b; Gerbner et al., 1977b, 1977c).

Soon after the first cultivation results were published (Gerbner & Gross, 1976), cultivation analysis became the focal point of the Cultural Indicators project. Message system analysis continued to be conducted each year, but the industry's critiques abated. The lull in the Cultural Indicators (CI) storm was brief, however, and a period of intense debate over cultivation soon began.

One of the first critiques of cultivation (Newcomb, 1978) in part was based on some supposed differences between a quantitative and qualitative approach and again reflected differences in definitional perspectives (see also Gerbner & Gross, 1979). Around the same time, research conducted by the Independent Broadcasting Authority in the United Kingdom was reported as failing to replicate what was called the "paranoid effect of television" (Wober, 1978). This research, however, can be seen more as serving to point out the cultural and institutional differences between the United States and Great Britain than as disconfirmation of cultivation (Gerbner, Gross, Morgan, & Signorielli, 1979; see also Neville, 1980; Wober, 1979).

The early 1980s brought a new, massive, unprecedented round of attacks, responses, and rejoinders. The regular publication of cultivation findings in several annual Violence Profiles (Gerbner et al., 1977a; Gerbner et al., 1978; Gerbner, Gross, Signorielli, Morgan, & Jackson-Beeck, 1979) had set the stage for the onslaught that was to come. And come it did. Fierce, prolonged battles (occasionally acrimonious and vaguely ad hominem at times) consumed hundreds of pages of scholarly and research journals; their repercussions were vividly felt at academic conferences and the controversies even spilled over into such popular media as *Time* magazine. The conflicts grew harsher and louder, and the rivers ran red with dead data and mutilated statistical techniques.

Why all the fighting? It is not possible to review all the arguments and counterarguments here (but see Doob & Macdonald, 1979; Hughes, 1980; Gerbner et al., 1980a, 1980b; Hirsch, 1980b; Gerbner et al., 1981c; Hirsch, 1980a, 1981b; Gerbner et al., 1981b; Hirsch, 1981a; Gerbner et al., 1981a — preferably in that order — for a relatively complete account). Among many other charges and countercharges, it is safe to say that the major issues revolved around questions of spuriousness and controls.

All at around the same time, Hirsch, Hughes, the Cultural Indicators research team, and others were independently finding that many of the relationships reported earlier using the National Opinion Research Center's (NORC) General Social Surveys looked different under multiple controls. For the most part, cultivation analyses had been implementing controls by examining associations between amount of viewing and attitudes within subgroups, one at a time. That is, the results were presented for males, older people, those with less education, and so on, separately. On reanalysis of those same data, it was found that *multiple* controls (i.e., controlling for age, sex, education, etc., all at once), tended to reduce or completely eliminate those relationships.

Yet, we found that the absence of an overall relationship under multiple controls did *not* mean that there were not nonspurious and theoretically meaningful associations *within* specific subgroups (Gerbner et al., 1980b). This discovery had profound conceptual and analytical implications for cultivation theory, and ultimately led to important refinements and enhancements. The most central of these was the idea of mainstreaming, first noted in research relating to conceptions about sex roles (Signorielli, 1979); it has been found since in more and more substantive areas, including interpersonal mistrust (Mean World Syndrome), alienation/gloom (Anomie), political orientations, and many other issues.

In sum, these battles have been characterized as everything from "healthy scholarly exchanges" to "scathing exposees" to "vicious and unprofessional spats." They were challenging, unpleasant, and in some ways, fun. They attest to the importance of cultivation theory in the discipline and to the fact that cultivation analysis has not been a static research approach, but one that has evolved and developed in numerous ways, making it not only more complex and intricate but also more dynamic and intriguing. Arguments concerning cultivation analysis did produce significant new issues and questions, many of which are addressed in the chapters in this book.

Current Issues in Cultivation Analysis

As cultivation analysis has evolved it has continued to raise more and more questions about underlying processes and broader consequences. There is general (though not universal) acceptance of the conclusion that there *are* statistical relationships between how much people watch television and what they think and do; there is far less consensus on a host of related questions and problems. Space does not permit a full and comprehensive review of all of these questions and relevant research, but this section outlines some of the major issues that have evolved from cultivation analysis and which numerous independent investigators are pursuing.

How does cultivation occur? What are the psychological processes and cognitive mechanisms that best explain the ways in which heavy viewers incorporate television content into their conceptions of social reality? What principles of learning, if any, are relevant? These have turned out to be challenging and complex questions. While some conceptual and empirical answers are beginning to emerge (see D'Alessio, 1987; Hawkins & Pingree, 1980, 1982; Hawkins et al., 1987; Hawkins & Pingree, this volume; Pingree, 1983), much work in this area remains to be done.

What demographic subgroups are more likely to show evidence of cultivation? As previously noted, cultivation patterns are rarely uniform across all subgroups in a sample. Many differential conditional associations suggest mainstreaming, in which the heavy viewers of a subgroup that is relatively "out" of the mainstream tend to express views that match those of their counterparts (Gerbner, Gross, Morgan, & Signorielli, 1980b, 1982, 1984; Morgan, 1986; see also Perry, 1987, for an account of some possible statistical artifacts). Other patterns of results sometimes suggest "resonance," in which cultivation is enhanced among those for whom a certain issue has some special salience. More work needs to be done to determine if certain socio-demographic groups are consistently and systematically more likely to be vulnerable to television, and to explore why they are (Morgan, 1983).

How is cultivation mediated by interpersonal and family relations? Television viewing is often a family activity; family members may influence each others' interpretation of television content in direct and intentional as well as indirect and unintentional ways, and the nature of the family's interactions apart from the television viewing context can also relate to variations in vulnerability to cultivation (Gross & Morgan, 1985; Rothschild & Morgan, 1987). Again, differences in children's levels of peer integration also indicate differences in susceptibility to cultivation (Rothschild, 1984), and such factors as "sociability" may plan important roles (Geiger, 1987). Overall, further research is needed to understand how the dynamics of interpersonal interaction mediate cultivation.

What are the levels of cultivation? Explorations of cultivation have suggested that there are important differences between the cultivation of (1) conceptions of the "facts of life," such as estimates of how many people are involved in violence, how many people work in different occupations, and so on (sometimes referred to as *first-order cultivation*), and (2) the cultivation of more global extrapolations from those facts, such as degree of interpersonal mistrust, or some political orientations (a kind of *second-order cultivation*) (Gerbner et al., 1986; Hawkins, et al., 1987). Similarly, there are potential differences between societal-level beliefs and personal-level beliefs; for example, images of the amount of violence in society may or may not be related to perceived chances of personal victimization, or fear in one's own home or neighborhood (Geiger, 1987; Gerbner et al., 1981a; Tyler, 1984). Finally, there may be differences between the cultivation of various attitudes and their specific behavioral manifestations (Morgan, 1987). Conceptions of social reality have branched off in various directions, and future work should provide greater specificity of the level(s) at which such conceptions apply.

What is the role of personal experience in cultivation? It is a truism that media effects will be greater for issues about which we have less direct personal experience. But this need not be the case; it is indeed possible for one to assume that his or her own experience is atypical, and that the television version or the cultural stereotype is more accurate. In any case, the issue of personal experience is closely tied in with the issue of perceived reality of television content. Studies of these issues have produced some useful findings, but for the most part they have only focused on violence (Geiger, 1987; Potter, 1986; Elliott & Slater, 1980; Slater & Elliott, 1982; Weaver and Wakshlag, 1986). Research should be undertaken to explore the implications of both personal experience and perceived reality as they might relate to other substantive areas besides violence.

How do viewers' orientations toward television influence cultivation? By "orientations toward television," we mean such phenomena as "active" vs. "passive" viewing, "selective" viewing, uses, and gratifications, "involvement" with television, and conscious interpretations of television content as well as perceived reality. All these have been the focus of numerous studies of cultivation (Carveth & Alexander, 1985; Gunter & Furnham, 1984; Perse, 1986; Perse, this volume; Rouner, 1984; Rubin et al., 1988; Wakshlag et al., 1983). Some of these issues need more work in terms of conceptualization and operationalization, and too often they are used as independent variables along with amount of viewing; they are more likely to offer further understanding of cultivation when they are implemented as intervening variables in order to explore the within-group conditional associations they might produce.

What are the roles of specific programs and genres in cultivation? A frequent concern raised about cultivation analysis is the focus on overall amount of viewing without regard to exactly what programs people watch. Cultivation theory insists that the message elements that are likely to lead to cultivation (as opposed to other effects) are those that cut across most programs and are inescapable for heavy viewers, and therefore how much is far more important than what. Many researchers, however, believe that cultivation must be traced to exposure to specific types of programs. For example, some have explored the cultivation potential of soap operas (Buerkel-Rothfuss & Mayes, 1981; Carveth & Alexander, 1985; Perse, 1986), family programs (Buerkel-Rothfuss et al., 1982), or have partitioned cultivation relationships according to specific viewing patterns (Hawkins & Pingree, 1981; Potter, 1986). Yet, except when VCRs are used to time-shift, viewing is limited by what is on at a particular time. More specifically, in the case of network programming, situation comedies usually are seen in the early evening while action adventure programs are shown during the late evening (Signorielli, 1986). Certainly, there may be *some* heavy viewers who only watch news, or sitcoms, etc. But by and large, to the extent that common economic imperatives and production influences mean that most programming conveys complementary cultural values, and if *most* heavy viewers indeed see more of everything, then idiosyncratic viewing patterns are less relevant. Most of all, while specific programs and genres may certainly have effects, those effects are indications of cultivation *only* if they occur at the aggregate level. Researchers who wish to explore genre-specific relationships should not neglect to consider overall viewing as an important theoretical construct and as an empirical measure.

How and what do other media cultivate? Little cultivation work has explicitly compared the relative contributions of television and other media. In terms of political self-designation, a greater tendency to describe oneself as moderate was associated with greater viewing, but not with newspaper reading or radio listening (Gerbner, Gross, Morgan, & Signorielli, 1982); movies, music, and magazines (Preston, this volume) offer important avenues for future cultivation analysis. Extensive typologies of media exposure profiles would allow for more precise understanding of the degree of interaction among various media.

How will new technologies influence cultivation? Television is not the same institution it was when the Cultural Indicators project began, when commercial-network, over-the-air broadcasting essentially had the medium to itself. But more channels do not necessarily mean more diversity, especially given increasing concentration of ownership and the relatively small number of production companies. In fact, Morgan and Rothschild (1983) found greater cultivation among cable-viewing adolescents. The rapid proliferation of VCRs may have similar implications for cultivation (Dobrow, this volume).

Does cultivation occur in other countries? The extension of cultivation analysis to other countries and cultures represents a major development in the approach (Morgan, this volume). Just as cultivation patterns are not uniform across subgroups in the United States, they vary tremendously across different cultural contexts. As evidence from cross-cultural replications of cultivation continues to accumulate, it will be necessary to begin to analyze and explain what accounts for these differences. International cultivation analysis will also need to differentiate between the contributions of domestic and imported programming (Pingree & Hawkins, 1981).

These are just some of the conceptual issues that have been developing from cultivation analysis. In addition, there are many methodological issues that cultivation analyses must continue to explore. These include the appropriateness of the samples used (too many studies present data from undergraduate communication majors, which raises severe problems of external validity); problems of question order and sensitization of respondents (too often respondents are clued in to the fact that the survey they're filling out is about the effects of television); and the use of simultaneous multiple controls, both overall and within groups, coupled with persistent problems of neglected potential sources of spuriousness and curtailment of variance within groups (Carlson, 1985; Hawkins & Pingree, 1982). This list could be expanded considerably; the point is that these methodological concerns are as complex, critical, and challenging as are the more substantive issues previously described.

The Future of Cultivation Analysis

As the above list demonstrates, our knowledge of the cultivation process is by no means complete. A great deal of work is underway on exploring the conceptual and methodological implications of cultivation on numerous levels, from the micro to the macro. The development of cross-cultural studies (including an ongoing global-level international cooperative venture) will provide even more information about the generalizability of cultivation as a phenomenon.

New technologies, alternative delivery systems, new program genres, and changes in institutional structures may have varied consequences for cultivation theory in the future. Predicting the future is always dangerous, but we believe that the likely-to-continue decline in the dominance of network broadcasting will not reduce the relevance of cultivation analysis. All current (and historical) indications point to increasing concentration and interdependence in media industries, imitation of successful formats and styles, and greater competition for the broadest, most attractive, mainstream audiences. These are conditions that enhance, rather than fragment, the cultivation of standardized values and ideologies. The hymn is likely to be the same, even if the choir is larger.

There are many additional substantive areas to address. We have barely scratched the surface of the 20-year archives of message system analysis. While cultivation analysis has already clearly moved well beyond violence, the range of issues and dimensions that may be fruitful areas for cultivation analysis will continue to expand.

In sum, the chapters in this volume make it abundantly clear that whatever advances we are making, cultivation analysis will lead to more and more questions about the role of television in our lives. We expect cultivation research to continue to flourish and to provoke lively controversy about media effects and how to study them. While much work has been done, there is far more to do. The arguments, findings, and issues raised in this book are intended to contribute to the further development, elaboration, and refinement of the theory and method of cultivation analysis.

References

Baker, R. K., & Ball, S. J. (Eds.). (1969). *Violence in the media*. Staff report to the National Commission on the Causes and Prevention of Violence. Washington, DC: U.S. Government Printing Office.

Blank, D. M. (1977a). Final comments on the violence profile. *Journal of Broadcasting, 21*(3), 287-296.

Blank, D. M. (1977b). The Gerbner violence profile. *Journal of Broadcasting, 21*(3), 273-279.

Bogart, L. (1956). *The age of television: A study of viewing habits and the impact of television on American life*. New York: Ungar.

Buerkel-Rothfuss, N. L., Greenberg, B. S., Atkin, C. K., & Neuendorf, K. (1982). Learning about the family from television. *Journal of Communication, 32*(3), 191-201.

Buerkel-Rothfuss, N. L., & Mayes, S. (1981). Soap opera viewing: The cultivation effect. *Journal of Communication, 31*(3), 108-115.

Carlson, J. M. (1985). *Prime time law enforcement*. New York: Praeger.

Carveth, R., & Alexander, A. (1985). Soap opera viewing motivations and the cultivation process. *Journal of Broadcasting and Electronic Media, 29*, 259-273.

Coffin, T. E., & Tuchman, S. (1972-73a). A question of validity: Some comments on "Apples, oranges, and the kitchen sink." *Journal of Broadcasting, 17*(1), 31-33.

Coffin, T. E., & Tuchman, S. (1972-73b). Rating television programs for violence: A comparison of five surveys. *Journal of Broadcasting, 17*(1), 3-20.

D'Alessio, D. (1987, May). *A psychophysiological model of television viewing*. Paper presented to the International Communication Association, Montreal.

Doob, A. N., & Macdonald, G. E. (1979). Television viewing and fear of victimization: Is the relationship causal? *Journal of Personality and Social Psychology*, *37*(2), 170-179.

Eleey, M., Gerbner, G., & Signorielli (Tedesco), N. (1972-73a). Validity indeed! *Journal of Broadcasting*, *17*(1), 34-35.

Eleey, M., Gerbner, G., & Signorielli (Tedesco), N. (1972-73b). Apples, oranges, and the kitchen sink: An analysis and guide to the comparison of 'violence ratings.' *Journal of Broadcasting*, *17*(1), 21-31.

Elliott, W. R., & Slater, D. (1980). Exposure, experience, and perceived TV reality for adolescents. *Journalism Quarterly*, *57*(3), 409-414, 431.

Geiger, S. F. (1987, May). *Social reality and mass media effects: Source dependencies, issues relevance, and levels of signficance.* Paper presented to the International Communication Association, Montreal.

Gerbner, G. (1969). Dimensions of violence in television drama. In R. K. Baker & S. J. Ball (Eds.), *Violence in the media.* Staff report to the National Commission on the Causes and Prevention of Violence (pp. 311-340). Washington, DC: U.S. Government Printing Office.

Gerbner, G. (1972). Violence and television drama: Trends and symbolic functions. In G. A. Comstock & E. Rubinstein (Eds.), *Television and social behavior, Vol. 1, Content and control* (pp. 28-187). Washington, DC: U.S. Government Printing Office.

Gerbner, G., & Gross, L. (1976). Living with television: The violence profile. *Journal of Communication*, *26*(2), 173-199.

Gerbner, G., & Gross, L. (1979). Editorial response: A reply to Newcomb's "Humanistic critique." *Communication Research*, *6*(2), 223-230.

Gerbner, G., Gross, L., Eleey, M., Jackson-Beeck, M., Jeffries-Fox, S., & Signorielli, N. (1977a). TV violence profile no. 8: The highlights. *Journal of Communication*, *27*(2), 171-180.

Gerbner, G., Gross, L., Eleey, M., Jackson-Beeck, M., Jeffries-Fox, S., & Signorielli, N. (1977b). One more time: An analysis of the CBS 'Final comments on the violence profile.' *Journal of Broadcasting*, *21*(3), 297-303.

Gerbner, G., Gross, L., Eleey, M., Jackson-Beeck, M., Jeffries-Fox, S., & Signorielli, N. (1977c). The Gerbner violence profile—An analysis of the CBS report. *Journal of Broadcasting*, *21*(3), 280-286.

Gerbner, G., Gross, L., Hoover, S., Morgan, M., Signorielli, N., & Wuthnow, R. (1984). *Religion and television.* Philadelphia: The Annenberg School of Communications, University of Pennsylvania.

Gerbner, G., Gross, L., Jackson-Beeck, M., Jeffries-Fox, S., & Signorielli, N. (1978). Cultural indicators: Violence profile no. 9. *Journal of Communication*, *28*(3), 176-207.

Gerbner, G., Gross, L., Morgan, M., & Signorielli, N. (1979). On Wober's 'Televised violence and paranoid perception: The view from Great Britain.' *Public Opinion Quarterly*, *43*(1), 123-124.

Gerbner, G., Gross, L., Morgan, M., & Signorielli, N. (1980a). Some additional comments on cultivation analysis. *Public Opinion Quarterly*, *44*(3), 408-410.

Gerbner, G., Gross, L., Morgan, M., & Signorielli, N. (1980b). The 'mainstreaming' of America: Violence profile no. 11. *Journal of Communication*, *30*(3), 10-29.

Gerbner, G., Gross, L., Morgan, M., & Signorielli, N. (1980c, April). *Media and the family: Images and impact.* Paper for the National Research Forum on Family Issues, White House Conference on Families.

Gerbner, G., Gross, L., Morgan, M., & Signorielli, N. (1981a). Final reply to Hirsch. *Communication Research*, *8*(3), 259-280.

Gerbner, G., Gross, L., Morgan, M., & Signorielli, N. (1981b). A curious journey into the scary world of Paul Hirsch. *Communication Research, 8*(1), 39-72.

Gerbner, G., Gross, L., Morgan, M., & Signorielli, N. (1981c). On the limits of 'The limits of advocacy research': Response to Hirsch. *Public Opinion Quarterly, 45*(1), 116-118.

Gerbner, G., Gross, L., Morgan, M., & Signorielli, N. (1981d). Scientists on the TV screen. *Society*, May/June, 41-44.

Gerbner, G., Gross, L., Morgan, M., & Signorielli, N. (1982). Charting the mainstream: Television's contribution to political orientations. *Journal of Communication, 32*(2), 100-127.

Gerbner, G., Gross, L., Morgan, M., & Signorielli, N. (1984). Political correlates of television viewing. *Public Opinion Quarterly, 48*, 283-300.

Gerbner, G., Gross, L., Morgan, M., & Signorielli, N. (1986). Living with television: The dynamics of the cultivation process. In J. Bryant & D. Zillmann (Eds.), *Perspectives on media effects* (pp. 17-40). Hillsdale, NJ: Lawrence Erlbaum.

Gerbner, G., Morgan, M., & Signorielli, N. (1982). Programming health portrayals: What viewers see, say and do. In D. Pearl, L. Bouthilet, & J. Lazar (Eds.), *Television and behavior: Ten years of scientific progress and implications for the 80's, Volume II, Technical reviews* (pp. 291-307). Rockville, MD: National Institute of Mental Health.

Gerbner, G., Gross, L., Signorielli, N., & Morgan, M. (1980). Aging with television: Images on television drama and conceptions of social reality. *Journal of Communication, 30*(1), 37-47.

Gerbner, G., Gross, L., Signorielli, N., Morgan, M., & Jackson-Beeck, M. (1979). The demonstration of power: Violence profile no. 10. *Journal of Communication, 29*(3), 177-196.

Gerbner, G., & Signorielli, N. (1979, October). Women and minorities in television drama, 1969-1978. Philadelphia: The Annenberg School of Communications, University of Pennsylvania.

Glynn, E. D. (1956). Television and the American character: A psychiatrist looks at television. In W. Y. Elliot (Ed.), *Television's impact on American culture* (pp. 175-182). East Lansing: Michigan State University Press.

Gross, L., & Morgan, M. (1985). Television and enculturation. In J. Dominick & J. Fletcher (Eds.), *Broadcasting research methods* (pp. 221-234). Boston: Allyn & Bacon.

Gunter, B., & Furnham, A. (1984). Perceptions of television violence: Effects of programme genre and type of violence on viewers' judgements of violent portrayals. *British Journal of Social Psychology, 23*(2), 155-164.

Hawkins, R. P., & Pingree, S. (1980). Some processes in the cultivation effect. *Communication Research, 7*(2), 193-226.

Hawkins, R. P., & Pingree, S. (1981). Uniform content and habitual viewing: Unnecessary assumptions in social reality effects. *Human Communication Research, 7*, 219-301.

Hawkins, R. P., & Pingree, S. (1982). Television's influence on social reality. In D. Pearl, L. Bouthilet, & J. Lazar (Eds.), *Television and behavior: Ten years of scientific progress and implications for the 80's, Volume II, Technical reviews* (pp. 224-247). Rockville, MD: National Institute of Mental Health.

Hawkins, R. P., Pingree, S., & Adler, I. (1987). Searching for cognitive processes in the cultivation effect. *Human Communication Research, 13*(4), 553-577.

Himmelweit, H. T., & Swift, B. (1976). Continuities and discontinuities in media usage and taste: A longitudinal study. *Journal of Social Issues, 32*(4), 133-156.

Hirsch, P. M. (1980a). The 'scary world' of the nonviewer and other anomalies: A reanalysis of Gerbner et al.'s findings of cultivation analysis, part I. *Communication Research, 7*(4), 403-456.

Hirsch, P. M. (1980b). On Hughes' contribution: The limits of advocacy research. *Public Opinion Quarterly, 44*(3), 411-413.

Hirsch, P. M. (1981a). Distinguishing good speculation from bad theory: Rejoinder to Gerbner et al. *Communication Research, 8*(1), 73-95.

Hirsch, P. M. (1981b). On not learning from one's own mistakes: A reanalysis of Gerbner et al.'s findings on cultivation analysis, part II. *Communication Research, 8*(1), 3-37.

Hughes, M. (1980). The fruits of cultivation analysis: A re-examination of the effects of television watching on fear of victimization, alienation, and the approval of violence. *Public Opinion Quarterly, 44*(3), 287-302.

Lazarsfeld, P., & Merton, R. (1948, reprinted 1974). Mass communication, popular taste, and organized social action. In W. Schramm & D. F. Roberts (Eds.), *The process and effects of mass communication, 2nd ed.* (pp. 554-578). Urbana: University of Illinois Press.

Morgan, M. (1982). Television and adolescent's sex-role stereotypes: A longitudinal study. *Journal of Personality and Social Psychology, 43*(5), 947-955.

Morgan, M. (1983). Symbolic victimization and real world fear. *Human Communication Research, 9*, 146-157.

Morgan, M. (1986). Television and the erosion of regional diversity. *Journal of Broadcasting and Electronic Media, 30*(2), 123-139.

Morgan, M. (1987). Television, sex role attitudes, and sex role behavior. *Journal of Early Adolescence, 7*(3), 269-282.

Morgan, M., & Gross, L. (1982). Television and educational achievement and aspiration. In D. Pearl, L. Bouthilet, & J. Lazar (Eds.), *Television and behavior: Ten years of scientific progress and implications for the 80's*, Volume II, *Technical reviews* (pp. 78-90). Rockville, MD: National Institute of Mental Health.

Morgan, M., & Rothschild, N. (1983). Impact of the new television technology: Cable TV, peers, and sex-role cultivation in the electronic environment. *Youth and Society, 15*, 33-50.

Neville, T. J. (1980). More on Wober's "Televised violence..." *Public Opinion Quarterly, 44*(1), 116-117.

Newcomb, H. (1978). Assessing the violence profile of Gerbner and Gross: A humanistic critique and suggestion. *Communication Research, 5*(3), 264-282.

Perry, D. K. (1987, May). *Uniform media effects and uniform audience responses.* Paper presented to the International Communication Association, Montreal.

Perse, E. M. (1986). Soap opera viewing patterns of college students and cultivation. *Journal of Broadcasting and Electronic Media, 30*(2), 175-193.

Pingree, S. (1983). Children's cognitive processes in constructing social reality. *Journalism Quarterly, 60*(3), 415-422.

Pingree, S., & Hawkins, R. P. (1981). U.S. programs on Australian television: The cultivation effect. *Journal of Communication, 31*(1), 97-105.

Potter, W. J. (1986). Perceived reality and the cultivation hypothesis. *Journal of Broadcasting and Electronic Media, 30*(2), 159-174.

Rothschild, N. (1984). Small group affiliation as a mediating factor in the cultivation process. In G. Melischek, K. E. Rosengren, & J. Stappers (Eds.), *Cultural indicators: An international symposium* (pp. 377-387). Vienna: Verlag der Osterreichischen Akademie der Wissenschaften.

Rothschild, N., & Morgan, M. (1987). Cohesion and control: Adolescents' relationships with parents as mediators of television. *Journal of Early Adolescence, 7*(3), 299-314.

Rouner, D. (1984). Active television viewing and the cultivation hypothesis. *Journalism Quarterly, 61*(1), 168-174.

Rubin, A. M., Perse, E. M., & Taylor, D. S. (1988). A methodological investigation of cultivation. *Communication Research, 15*(2), 107-134.

Signorielli, N. (1979, April). *Television's contribution to sex role socialization.* Paper presented to the Seventh Annual Telecommunications Policy Research Conference, Skytop, PA.

Signorielli, N. (1986). Selective television viewing: A limited possibility. *Journal of Communication, 36*(3), 64-75.

Signorielli, N. (1989). Television and conceptions about sex-roles: Maintaining conventionality and the status quo. *Sex Roles, 21*(5/6), 337-356.

Slater, D., & Elliott, W. R. (1982). Television's influence on social reality. *Quarterly Journal of Speech, 68*(1), 69-79.

Tyler, T. R. (1984). Assessing the risk of crime victimization: The integration of personal victimization experience and socially transmitted information. *Journal of Social Issues, 40*(1), 27-38.

Wakshlag, J. J., Val, V., & Tamborini, R. (1983). Selecting crime drama and apprehension about crime. *Human Communication Research, 10*(2), 227-242.

Weaver, J., & Wakshlag, J. (1986). Perceived vulnerability to crime, criminal victimization experience, and television viewing. *Journal of Broadcasting and Electronic Media, 30*(2), 141-158.

Wober, J. M. (1978). Televised violence and paranoid perception: The view from Great Britain. *Public Opinion Quarterly, 42*(3), 315-321.

Wober, J. M. (1979). Televised violence and viewers' perceptions of reality: A reply to criticisms of some British research. *Public Opinion Quarterly, 43*(2), 271-273.

2

Divergent Psychological Processes in Constructing Social Reality from Mass Media Content

ROBERT P. HAWKINS
and
SUZANNE PINGREE

The cultivation hypothesis, the proposal that television's presentation of social reality influences the social reality beliefs of its viewers, has been characterized by two research orientations: (1) investigations into the simple existence or robustness of the effect, and (2) its integration with sociological theories in work examining group and social setting differences in the effect. We have argued at various times (Hawkins & Pingree, 1980, 1982; Hawkins, Pingree, & Adler, 1987; Pingree, 1983) for research into the psychological processes that may underlie cultivation effects. That is, how is it that watching television contributes to certain social reality beliefs and not others? What are the psychological processes that lead individuals to construct their own social reality in ways that mirror both the facts and the ostensible meaning of television's social reality?

We think that these questions are crucial to research on cultivation as well as to our understanding of social reality construction. Unless such questions can be successfully addressed, *cultivation* runs the risk of being dismissed as a label for a single correlate (television time) masquerading as a program of research, and as an ideological position more than as a focus for social scientific research. The problem is that without evidence for psychological processes, the cultivation hypothesis stands on a tenuous foundation.

Even though years of research have provided considerable evidence of a small but consistent relationship between television viewing and beliefs about the social world that are similar to or plausibly implied by the images in television programs (see Hawkins & Pingree, 1982, for a review), the research community still does not understand how this relationship occurs. And since most evidence of cultivation is based on cross-sectional survey research (although supported by an occasional experiment or panel survey), as long as these effects occur within a "black box," the whole enterprise remains vulnerable to questions of spuriousness. That is, even though attempts to ascribe the relationship between viewing and beliefs as the spurious result of third variables have generally ended with some irreducible effect remaining, the effect explanation logically (as in all survey research) remains in competition with unexamined third variables.

On the other hand, if a psychological mechanism or mechanisms through which television content viewed becomes social reality beliefs could be demonstrated, then the effect explanation for the cultivation correlations becomes more plausible. In other words, if we can demonstrate psychological processes through which people turn the television messages they watch into social reality beliefs, then the field can have much more confidence in what the correlational results tell us about differences among population subgroups and among different kinds of beliefs.

This situation can also usefully be viewed in terms of "internal" and "external" validity (Campbell & Stanley, 1963). We have considerable research addressing external validity, or generalizability, of a weak but persistent cultivation *relationship*, but very little evidence that provides these findings with internal validity, or the assurance that they do in fact represent television effects. That this is the reverse of the situation for many other debates over media effects (e.g., violence and aggression, pornography and violence against women) does not detract from the essential requirement that effects research attain *both* internal and external validity to be compelling.

Demonstrating a plausible psychological process for cultivation results has proved surprisingly difficult. Sociologically oriented cultivation research typically sums up the psychology involved as "learning": viewers learn the actions and characteristics of television, and heavy viewers, who see so many television examples, come to accept television images as representative of the real world. But this is a label, not an explanation. Just what is it that is learned? How is that learning stored in memory? What kind of processing translates learning into generalizations about social reality?

To begin with, the meaningful message units for television effects on social reality beliefs are not individual television actions, characters, or messages. The messages that lead to cultivation are aggregate *patterns* of action and characterization across many programs or even seasons of entertainment television. For example, the frequency that violence is shown or the proportion of males portrayed as employed in law enforcement is what constitutes the message. Thus, individual actions in television content (and learning these actions) may be quite insignificant. Individual actions may or may not be learned on the way to constructing social reality beliefs (this is a process question in itself), but because the relevant television content that forms the message is aggregate patterns, any processes posited need to address the way in which individuals track and use these patterns.

Furthermore, because the relevant messages are aggregates of television presented over time, the processes involved must be long-term themselves. If the relationship between viewing and beliefs does represent an effect, the time involved must be weeks at the least and more likely months and years. We do not mean simply that learned individual stimuli must be remembered over time, although such memory may in fact be necessary. Rather, any psychological process explanations offered must address questions about *when* encoding and abstraction processes occur.

The kinds of questions this poses for cultivation process research — how messages are encoded, what exactly is stored, and how individuals abstract or form decisions from remembered material — sound very much like those typical of cognitive psychology, which has well-developed research paradigms for addressing such questions (see Markus & Zajonc, 1985). However, these research paradigms are set up for use with very small messages and immediate tasks. Thus, while we can see what people remember from *a* message that seems relevant to the cultivation hypothesis, single messages do not influence social reality beliefs at all. The more difficult problem is linking particular encodings and memory of details to the long-term outcome of beliefs.

Thus, the label *learning* must be broken into a number of separate questions, each of which deserves an answer. Do we acquire and remember a store of fragments that together might provide a symbolic message? If so, what kind of averaging or abstraction process is applied to this store in order to draw the conclusions of social reality beliefs? On the other hand, perhaps the fragments are encoded for their relevance to various social reality beliefs when originally viewed, and it is this coding that is tallied when a social reality belief is formed. Perhaps learning is the wrong paradigm altogether: the relevant mechanisms may be more akin to reinforcement than learning. That is, observing individual characters and behaviors on television may instantiate prototypes already known, and the social reality beliefs may reflect the frequency of instantiation of the various prototypes. In all this, however, one must ask whether the social reality beliefs exist on their own, or appear only in response to a researcher's questions.

Current Process Research

A number of studies have begun to address questions of psychological processes in constructing social reality based on television content. In reviewing them, we will divide them into three groups (long inference, short inference, and intermediate products), according to the type of evidence they bring to bear on the problem. Unfortunately, we have less and less evidence as we move from weaker to stronger methods.

Long Inferences

Most evidence of psychological processes is inferred from conditional or subgroup effects of variables that have nothing to do with the processes inferred. For example, education, social class, and race often locate cultivation relationships more strongly or even entirely within one subgroup (Gerbner et al., 1980; Signorielli, this volume). The resulting findings are usually labeled *mainstreaming*, a situation in which light television viewers from two or more subgroups (e.g., high school vs. college educated) hold different social reality beliefs while the heavy viewers in the subgroups hold more similar beliefs. For example, members of one group, such as the less educated, hold a pessimistic Mean World view regardless of amount of viewing, while the beliefs of the college-educated group are correlated with television viewing: light viewers are much less pessimistic, while heavy viewers hold views similar to those of those with only high school educations. ("Resonance" is a less common result in which a group whose real world situation is more similar to television's portrayals shows a stronger relationship between viewing and beliefs than do other groups.

On a societal level, mainstreaming describes a process whereby television viewing acts to homogenize groups who would otherwise be disparate, by bringing the heavy viewers of the divergent group back to the mainstream of the rest of society. Psychologically, however, it is implicit that shared experiences are central in determining social reality beliefs. The less educated have a bleaker pool of experiences regardless of their television viewing (and it would seem that television content matches their own experience so well as to have no effect); the experience pool of the well educated is different and more positive unless they watch large amounts of entertainment television and thus share in the same experiences as the less educated.

This explanation is certainly plausible, but it requires a great deal of assumption and inference beyond the evidence at hand. The real-world experiences of the two groups are *assumed* to be different, and the television world is implicitly *assumed* to match the real-world experience of the less educated. Beyond that, there is a *presumption* that social reality beliefs are somehow constructed based on one's total experience pool, with little or no attention to the television vs. real-world source of the experiences. Thus, while conditional effects based on demographic variables may appear striking, they actually provide reason for speculation, not explanations, about psychological processes.

Similarly, there is considerable theorizing, and some evidence, bearing on the role of personal experience in cultivation (Adoni & Mane, 1984; Tyler & Cook, 1984; Weaver & Wakshlag, 1986). These are not strictly speaking conditional relationships, since the differences are between dependent variables rather than subgroups. That is, it seems that the effect occurs for beliefs about society in general but not about personal concerns. This research is more explicit in its posited psychological process: television content will have more influence where it does not compete with an individual's own experience. Presumably, there is some labeling of the source of one's experiences or else an evaluation of the truth or reality of television as a source of experience. Nonetheless, there is no direct evidence of process available, leaving us once again with "long inference."

Shorter Inference: Cognitive Traits

There are several research tracks that attempt to shorten the chain of inference by reference to cognitive trait variables. That is, if cultivation occurs in the presence of some enduring cognitive trait or habit, then that trait may locate an important process. The link between the cognitive trait and the actual operation of the process is presumably much closer and less problematic than those in the previous section, thus the label *shorter inference*. The remaining problem is differing time frames: does the enduring trait produce the necessary, probably short-term or momentary, cognitive processes?

For example, Hawkins et al. (1987) found that subgroups based on school achievement scores or current events knowledge differed in the size of various cultivation relationships, especially for second-order social reality belief measures (those that lack a direct, quantifiable referent in television content, and thus are linked to content only in that it implies them[1]). To interpret those results, we argued that school achievement and knowledge of current events were surrogates tapping some portion of either cognitive activity, cognitive effort, or both. The point here is that while this still requires an inference between measurement and process, the inferential chain is considerably shorter than with demographic subgroups or differences in dependent variables. These studies cannot claim to measure the action of their posited cognitive processes, but what they do measure is at least itself plausibly a result of the posited process as well.

Several other studies attempt to measure a cognitive process directly as a trait variable, but in fact are similar in their logical relation to processes. For example, Potter (1986) assessed adolescents' and adults' beliefs about the reality of television on several dimensions (their perceived reality). Correlations between amount of viewing and social reality beliefs occurred for those who believed television to be an accurate representation of actual life, and not for those skeptical of television. Potter's argument is that people who believe entertainment television to be realistic accept its messages as more applicable to their social reality judgments. (See also Perse, this volume, on involvement.)

While the measurement of perceived reality as a cognitive trait was far removed from the time any effects occurred, the assumption is that this cognitive characteristic is traitlike: cognitive orientations are stable over time so that those who say they perceive television to be real will also see it as real when watching or when constructing social reality beliefs. Still, perceived reality, while relatively close, is not itself the process it implicates as constructing social reality. As with grade point average or achievement test scores, perceived reality is argued to be a surrogate for skeptical or accepting evaluations of television content, or more or less active, rational processing of television. It is the hypothesized evaluation or activity that determines the degree to which television influence occurs.

Intermediate Products

Lest the idea of assessing processes more directly seems unrealistically demanding, we should say that while such research faces formidable challenges both theoretically and methodologically, it is still possible. So far, we are aware of only one real attempt to measure process, and it did so by trying to tap an intermediate product of viewing (and other sources of information) and tying it to social reality beliefs.

Shapiro (1987, 1988) pursued the implications for social reality beliefs of memory models that assume independent memory traces of each event observed (that is, traces of individual events are individually stored in memory). These models are responding to evidence that people are relatively good at judging the frequency of events, and seem to also encode the context or source of such traces, because instructions to base these estimations only on certain sources produce accurate changes in the frequency estimations (Hintzman, 1986; Hintzman & Block, 1971). Social reality construction based on television might be based on two steps: (1) learning incidental content from viewing, and (2) constructing beliefs from that store of memories (Hawkins & Pingree, 1981, 1982). Shapiro reasoned that if cultivation occurs by abstraction from a memory store, it should be possible to assess the relevant stored memories and their individual sources directly, and find them more closely associated with social reality beliefs than is any measure of television viewing.

That is, he argued that what people have seen (the implicit construct behind any amount-of-viewing measure) is less important than the relevant events and people remembered, from whatever source. If frequency registration and prototype abstraction are the central processes in the construction of social reality beliefs, it is the nature of the contents of one's memory, perhaps qualified by the source encoding of traces that allows reality monitoring discriminations, that should determine what social reality beliefs are actually constructed and held.

Thus, Shapiro (1987, 1988) asked college students to provide "memory dumps": listing all examples they could think of in a category, such as "victims of crime" or "law enforcement personnel." After a fixed period for the memory dump ended, respondents went back and marked one of eight communication sources (a mix of direct, interpersonal, and mediated) for each exemplar. The number of exemplars remembered from each of the eight different sources, taken as a block of variables in a multiple regression, accounted for much more variance in two social reality indices (dealing with the prevalence of crime and the proportion of the population accounted for by various subgroups) than did television viewing or any or all of a group of media-use variables. That is, the number of relevant exemplars recalled from various sources (arguably an indicator of the number of exemplars in memory) was a much better predictor of beliefs than were media-use variables, although media use was generally correlated with the number of exemplars produced.

While these results provide support for a model in which social reality beliefs are constructed from multiple memory traces of individual events, it is not clear that this process is the one responsible for the results generally reported. Exemplars are clearly not just a better measure of exposure to television, and in fact, exemplars from television sources were unrelated to beliefs. Reporting more exemplars from books and movies was associated with beliefs that would generally be regarded as less "TV-biased." In other words, Shapiro's research may tell us something about the origins of social reality beliefs, but it is not clear that this process is the one responsible for relationships between viewing and beliefs. Given the predictive strength of the memory dump procedure and its robustness facing controls for mental abilities and other explanations, further work attempting to link the dump back to media use is clearly in order, as is work addressing the belief direction implied by the exemplars.

Still, for the present argument, the point is that if one posits a specific psychological mechanism to account for or explain cultivation relationships, it is possible to provide a test of that mechanism. That Shapiro's results are uncertain in their application to the cultivation hypothesis does not detract from the power inherent in approaching the problem in like ways.

Toward A Solution: Divergent Processes

Perhaps the above discussion of different approaches to process questions is unnecessarily pessimistic. It is certainly true that we know a great deal more about psychological processes in cultivation than we did a few years ago, even though much of what we have learned is negative — the ruling out of what had seemed plausible processes. For example, one plausible process was derived from the logical connection between first- and second-order cultivation beliefs: while first-order beliefs could be regarded as matching the demographic characteristics of television or the real world, second-order beliefs would only be *implied* by television content. Thus, we hypothesized that second-order beliefs might be derived by inference from an individual's first-order beliefs (Hawkins et al., 1987). However, we found no evidence to support such a process; first- and second-order beliefs were minimally correlated, and controlling for or subgrouping on first-order beliefs did not indicate they were an intervening step between television viewing and second-order beliefs. The two types of beliefs seem to be independently influenced by viewed television content.

This leads to what may be an important insight: that the two types seem to be constructed independently of each other opens the possibility that they are constructed in different ways. In fact, it is possible that research on processes has been hampered by the implicit assumption that similar processes apply to both. The different cognitive demands of the two, recent work in cognitive psychology, and the available evidence on processes in social reality effects all point toward very different ways of constructing social reality in first- and second-order beliefs.

First Order

For first-order beliefs (estimates of the concrete demographics of the world) the nature of the cognitive problem for an individual who must form a social reality belief constrains the possible processes. Given that the social reality beliefs in question are themselves estimates of likelihood (either explicitly or slightly removed as forced choices of the most likely value), some direct use of individual events and characters is required, even though the estimates themselves are at a higher level of aggregation. And the evidence thus far on the construction of first-order social reality beliefs points us in some directions and not others.

We know that correlations between television viewing and first-order beliefs seem to be more robust and less affected by third-variable controls than correlations for second-order beliefs; they also seem less likely to be involved in conditional relationships based on demographic characteristics of respondents (Hawkins & Pingree, 1982). Academic achievement and current events knowledge, which arguably may index mental abilities and/or amount of effort expended processing, do not mediate these relationships, although they do affect correlations between viewing and second-order beliefs (Hawkins et al., 1987; Pingree, 1983; Shapiro, 1987, 1988). On the other hand, an individual's perceptions of the reality of television do make a difference in whether their first-order beliefs are correlated with their television viewing (Potter, 1986), indicating the importance of the source of information. And a variety of evidence suggests that the perceived proximity of the judgment may change what information is used, with television content more relevant to judgments of societal or distal phenomenon (Adoni & Mane, 1984; Cohen, Adoni & Drori, 1983; Tyler & Cook, 1984).

Given this relative consistency of relationship, lack of sensitivity to mental abilities, and sensitivity to source of information and the proximity of the judgment to be made, we may be relatively close to understanding how first-order beliefs are constructed. Our earlier model—that a great deal of incidental information about characters and events is learned, and that beliefs are somehow constructed from this memory pool (Hawkins & Pingree, 1982)—may still be a useful beginning. More specifically, the multiple memory trace models, such as those used by Shapiro (1987, 1988), posit that each event produces a separate trace in memory. While these traces vary in strength and are subject to forgetting, people are relatively good at estimating the frequency of occurrence of particular types of events (Hintzman, 1976). Frequency estimation and prototype extraction (finding the central tendency or best representative of multiple exemplars; Hintzman, 1986) are then plausible mechanisms to move from the separate traces of different events in memory to an overall summary belief that corresponds to experiences.

Such estimations seem relatively, although not completely, automatic, and this is consistent with the lack of mental ability or effort effects for first-order beliefs. On the other hand, a number of studies suggest that context or source information is an important and accessible part of these memory traces that could be used to produce the perceived reality or proximity results noted above. The use of television exemplars by heavy viewers might then reflect not just the relative amount of television content in memory, but the gradual dissociation of the trace from its source, so that the event traces cannot be separated into those from relevant and irrelevant sources (Shapiro, 1987).

While this model has some internal consistency, fits into a coherent stream of cognitive psychology research, and is consistent with the data so far on first-order social reality construction, it should not be taken as conclusive yet. An alternate model might involve memory not of individual events, but of one's reactions to them. That is, events with relevance to social reality issues might be processed immediately as bearing on and reinforcing or changing one or more already-existing social reality beliefs. This is certainly at odds with the multiple trace models and with the ability of subjects to make multiple, different uses of the same memory trace depending on the estimate demanded (Hintzman & Block, 1971), but the stimuli involved are quite different. In addition, Shapiro's work (1987, 1988) links the memory store to beliefs, but it is not clear that the social reality beliefs measured contained much, if any, relation to television viewing in the first place. Thus, as noted earlier, Shapiro provides evidence of one side of belief construction, but does not yet link this to media use.

In addition, it is a separate but still important question whether constructing first-order social reality beliefs occurs spontaneously or only in response to unusual situations or demands for such estimates by researchers. That is, what is the importance of television affecting first-order social reality beliefs if these effects occur only for survey respondents? If first-order beliefs do not lead to second-order beliefs, what do they lead to? Thus, while we may be close to explaining the observed relation between viewing and first-order beliefs, it is still possible that this relationship is of no practical significance; first-order beliefs are trivial if there is no further connection to other beliefs or behavior.

Second Order

The relevance and importance of second-order beliefs are not generally in question. Researchers seem to accept the idea that people have ongoing beliefs about the meanness of society, their own fearfulness, sex role stereotypes, and so on, and that these beliefs have some important consequences for social behavior. On the other hand, we have much less understanding of what processes might produce these beliefs, especially processes that might produce them from viewing television content that is biased and patterned in the aggregate.

While these beliefs may be implied by the patterns of television content, they are not constructed from first-order beliefs isomorphic with that content. Relationships are often weaker than those for first-order beliefs, and have in some cases proved to be spurious (Hawkins & Pingree, 1982; Hirsch, 1980). The effects are quite frequently confined to one population subgroup, or even reversed for two different subgroups (this can still be called cultivation if television content can be shown to imply beliefs intermediate to those of the two groups).

Given the extent of differences in these relationships, we suggest it may be time to look for an entirely different set of processes to account for relationships between television viewing and second-order beliefs. Perhaps individual memory traces are simply irrelevant for second-order beliefs. The processes might instead involve something like construct instantiation — an experienced event "fits" or "activates" an already existing idea. In this case, we would start with the idea that all the social reality beliefs that might be cultivated are enough a part of our culture that television viewers already possess all of them, at least as potentials. Some or all events experienced through television or other sources would be recognized as matching or implying certain of these beliefs and not others (this is similar to the alternate process offered for first-order beliefs, in which it is the consequence for the prototype that is relevant rather than the original memory trace), thus strengthening some beliefs and not others.

Such a recognition or instantiation process would draw on a very different literature in cognitive psychology. For example, one might draw on construct accessibility (Higgins & King, 1981; Bargh & Thein, 1985) to account for which constructs are available and called up by experiences and used to make judgments. Priming effects (Higgins, Bargh, & Lombardi, 1985; Iyengar & Kinder, 1987) and other models of spreading activation through an associative net of memory or world view (Berkowitz & Rogers, 1986) could provide the diffusion by which specific but salient events might affect several more general beliefs. Automaticity (Bargh, 1984), that we cannot help use some constructs or apply some processes in given situations, will be an issue regardless of the resolution of the ability/effort conditional effects. Automaticity, however, should mean more than Bargh's narrow definition. The use and perception of mass communication probably involves behaviors that are intended and controlled in the long run (as in the formation of habits), but automatic in the short run.

In all this, a central issue will be the conditions under which, or the extent to which, information consistent or inconsistent with expectations takes precedence. Higgins and Bargh (1987), in reviewing this literature, suggest that impression formation may be more open to inconsistent information than is impression testing, where the prior belief may take precedence. Obviously, the question for social reality beliefs is whether these beliefs are constructed fresh, as we believe may well be the case with first-order beliefs, or instead further activated and elaborated. Of course, as Higgins and Bargh also point out, there is no real reason for us to pose a dichotomous choice between theory-driven and data-driven approaches. In fact, there is considerable evidence that we can remember both the original data and our responses to it.

It is also possible that the construction of second-order social reality beliefs might be a two step process involving experiential strengthening or highlighting of some constructs in an associate net of subjective beliefs, and the subsequent implication of the social reality beliefs themselves. This would place both instantiation and construction together within the same overall process.

Conclusions

One problem in applying cognitively oriented psychology to problems of psychological processes in effects on social reality beliefs is that there is a mismatch between the narrow, particularistic research paradigms of cognitive psychology and the long-term, television-content-as-a-whole nature of the potential stimulus here. That problem has not been resolved in this chapter; there will have to be many creative solutions, each devised to match an individual problem of time-order, duration, and the particular constructs and processes involved. We do think that research should explicitly treat first- and second-order beliefs separately, propose specific theory-based processes for each, and test them as directly as possible. Of course, the distinction between first- and second-order beliefs may itself prove fuzzy in some domains or need elaboration in others, and this will further theory building as well.

But there is another issue in applying the psychological literature. In general, social psychological theory is complex and conditional because "most social information is at least somewhat ambiguous and open to multiple interpretations" (Higgins & Bargh, 1987, p. 374). But in a fundamental way, television is not ambiguous as a social stimulus. True, viewers have differences of perception and can form multiple meanings for the same television stimulus (Livingston, 1988). But the point of television as a dramatic entertainment medium is to form substantial agreement and consensus of meaning; there is clearly a preferred reading of most television content. Even if there are momentary variations in interpretation, viewers probably get brought back to the point through redundancy in the story line (see Hawkins & Daly, 1988).

In many ways, the stories of episodic television are much more like lessons than social situations (see Pingree & Thompson, in press, for an argument that soap operas are not). There *is* a point to a story; writers, directors, story editors, producers, and others who share the content have a point to make, even if that point is trite and formulaic. Obviously, this makes it possible to look for mass media effects on social reality beliefs at all, since there is some reason to look for consistency of intended messages across stories and for consistency of interpretation across receivers. That stories are lessons makes the linkage of exemplar and belief likely to be clearer and less problematic.

But there is a further implication for our attempts to incorporate cognitive social psychological theories here as well. We see an analogy to the social situation of evaluating a person whose strong self-concept contradicts one's prior expectancy, and thus the data (the immediate experience) gain some advantage over theory or expectation (Swann & Ely, 1984). Given the relative lack of ambiguity in television when compared to interpersonal social interaction, the lessons from psychology about the balance of data and theory (or of construction vs. instantiation) will probably have to be tipped at least somewhat toward the data and fresh construction (that is, toward effects) in the case of television than what one might expect solely on the basis of the psychological literature.

More psychological process research on the cultivation hypothesis would be necessary to establish some internal validity and explanation for the relationship between television viewing and social reality beliefs. The research community is in a much better position to do this than it was 5 or 10 years ago. The advances in theory and operationalization in cognitive social psychology, recognizing the importance of the first-order vs. second-order distinction in social reality beliefs, and the pioneering process studies cited here all combine to provide a full but clear research agenda for future studies.

Notes

1. *First-order* (also called *demographic*) beliefs are estimates of the frequency or probabilities or characterization of events, and one can clearly distinguish a "television" answer from a "real-world" answer. That is, one can measure the frequency of violent crime in both the real and television worlds, and compare respondent estimates to these two measures. Second-order beliefs, such as fear of walking alone or mistrusting strangers, have no quantifiable referent in television content, but one can argue that the prevalence of violence between strangers *implies* that one should fear and mistrust strangers. Thus, the second-order beliefs are further removed from content in any argument that correlations of beliefs with viewing represent effects.

References

Adoni, H., & Mane, S. (1984). Media and the social construction of reality: Toward an integration of theory and research. *Communication Research, 11* (3), 323-340.

Bargh, J. A. (1984). Automatic and conscious processing of social information. In R. S. Wyer & T. K. Srull (Eds.), *Handbook of social cognition, Vol. III* (pp. 1-43). Hillsdale, NJ: Lawrence Erlbaum.

Bargh, J. A., & Thein, R. D. (1985). Individual construct accessibility, person memory, and the recall-judgment link: The case of information overload. *Journal of Personality and Social Psychology, 49*(5), 1129-1146.

Berkowitz, L., & Rogers, K. H. (1986). A priming effect analysis of media influences. In J. Bryant & D. Zillmann (Eds.), *Perspectives on media effects*. Hillsdale, NJ: Lawrence Erlbaum.

Campbell, D., & Stanley, J. (1963). *Experimental and quasi-experimental designs for research*. Chicago: Rand McNally.

Cohen, A. A., Adoni, H., & Drori, G. (1983). Adolescents' perceptions of social conflicts in television news and social reality. *Human Communication Research, 10*(2), 203-225.

Gerbner, G., Gross, L., Morgan, M., & Signorielli, N. (1980). The "mainstreaming" of America: Violence profile no. 11. *Journal of Communication, 30*, 10-39.

Hawkins, R. P., & Daly, J. (1988). Cognition and communication. In R. P. Hawkins, J. M. Wiemann, & S. Pingree (Eds.), *Advancing communication science: Merging mass and interpersonal processes*. Newbury Park, CA.: Sage.

Hawkins, R. P., & Pingree, S. (1980). Some processes in the cultivation effect. *Communication Research, 7*, 193-226.

Hawkins, R. P., & Pingree, S. (1981). Using television to construct social reality. *Journal of Broadcasting, 25*(4), 347-364.

Hawkins, R. P., & Pingree, S. (1982). Television's influence on social reality. In D. Pearl, L. Bouthilet, & J. Lazar (Eds.), *Television and behavior: Ten years of scientific progress and implications for the eighties* (DHHS Publication No. ADM 82-1196, Vol. 2, pp. 224-247). Washington, DC: U.S. Government Printing Office.

Hawkins, R. P., Pingree, S., & Adler, I. (1987). Searching for cognitive processes in the cultivation effect: Adult and adolescent samples in the United States and Australia. *Human Communication Research, 13*(4), 553-577.

Higgins, E. T., & Bargh, J. A. (1987). Social cognition and social perceptions. *Annual Review of Psychology, 38*, 369-425.

Higgins, E. T., Bargh, J. A., & Lombardi, W. (1985). Nature of priming effects on categorization. *Journal of Experimental Psychology, 11*(1), 59-69.

Higgins, E. T., & King, G. (1981). Accessibility of social constructs: Information processing consequences of individual and contextual variability. In N. Cantor & J. F. Kihlstrom (Eds.), *Personality, cognition and social interaction*. Hillsdale, NJ: Lawrence Erlbaum.

Hintzman, D. L. (1976). Repetition and memory. In G. H. Bower (Ed.), *The psychology of learning and motivation* (pp. 47-91). New York: Academic Press.

Hintzman, D. L. (1986). "Schema abstraction" in a multiple-trace memory model. *Psychological Review, 93*(4), 411-428.

Hintzman, D. L., & Block, R. A. (1971). Repetition and memory: Evidence for a multiple-trace hypothesis. *Journal of Experimental Psychology, 88*(3), 297-306.

Hirsch, P. M. (1980). The 'scary world' of the nonviewer and other anomalies: A reanalysis of Gerbner et al.'s findings on cultivation analysis, Part I. *Communication Research, 7*(4), 403-456.

Iyengar, S., & Kinder, D. R. (1987). *News that matters*. Chicago: University of Chicago Press.

Livingston, S. (1988). Viewers' interpretations of soap opera characters. In P. Drummond & R. Paterson (Eds.), *Television and its audience: International research perspectives*. London: BFI.

Markus, H., & Zajonc, R. B. (1985). The cognitive perspective in social psychology. In G. Lindzey and E. Aronson (Eds.), *Handbook of social psychology*. New York: Newbury Award Records.

Perse, E. M. (in press). Cultivation and involvement with local television news. In N. Signorielli & M. Morgan (Eds.), *Cultivation analysis*. Newbury Park, CA: Sage.

Pingree, S. (1983). Children's cognitive processes in constructing social reality. *Journalism Quarterly, 60*, 415-422.

Pingree, S., & Thompson, M. (in press). Families in daytime serials. In J. Bryant (Ed.), *Mass media and the family*. Hillsdale, NJ: Lawrence Erlbaum.

Potter, W. J. (1986). Perceived reality and the cultivation hypothesis. *Journal of Broadcasting and Electronic Media, 30*(2), 159-174.

Shapiro, M. A. (1987). *The influence of communication-source coded memory traces on world view*. Unpublished doctoral dissertation, University of Wisconsin, Madison.

Shapiro, M. A. (1988). *The influence of communication-source coded memory traces on world view*. Paper presented to the International Communication Association, New Orleans.

Signorielli, N. (1990). Television's mean and dangerous world: A continuation of the cultural indicators perspective. In N. Signorielli & M Morgan (Eds.), *Cultivation analysis*. Newbury Park, CA: Sage.

Swann, W. B., Jr., & Ely, R. J. (1984). A battle of wills: Self-verification versus behavioral confirmation. *Journal of Personality and Social Psychology, 46*, 12887-1302.

Tyler, T. R., & Cook, F. L. (1984). The mass media and judgments of risk: Distinguishing impact on personal and societal level judgments. *Journal of Personality and Social Psychology, 47* (4), 693-708.

Weaver, J., & Wakshlag, J. (1986). Perceived vulnerability to crime, criminal victimization experiences, and television viewing. *Journal of Broadcasting and Electronic Media, 30*, 141-158.

3

Cultivation and Involvement with Local Television News

ELIZABETH M. PERSE

Over the past decade, researchers have uncovered a consistent societal-level link between television exposure and social reality beliefs. Many studies using a variety of methods have observed that television cultivates a wide range of social perceptions, such as fear of crime, anomie, mistrust, and images of races, sexes, female beauty, and the elderly (e.g., Gerbner, Gross, Morgan, & Signorielli, 1980; Gerbner, Gross, Signorielli, & Morgan, 1980; Tan, 1979; Volgy & Schwartz, 1980).

Research has also examined cultivation at an individual level to understand the process by which television exposure and perceptions of social reality are linked in people. Although it is clear that numerous variables, including life situation, television exposure, and personality variables, influence cultivation, researchers have not discovered how cultivation occurs at the individual level. This study focused on individual-level cultivation to examine how television exposure and perceptions of personal risk become linked. Because research has observed that involvement clarifies many other communication effects, such as voting decisions (Rothschild & Ray, 1974) and persuasion (Petty & Cacioppo, 1984), this study investigated the relationship between local television news viewing, involvement, and perceptions of personal safety.

The Cultivation Process

Cultivation was originally described as incidental, or unintentional, learning where television viewers unconsciously acquire the demographic "facts" of television drama (Gerbner & Gross, 1976, p. 179). According to Gerbner and his associates, these facts become the basis for images and values about the real world. The cognitive process linking the television facts and second-order cultivation of images and values (Gerbner, Gross, Morgan, & Signorielli, 1986), though, was unspecified.

Hawkins and Pingree (1982) suggested that individual-level cultivation is a two-part learning process based on viewing attention, incidental learning, and cognitive inference skills (also see Hawkins & Pingree, this volume). According to Hawkins and Pingree, attention during exposure leads to learning television facts and values. Through cognitive action, these television facts become a source of information for social reality perceptions. Extensive tests, though, find little support for this hypothesis (Hawkins, Pingree, & Adler, 1987). The acquisition of television facts seems unrelated to perceptions of social reality.

Other writers have proposed that cultivation is based on cognitive processing of television content. Weaver and Wakshlag (1986), for example, concluded that people actively interpret televised information and relate that information to their own personal experiences when using television as a basis for social reality beliefs. Other writers observed that perceptions of television realism were substantial contributors to cultivation (Perse, 1986; Potter, 1986; Slater & Elliott, 1982). People apparently evaluate the veracity of television content before using it as a basis for social reality.

Finally, Tamborini, Zillmann, and Bryant (1984) argued that cultivation is the result of a cognitive priming process. According to this perspective, television exposure provides salient information about facts, images, and values. Frequent television exposure makes television information easy to retrieve from memory. Because people make judgments based on the most available information (Tversky & Kahneman, 1973), judgments about social reality are based on television content. Tamborini and his associates' (1984) support for the priming process, though, was drawn on indirect experimental evidence, not direct observation of cognitive processes. Hawkins and his associates (1987) suggested that a direct measure of cognitive activity is needed to uncover the cultivation process.

Involvement

Communication researchers hold two different views of involvement. On one hand, involvement in persuasion research is thought to be a sense of importance attached to an object, person, or issue (e.g., Salmon, 1986). On the other hand, in mass communication research involvement is seen as intellectual and emotional participation during message reception (e.g., Gans, 1980; Levy & Windahl, 1985). Both views, though, hold that involvement is shown in cognitive activity.

Petty and Cacioppo (1984), for example, found that issue involvement is reflected in more intense cognitive activity. When people encounter messages about topics important to them, they pay attention to and evaluate the content. The researchers concluded that involved individuals process information more deeply. Involvement, then, has a dimension of intensity. As involvement becomes more intense, processing moves through three stages: (a) attention, or allocating cognitive effort to process the information; (b) recognition, or categorizing the information as familiar or unfamiliar; and (c) elaboration, or relating the information to prior knowledge (Greenwald & Leavitt, 1984; Perse, 1987).

According to persuasion research, though, involvement has only a single orientation or direction: informational message elements. Any response that focuses on other message elements, such as message structure or source, is considered a low-involvement response. Moreover, emotional reactions are not considered signals of involvement because affective responses require less effort than cognitive responses.

Mass communication research, however, points out that involved message responses may be oriented toward any aspect of a message. Media involvement may have several orientations beyond the informational content of messages. People may react interpersonally to news anchors (Rubin, Perse, & Powell, 1985). Soap opera viewers may become emotional over story lines (Lemish, 1985). Or, sports viewers may get caught up in the excitement of the audience (Hocking, 1982). Because different message elements may lead to involvement, involvement may have several different orientations.

Psychological theory points out that emotional reactions are also an important aspect of audience involvement. Emotion and cognition are interrelated because emotions are the result of a cognitive, attributional process where emotional meaning is ascribed to perceptions. In his two-factor theory of emotion, Schachter (1964) proposed that feelings of arousal determine the intensity of emotional response, but assigning meaning to that arousal leads to emotional reactions.

Involvement, then, is an information-processing response to messages that has two dimensions: orientation and intensity. *Orientation* marks the direction of the cognitive-emotional processing. People may become involved with any aspect of the message: issue information, personalities, plot, music, or audience. *Intensity* marks the depth of the processing. As people become more involved, they process the information more deeply, moving from paying attention to the information, categorizing it as familiar or unfamiliar, relating the information to prior knowledge, and reacting emotionally to it.

Local Television News

Most cultivation research has focused on the relationship between overall levels of television viewing and conceptions of social reality reflected in prime-time entertainment programming (Gerbner et al., 1986) because incidental learning grows out of entertainment viewing motives (Windahl, 1981). Local television news, though, also may be associated with cultivation because local news focuses on violence acts and may bear little resemblance to reality.

Just as prime-time television is filled with scenes of violence, local news often focuses on conflict and uses graphic visuals of crime, accidents, and disasters (e.g., Dominick, Wurtzel, & Lometti, 1975). Levine (1986), for example, found that 59.3% of the news stories on local New York City newscasts highlighted accidents and crime victims unable to control their own fate. Moreover, just as prime-time depictions of violence bear little resemblance to actuality (Gerbner & Gross, 1976), crime news reporting often deviates from reality. Sheley and Ashkins (1981), for example, found that local crime news in New Orleans media bore little relationship to police records. Eighty percent of crime stories on local television newscasts focused on murder and robbery although these crimes made up only 12.4% of crimes reported by police. Graber (1980) found that crime news exposure was linked to fear of becoming a crime victim.

There are several other reasons that local news may be the basis for social reality perceptions. First, local news is dramatic and often watched for entertainment reasons (Bogart, 1980; Rubin et al., 1985).

Second, local news is heavily watched (Comstock, Chaffee, Katzman, McCombs, & Roberts, 1978) and is part of some viewers' regular daily activities (Levy, 1978). Third, local news is perceived as realistic by much of its audience (Rubin et al., 1985).

All news viewing, though, may not be associated with cultivation. Jaehnig, Weaver, and Fico (1981), for example, observed that different news content may be interpreted differently. The researchers found a weak correlation between watching television news and fear of becoming a crime victim, but no relationship between using television news for political information and fear of victimization. The kinds of news stories that viewers process (i.e., the orientation of news use) may influence cultivation. Those heavier local news viewers who are oriented toward seeking drama and excitement may pay more attention to crime news, become more involved with crime news, and become more fearful of the real world.

Thus, the present study tested the following hypothesis: Perceptions of less personal safety will be predicted by:

1. higher levels of local news exposure and nonnews television exposure,
2. more salient diversionary local television news viewing motives,
3. higher levels of local news perceived realism,
4. higher levels of attention to local television crime news,
5. higher levels of recognition of local television crime news,
6. higher levels of elaboration on local television crime news, and
7. more emotional reactions to local television news.

Method

Undergraduate students enrolled in communication courses at a branch campus of a large midwestern university were given extra credit for collecting the data for this study.[1] The volunteers were trained in data collection and ethics. The trained assistants were assigned age and gender quotas and instructed to gather data from adults at least 18 years old who watched local news at least once a week and were not enrolled in college. All data were collected during a 1-week period in Winter, 1987. Of the 309 questionnaires returned, 4 were discarded because they were completed by adults who did not watch local news at least once a week.

The sample (N = 305) ranged in age from 17 to 92 years (M = 40.90, SD = 15.82) and was 53.1% female. Most of the respondents were high school graduates (42.3%), 29.5% had completed some college, and 10.2% were college graduates. Average socioeconomic status (SES), using the Duncan scale (Reiss with Duncan, Hatt, & North, 1961) was 30.64 (SD = 22.70). Zip codes recoded to reflect population density (U.S. Department of Commerce, 1980) indicated that most of the sample (93.4%) lived in areas under 25,000 in population.

Perceptions of Personal Safety

To measure the dependent variable of perceptions of personal safety, respondents were presented with four hypothetical situations adapted from Weaver and Wakshlag (1986) and asked to express their concern for their own personal safety in each situation on 7-point scales anchored by "extremely concerned" (7) and "not at all concerned" (1).[2] Responses to the four items were averaged. Perceptions of Personal Safety scores ranged from 1.00 to 7.00 (M = 4.78, SD = 1.64, Cronbach alpha = .80).

Media Behaviors

Two television exposure measures were used to assess viewing. First, respondents indicated the number of times during a week they typically watched local news programs. Estimated local news exposure ranged from 1 to 21 times a week (M = 5.78, SD = 3.74). Second, television exposure was measured with two questions about exposure "yesterday" and on a typical weekday that have been used reliably in previous research (e.g., Rubin et al., 1985). The two questions (Cronbach alpha = .69) were averaged to provide an index of television exposure. Estimated daily television exposure ranged from 0.50 to 12.00 hours (M = 3.93, SD = 2.05).

Next, several steps were taken to create a measure of nonnews television exposure to control for any effects that are due to general television viewing. First, estimates of daily television exposure were multiplied by 7 to create an estimate of weekly television viewing. Second, because most local news programs are 30 minutes in length, weekly local news exposure was multiplied by .5 to create an estimate of the number of local news hours watched during a typical week. Third, the weekly local news measure was subtracted from the weekly television exposure measure to create an estimate of weekly nonnews television exposure. Estimated nonnews television exposure ranged from 0.50 to 81.50 hours per week (M = 24.67, SD = 13.98).

Local News Viewing Motives

This study examined two orientations toward local television news: information and diversion. Local television news viewing motives were assessed by asking respondents to compare their reasons for watching local television news (5 = exactly to 1 = not at all) to 12 statements, three items to assess information, social utility, entertainment, and excitement (Palmgreen, Wenner, & Rayburn, 1980; Rubin et al., 1985).

Because previous research suggests that viewing motives are interrelated (e.g., Rubin, 1983), the 12 local news viewing motives were subjected to principal factor analysis with oblique rotation (SPSS, 1986). Two factors, accounting for 48.3% of the total variance, were identified. Using the criteria of an eigenvalue greater than 1.0 and three primary loadings above .50 with no secondary loadings above .30, both factors were retained. The factor analysis is summarized in Table 3.1. Local news viewing motives were constructed using factor scores derived by the regression method (SPSS, 1986).

Factor 1, *Exciting Entertainment* (eigenvalue = 4.60), accounted for 25.3% of the total variance. It included all six items reflecting entertainment and excitement. Factor 2, *Social/Personal Utility* (eigenvalue = 1.20), accounted for 20.9% of the variance. It included all three social utility items and two information items. As instrumental orientations toward the news, the two factors were related positively ($r = .61$, $p < .001$).

Perceived Realism of Local Television News

Perceived realism of local television news was measured with six 5-point Likert scale items also drawn from previous local television news and soap opera research (Rubin & Perse, 1987; Rubin et al., 1985).[3] Responses to the six items were averaged. Perceived realism scores ranged from 1.00 to 5.00 (M = 3.30, SD = 0.61, Cronbach alpha = .80).

Table 3.1 Local Television News Viewing Motives Oblique Factor Solution

I watch local news on television . . .	Exciting Entertainment	Social/Personal Utility
Because it amuses me (2.16, 1.01)	.72	−.13
Because it entertains me (2.66, 1.04)	.72	−.03
Because it's dramatic (2.03, 1.00)	.71	.06
Because it's thrilling (2.00, 0.98)	.70	.15
Because it's enjoyable (2.70, 1.08)	.70	.11
Because it's exciting (2.35, 0.99)	.69	.06
So I can talk with others about what's on the program (2.91, 1.13)	−.09	.78
So I can pass the information on to other people (2.88, 1.10)	−.02	.71
To learn about issues affecting people like me (3.81, 1.05)	−.06	.66
To support my own viewpoints to other people (2.78, 1.14)	.14	.62
So I can learn about what could happen to me (3.20, 1.17)	.10	.61
Because it helps me learn things about myself and others (3.29, 1.05)	.18	.38
Eigenvalue	4.60	1.20
Variance Explained	25.3%	20.9%
Cronbach Alpha	.87	.81
Mean	2.32	3.14
Standard Deviation	.79	.80

NOTE: $N = 305$. The numbers in parentheses are the mean and standard deviation for each item.

Local News Involvement

To measure attention, recognition, and elaboration on news content, respondents were asked to consider how often each of 15 statements described their typical thoughts or feelings when watching government and crime local news reports (very often = 5 to never = 1). To help respondents understand the types of news stories included in those two categories, brief descriptions were provided (Adams, 1978; Bush, 1960). For each type of news report, scale items were averaged to create indices of attention, recognition, and elaboration.

Attention

Attention to government and crime reports were each measured with a five-item scale adapted from Cegala's (1981) interaction involvement scale. The items assess overall attention as well as attention to visual and audio aspects of the news programs.[4] Attention to government reports ranged from 1.00 to 5.00 (M = 3.35, SD = 0.92, Cronbach alpha = .89). Attention to crime reports ranged from 1.00 to 5.00 (M = 3.64, SD = 0.76, Cronbach alpha = .85).

Recognition

A five-item recognition scale was developed from previous research on news exposure to measure recognition of government reports and recognition of crime reports. Drawing from Garramone (1983b) and Graber (1984), five items were generated that reflect understanding, recognizing, and confusion about news stories.[5] Recognition of government reports ranged from 1.00 to 5.00 (M = 3.23, SD = 0.79, Cronbach alpha = .83). Recognition of crime reports ranged from 1.80 to 5.00 (M = 3.43, SD = 0.57, Cronbach alpha = .63).

Elaboration

To operationalize elaboration on government and crime reports, five items were generated that concern relating the news information to previous knowledge, considering the interpersonal and social consequences of the information, and thinking about the information.[6] Elaboration on government reports ranged from 1.00 to 5.00 (M = 3.41, SD = 0.80, Cronbach alpha = .85). Elaboration on crime reports ranged from 1.20 to 5.00 (M = 3.24, SD = 0.66, Cronbach alpha = .83).

Emotional Reactions

To assess the intensity of emotional reactions to news reports, 12 items were adapted from Davitz (1969) that concern the emotions of happiness, anger, and sadness. Three additional statements were created that were more explicit measures of the three emotions: "I feel happy," "I feel angry," and "I feel sad."[7] Respondents were asked to indicate how often they shared the feelings expressed in each of the 15 statements when watching local news (very often = 5 to never = 1).

The 15 emotional reaction items were subjected to principal factor analysis with oblique rotation. Three factors accounting for 55.7% of the variance were identified that supported the conceptualization of the three scales. Thus, responses to the three 5-item emotional reaction scales were averaged. Happiness scores ranged from 1.00 to 4.80 (M = 2.44, SD = 0.66, Cronbach alpha = .81). Anger scores ranged from 1.00 to 4.60 (M = 2.22, SD = 0.81, Cronbach alpha = .86). Sadness scores ranged from 1.00 to 4.80 (M = 2.30, SD = 0.82, Cronbach alpha = .88).

Statistical Analysis

Following factor and reliability analyses to construct the various measures of this investigation, the hypothesis of the investigation was assessed with two statistical tests. First, Pearson correlations were computed to examine the relationship between involvement orientation and the dependent variable, Perceptions of Personal Safety. Second, hierarchical multiple regression was used to assess the overall contribution of involvement orientation and intensity to Perceptions of Personal Safety. To control for the influence of demographics, demographic variables were entered on the first step. Because television viewing behaviors are important antecedents to cultivation, local news and nonnews television exposures were entered into the equation on the second step. The other variables were entered in the order specified by the hypothesis of the investigation.

Results

This study's hypothesis proposed that scores on the Personal Safety Scale would be explained by orientation and intensity of involvement. The first statistical test examined the univariate relationships between the Personal Safety Scale and measures of local news viewing motives, behaviors, and involvement measures. The correlations are presented in Table 3.2.

The partial correlations provided support for the prediction that a diversionary involvement orientation was linked to perceptions of

Table 3.2 Cultivation with Local News Viewing Motives, Exposure, and Involvement

Correlates	Perceptions of Risk of Assault	
	r	partial r
Viewing Motives		
Exciting Entertainment	.13*	.15**
Personal/Social Utility	.11	.07
News Perceived Realism	.15*	.10
Television Behaviors		
Local News Exposure	.06	.03
Nonnews Television Exposure	.15*	.08
Involvement		
Attention/Crime	.16**	.14*
Attention/Government	−.05	−.02
Recognition/Crime	−.21***	−.13*
Recognition/Government	−.19**	−.11*
Elaboration/Crime	.12*	.13*
Elaboration/Government	.03	.07
Emotions		
Happy	.13*	.09
Angry	.23***	.18**
Sad	.26***	.14*

NOTE: Partial correlations are controlled for age, gender, education, SES, and population density.

*$p < .05$.
**$p < .01$.
***$p < .001$.

greater hypothesized risk. In all cases, only those measures that indicate a diversionary orientation to local news viewing were related significantly to Perceptions of Personal Safety. The Exciting Entertainment viewing motive ($r = .15$, $p < .01$), attention to crime reports ($r = .14$, $p < .05$), elaboration on crime reports ($r = .13$, $p < .05$), feeling angry ($r = .18$, $p < .01$), and feeling sad ($r = .14$, $p < .05$) correlated with the dependent variable. The Personal/Social Utility viewing motive, and attention to and elaboration on government reports were not related significantly to hypothesized risk. Recognizing government and crime reports was correlated negatively to the Personal Safety index ($r = -.11$, $r = -.13$, respectively, both $p < .05$).

The second test of the hypothesis was hierarchical multiple regression. The variables were entered into the equation in the order specified in the hypothesis. To control for the demographic variables of age, gender, education, SES, and population density, those variables were entered at the first step. The regression is summarized in Table 3.3.

The final equation accounted for 27.6% of the variance in Perceptions of Personal Safety. The hypothesis was partially supported. Gender (male = 0, female = 1) (*beta* = .34, $p < .001$), the Exciting Entertainment viewing motive (*beta* = .18, $p < .03$), and attention to crime news (*beta* = .18, $p < .02$) were significant positive predictors. The Personal/Social Utility viewing motive (*beta* = -.17, $p < .04$) and recognition of crime news (*beta* = -.16, $p < .04$) were significant negative predictors of Perceptions of Personal Safety. Perceptions of Personal Safety were associated with indications of an entertainment orientation to the news, but not to evidence of more intense involvement.

Discussion

This study was an extension of societal-level cultivation research. This study investigated the individual-level process that links television exposure and individuals' perceptions of personal safety. Contrary to the predictions of the study, perceptions of decreased personal safety were not associated with more intense levels of involvement with local television news. Although previous research suggested that cognitive evaluation of television messages influences cultivation (e.g., Weaver & Wakshlag, 1986), the results demonstrate that only attention to the news is a significant positive contributor to the cultivation of perceptions of personal safety.

The orientation of involvement, though, was an important aspect to perceptions of personal safety. Higher levels of perceived personal risk were predicted by entertainment news viewing motives, attention to crime news stories, and lower levels of more utilitarian viewing motives. Consistent with cultivation writings (e.g., Gerbner et al., 1986) perceptions of personal safety were linked to an entertainment orientation to local news.

The consideration of the influence of involvement has added to knowledge about the individual-level cultivation process that is consistent with earlier speculations (e.g., Gerbner et al., 1986; Hawkins & Pingree, 1982). First, the regression results indicate that neither news nor nonnews exposure was linked to perceived risks. Similar to earlier research (Chaffee & Schleuder, 1986) measures of attention provide a

Table 3.3 Hierarchical Multiple Regression Summary: Regressing Cultivation

	Step Entered	R	R^2	R^2 Change	Final b	Final F	$p <$
Demographics	1	.44	.19	.19***			
Age					−.07	1.12	.30
Gender					.34	32.72	.001
Education					−.09	1.80	.19
SES					−.01	0.01	.93
Population Density					.09	2.58	.11
Television Behaviors	2	.44	.20	.00			
News Exposure					−.01	0.02	.90
Television Exposure					.04	0.56	.46
Perceived Realism	3	.45	.20	.01	.05	0.65	.42
Viewing Motives	4	.46	.21	.01			
Exciting Entertainment					.18	5.27	.03
Personal/Social Utility					−.17	4.51	.04
Attention	5	.48	.23	.01			
Crime					.18	6.61	.02
Government					.04	0.22	.64
Recognition	6	.51	.26	.04**			
Crime					−.16	4.49	.04
Government					−.12	1.71	.20
Elaboration	7	.52	.27	.01			
Crime					.00	0.00	.98
Government					.08	0.67	.42
Emotions	8	.53	.28	.00			
Happy					−.06	0.59	.45
Angry					.08	1.01	.32
Sad					.02	0.07	.79

NOTE: Step 1: $F(5, 273) = 12.90, p < .001$.
Step 2: $F(7, 271) = 9.43, p < .001$.
Step 3: $F(8, 270) = 8.53, p < .001$.
Step 4: $F(10, 268) = 7.34, p < .001$.
Step 5: $F(12, 266) = 6.55, p < .001$.
Step 6: $F(14, 264) = 6.80, p < .001$.
Step 7: $F(16, 262) = 6.10, p < .001$.
Step 8: $F(19, 259) = 5.20, p < .001$.
$N = 272$.
*$p < .05$.
**$p < .01$.
***$p < .001$.

better explanation of media effects. Consistent with the process proposed by Hawkins and Pingree (1982), individual-level cultivation depends on some base level of cognitive effort.

Second, the negative contribution of recognition to perceptions of personal safety may reflect the greater impact of mass media in areas where the individual does not have direct personal experience. Some have found that television's impact is greatest with perceptions of social reality most distant from everyday experience (Tyler, 1980; Weaver & Wakshlag, 1986). In other words, television becomes a source for social reality beliefs in the absence of other, more direct, experiences. When making social reality judgments, then, information provided by television may be the most readily available and top of mind (Tamborini et al., 1984).

Third, the findings support the view that cultivation is an incidental learning process (Gerbner & Gross, 1976; Hawkins & Pingree, 1982). Incidental learning occurs unintentionally without motivation to learn (McLaughlin, 1965). Perceptions of less personal safety are linked positively to an entertainment-oriented, local news viewing motive but negatively to a more learning-oriented local news viewing motive. Also, elaboration is not related to perceptions of personal safety, showing that perceptions of personal safety are learned at lower levels of intentionality. And, attention to news is a significant predictor of perceptions of personal safety. Research has shown that attention is necessary for incidental learning (McLaughlin, 1965). Finally, the significance of individual differences in cultivation is underscored in incidental learning research. Individual differences are particularly salient in incidental learning because people are not motivated to use their skills to learn (McLaughlin, 1965).

Fourth, because perceptions of personal safety were associated with lower levels of involvement, cultivation due to television exposure may not be long lasting. Previous research has shown that lower levels of cognitive activity result in less enduring effects because less intense information processing does not link the information very strongly to prior knowledge (Petty, Cacioppo, & Kasmer, 1987). Tamborini et al. (1984), for example, found that cultivation was evident immediately after exposure but diminished after 3 days. Future research should consider other influences that might make cultivation more enduring, such as reinforcement (Hawkins et al., 1987) or interaction with other individuals (Morgan, 1986).

There are some limitations to this study. The sample was not selected randomly, limiting generalizability of the study's results. And, most respondents were probably known to the students. The sample, however, was drawn from counties representative of the U.S. population (Bureau of the Census, 1983). And, sample characteristics are similar to earlier studies (Rubin et al., 1985).

This test of the role of involvement in the cultivation process supports the view that involvement is an important variable in media effects (Levy & Windahl, 1985; Salmon, 1986). Consideration of both the intensity and orientation dimensions of involvement increased understanding of individual-level cultivation from local news viewing. The results of this study also demonstrate the importance of viewing motives in media effects research. Motivation influences processing orientation (Garramone, 1983a).

In conclusion, this examination of the role of involvement in cultivation based on local television news viewing has added to the understanding of the individual-level cultivation process. As incidental learning, cultivation is linked to viewing local news for entertainment purposes. Some allocation of cognitive effort is necessary — attention to content. Lower stores of prior knowledge are associated with relying on more available television information to form perceptions of social reality.

Notes

1. This study is based on my doctoral dissertation completed at Kent State University. I'm grateful to Alan Rubin for directing the study and to Carole Barbato for arranging data collection.

2. The Perceptions of Personal Safety items and their means and standard deviations were:

(a) You've lived alone in a small community for many years and you know most of the people and places in the town. At 11 P.M. you arrive home and find your front door unlocked. You don't remember if you locked it the last time you left home. How concerned would you be that you might be assaulted? (4.72, 2.19)

(b) You are driving to visit friends in another city. On your way you get lost in a small rural town. It's dark out, and because there are no other lights on anywhere, you go into a bar to ask for directions. How concerned would you be that you might be assaulted? (4.51, 2.13)

(c) You are home alone at night watching television. It is a pleasant evening and your windows are open. You hear some whispering voices outside, but you don't know exactly where they came from. How concerned would you be that you might be assaulted? (4.49, 2.05)

(d) You're walking home from work at 1 A.M. Three men, obviously drunk, are walking toward you. No one else is around. How concerned would you be that you might be assaulted? (5.38, 1.94)

3. The six perceived realism items and their means and standard deviations were: Local television news presents things as they really are in life (3.33, 0.85); If I see something on local television news, I can be sure it really is that way (2.86, 0.94); Local television news lets me see how other people live (3.49, 0.85); Local television news shows life as it really is (2.95, 0.94); Local television news lets me see what happens in other places as if I were really there (3.34, 0.88); Local television news helps me understand some of the problems other people have (3.81, 0.74).

4. The five attention items and their means and standard deviations were: I pay close attention to [government/crime reports] (3.63, 1.09/3.85, 0.89); I listen carefully to [government/crime reports] (3.63, 1.06/3.88, 0.92); I watch carefully [government/crime reports] (3.55, 1.07/3.76, 0.99); My mind wanders during [government/crime reports] (2.97, 1.21/3.44, 1.01); I miss parts of [government/crime reports] (2.97, 1.07/3.29, 0.98). Negatively phrased items were recoded for further analysis.

5. The five recognition items and their means and standard deviations were: I understand [government/crime reports] (3.41, 1.01/3.90, 0.83); I recognize the places in [government/crime reports] (3.46, 0.98/3.35, 0.89); I recognize the names in [government/crime reports] (3.47, 0.95/2.75, 0.95); I get confused by [government/crime reports] (2.89, 1.08/ 3.53, 0.92); They seem too complicated to understand [government/crime reports] (2.93, 1.12/3.62, 0.92). Negatively phrased items were recoded for further analysis.

6. The five elaboration items and their means and standard deviations were: I think about what should be done [government/crime reports] (3.51, 1.09/3.70, 0.99); I think about the story over and over again [government/crime reports] (2.82, 1.07/3.06, 1.05); I think about what this will mean to me and my family [government/crime reports] (3.78, 0.91/3.60, 1.00); I think about what this will mean to other people [government/crime reports] (3.63, 0.99/3.60, 0.99); I think about how the story relates to other things I know [government/crime reports] (3.32, 1.01/3.28, 0.95).

7. The 15 emotional reaction items and their means and standard deviations were: *Happy*: I feel a warm inner glow (2.09, 0.91); I feel like smiling (2.81, 0.83); I feel a warm excitement (2.02, 0.86); I feel happy (2.56, 0.83); I feel like laughing (2.69, 0.92); *Angry*: I feel my blood pressure go up (2.13, 0.99); I feel like clenching my fists (2.25, 1.04); I feel like clenching my teeth (2.02, 0.97); I feel my face get tight, tense, and hard (1.94, 1.01); I get angry (2.77, 1.04); *Sad*: I feel a lump in my throat (2.21, 0.99); I feel myself getting choked up (2.17, 0.95); My heart seems to ache (2.23, 1.06); Tears come to my eyes (2.15, 1.06); I feel sad (2.73, 0.95).

References

Adams, W. C. (1978). Local public affairs content of TV news. *Journalism Quarterly, 55*, 690-695.

Bogart, L. (1980). Television news as entertainment. In P. H. Tannenbaum (Ed.), *The entertainment functions of television* (pp. 209-249). Hillsdale, NJ: Lawrence Erlbaum.

Bureau of the Census, U.S. Department of Commerce. (1983). *1980 census of population.* Washington, DC: U.S. Government Printing Office.

Bush, C. R. (1960). A system of categories for general news content. *Journalism Quarterly, 37,* 206-210.

Cegala, D. J. (1981). Interaction involvement: A cognitive dimension of communicative competence. *Communication Education, 30,* 109-121.

Chaffee, S. H., & Schleuder, J. (1986). Measurement and effects of attention to media news. *Human Communication Research, 13,* 76-107.

Comstock, G., Chaffee, S., Katzman, N., McCombs, M., & Roberts, D. (1978). *Television and human behavior.* New York: Columbia University Press.

Davitz, J. R. (1969). *The language of emotions.* New York: Academic Press.

Dominick, J. R., Wurtzel, A., & Lometti, G. (1975). Television journalism vs. show business: A content analysis of eyewitness news. *Journalism Quarterly, 52,* 213-218.

Gans, H. J. (1980). The audience for television — and in television research. In S. B. Withey & R. P. Abeles (Eds.), *Television and social behavior: Beyond violence and children* (pp. 55-81). Hillsdale, NJ: Lawrence Erlbaum.

Garramone, G. H. (1983a). Issue versus image orientation and effects of political advertising. *Communication Research, 10,* 59-76.

Garramone, G. M. (1983b). TV news and adolescent political socialization. In R. N. Bostrom (Ed.), *Communication yearbook 7* (pp. 651-669). Beverly Hills, CA: Sage.

Gerbner, G., & Gross, L. (1976). Living with television: The violence profile. *Journal of Communication, 26*(2), 173-199.

Gerbner, G., Gross, L., Morgan, M., & Signorielli, N. (1980). The "mainstreaming" of America: Violence profile no. 11. *Journal of Communication, 30*(3), 10-29.

Gerbner, G., Gross, L., Morgan, M., & Signorielli, N. (1986). Living with television: The dynamics of the cultivation process. In J. Bryant & D. Zillmann (Eds.), *Perspective on media effects* (pp. 17-40). Hillsdale, NJ: Lawrence Erlbaum.

Gerbner, G., Gross, L., Signorielli, N., & Morgan, M. (1980). Aging with television: Images on television drama and conceptions of social reality. *Journal of Communication, 30*(1), 37-47.

Graber, D. A. (1980). *Crime news and the public.* New York: Praeger.

Graber, D. A. (1984). *Processing the news: How people tame the information tide.* New York: Longman.

Greenwald, A. G., & Leavitt, C. (1984). Audience involvement in advertising: Four levels. *Journal of Consumer Research, 11,* 581-592.

Hawkins, R. P., & Pingree, S. (1982). Television's influence on social reality. In D. Pearl, L. Bouthilet, & J. Lazar (Eds.), *Television and behavior: Ten years of scientific progress and implications for the eighties* (DHHS Publication No. ADM 82-1196, Vol. 2, pp. 224-247). Washington, DC: U.S. Government Printing Office.

Hawkins, R. P., Pingree, S., & Adler, I. (1987). Searching for cognitive processes in the cultivation effect: Adult and adolescent sample in the United States and Australia. *Human Communication Research, 13,* 553-577.

Hocking, J. E. (1982). Sports and spectators: Intra-audience effects. *Journal of Communication, 32*(1), 100-108.

Jaehnig, W. B., Weaver, D. H., & Fico, F. (1981). Reporting crime and fearing crime in three communities. *Journal of Communication, 31*(1), 88-96.

Lemish, D. (1985). Soap opera viewing in college: A naturalistic inquiry. *Journal of Broadcasting & Electronic Media, 29,* 275-293.

Levine, G. F. (1986). Learned helplessness in local TV news. *Journalism Quarterly, 63,* 12-18, 23.

68   Cultivation and Involvement

Levy, M. R. (1978). The audience experience with television news. *Journalism Monographs, 55.*

Levy, M. R., & Windahl, S. (1985). The concept of audience activity. In K. E. Rosengren, L. A. Wenner, & P. Palmgreen (Eds.), *Media gratifications research: Current perspectives* (pp. 109-122). Beverly Hills, CA: Sage.

McLaughlin, B. (1965). "Intentional" and "incidental" learning in human subjects: The role of instruction to learn and motivation. *Psychological Bulletin, 63,* 359-376.

Morgan, M. (1986). Television and the erosion of regional diversity. *Journal of Broadcasting & Electronic Media, 30,* 123-139.

Palmgreen, P., Wenner, L. A., & Rayburn, J. D. (1980). Relations between gratifications sought and obtained: A study of television news. *Communication Research, 7,* 161-192.

Perse, E. M. (1986). Soap opera viewing patterns of college students and cultivation. *Journal of Broadcasting & Electronic Media, 30,* 175-193.

Perse, E. M. (1987). *Cognitive and affective involvement with local television news.* Unpublished doctoral dissertation, Kent State University, Kent, OH.

Petty, R. E., & Cacioppo, J. T. (1984). The effects of involvement on responses to argument quantity and quality: Central and peripheral routes to persuasion. *Journal of Personality and Social Psychology, 46,* 69-81.

Petty, R. E., Cacioppo, J. T., & Kasmer, J. A. (1987). The role of affect in the elaboration likelihood model of persuasion. In L. Donohue, H. E. Sypher, & E. T. Higgins (Eds.), *Communication, social cognition, and affect* (pp. 117-146). Hillsdale, NJ: Lawrence Erlbaum.

Potter, W. J. (1986). Perceived reality and the cultivation hypothesis. *Journal of Broadcasting & Electronic Media, 30,* 159-174.

Reiss, A. J., Jr., with Duncan, O. D., Hatt, P. K., & North, C. C. (1961). *Occupations and social status.* New York: Free Press of Glencoe.

Rothschild, M. L., & Ray, M. L. (1974). Involvement and political advertising effect: An exploratory experiment. *Communication Research, 1,* 264-283.

Rubin, A. M. (1983). Television uses and gratifications: The interactions of viewing patterns and motivations. *Journal of Broadcasting, 27,* 37-51.

Rubin, A. M., & Perse, E. M. (1987). Audience activity and soap opera involvement: A uses and effects investigation. *Human Communication Research, 14,* 246-268.

Rubin, A. M., Perse, E. M., & Powell, R. A. (1985). Loneliness, parasocial interaction, and local television news viewing. *Human Communication Research, 12,* 155-180.

Salmon, C. T. (1986). Perspectives on involvement in consumer and communication research. In B. Dervin & M. J. Voigt (Eds.), *Progress in communication sciences* (Vol. 7, pp. 243-268). Norwood, NJ: Ablex.

Schachter, S. (1964). The interaction of cognitive and physiological determinants of emotional state. In L. Berkowitz (Ed.), *Advances in experimental social psychology* (Vol. 1, pp. 49-80). New York: Academic Press.

Sheley, J. F., & Ashkins, C. D. (1981). Crime, crime news, and crime views. *Public Opinion Quarterly, 45,* 492-506.

Slater, D., & Elliott, W. R. (1982). Television's influence on social reality. *Quarterly Journal of Speech, 68,* 69-79.

SPSS, Inc. (1986). *SPSSX user's guide* (2nd ed.). New York: McGraw-Hill.

Tamborini, R., Zillmann, D., & Bryant, J. (1984). Fear and victimization: Exposure to television and perceptions of crime and fear. In R. N. Bostrom (Ed.), *Communication yearbook 8* (pp. 492-513). Beverly Hills, CA: Sage.

Tan, A. S. (1979). TV beauty ads and role expectations of adolescent female viewers. *Journalism Quarterly, 56,* 283-288.

Tversky, A., & Kahneman, D. (1973). Availability: A heuristic for judging frequency and probability. *Cognitive Psychology, 5,* 207-232.

Tyler, T. R. (1980). Impact of directly and indirectly experienced events: The origin of crime-related judgments and behaviors. *Journal of Personality and Social Psychology, 39,* 13-28.

U.S. Department of Commerce, Bureau of the Census. (1980). *County and city data book 1980* (10th ed.). Washington, DC: U.S. Government Printing Office.

Volgy, T. J., & Schwartz, J. E. (1980). TV entertainment programming and sociopolitical attitudes. *Journalism Quarterly, 57,* 150-155.

Weaver, J., & Wakshlag, J. (1986). Perceived vulnerability to crime, criminal victimization experience, and television viewing. *Journal of Broadcasting & Electronic Media, 30,* 141-158.

Windahl, S. (1981). Uses and gratifications at the crossroads. In G. C. Wilhoit & H. de Bock (Eds.), *Mass communication review yearbook* (Vol. 2, pp. 174-185). Beverly Hills, CA: Sage.

4

Patterns of Viewing and VCR Use:

Implications for Cultivation Analysis

JULIA R. DOBROW

Until recently, the bulk of cultivation research has been predicated on a distinction between those exposed to a great deal of television (the so-called heavy viewers), and those whose viewing hours are considerably fewer ("light viewers") (Gerbner, 1985; Gerbner & Gross, 1976; Gerbner, Gross, Morgan, & Signorielli, 1980; Gerbner, Gross, Morgan & Signorielli, 1986). Cultivation theory, itself, has been defined by and depends on the use of over-the-air television, a medium that disseminates a relatively stable set of images to large numbers of people. A considerable amount of empirical work has demonstrated that heavy exposure to these images tends to cultivate mainstream perspectives among otherwise divergent groups of viewers (Gerbner, 1985; Gerbner et al., 1986).

But what happens when a new technology enables people to view television more selectively, watching what they want to watch when they want to watch it? What happens when television has the potential to disseminate more than just the traditional mainstream messages? The videocassette recorder (VCR) presents precisely these new challenges to cultivation theory and analysis.

This chapter will explore some of the theoretical and empirical applications of VCR use for cultivation analysis. Does VCR use extend the relatively nonselective use of television, as we have known it, or does it enable people to use television in a manner more similar to the diverse and selective patterns of print use? Or does it, in fact, encourage both uses in different configurations among different groups?

There are two theoretical perspectives. First, some posit that VCR use diversifies the viewing ritual, taking viewers away from the centralized set of repetitive messages that dominates prime-time television to ones that might be more specialized. This view would posit that VCR use will contribute to the cultivation of diverse and varied perspectives. Conversely, there is the theory that VCR use intensifies existing viewing patterns, providing increased exposure to and extending the cultivation of mainstream images even further.

First released for commercial sale in the United States in 1963, the VCR's high retail price limited its use to a very small percentage of television-owning Americans for more than a decade (Lardner, 1987). But due to advances in technology and the Supreme Court ruling on home taping, the decline in retail price and subsequent growth of VCR households in the United States during the late 1970s and 1980s has been astonishing. From 50,000 units sold in 1976, comprising about 6% of all television households ("Technology versus tariffs," 1977), VCR penetration in 1987 was about 53% of all American television households ("VCR usage on fast forward," 1988). Forecasters project that VCR growth will continue, perhaps reaching 90% of all American homes by the turn of the century ("Video News," 1986). Such statistics clearly indicate that the VCR is a prevalent force that must be considered in any research involving television viewing, cultivation included.

The flexibility and versatility of the VCR enables viewers to view both prerecorded tapes (which might or might not match the messages of mainstream television), as well as to tape over-the-air television programs and play them back later (time shifting). Levy (1980, 1983) found that over 80% of his sample used their VCRs primarily to tape and play back television shows. Donohue and Henke (1985) found that among their respondents, taping television shows to play back at a more convenient time was ranked as the most valued function of the VCR. These data regarding the time-shifting function of VCRs raise a most important question: if the primary or most valued function of a VCR is its ability to play back television programs, are viewers being exposed to more of the same messages, thus concentrating their viewing even further around favorite programs or genres of program?

On the other hand, there are data that indicate that the primary and most highly rated function of the VCR for its users is not its ability to play back television shows but, rather, its ability to permit the viewing of prerecorded videocassettes. A recent study from AGB Television Research found that the majority of time spent using VCRs was spent in playing prerecorded tapes ("VCR usage on fast forward," 1988). Are viewers using their VCRs primarily to watch material other than mainstream television programming?

Still a third function of the VCR is often cited by its users as the primary or most highly valued function. This is the flexibility that the VCR engenders: the ability to permit viewing of whatever materials a viewer selects, whenever she or he selects them (Dobrow, 1987). Does VCR use then pose a challenge to the contention of Gerbner et al. (1986) that "the audience is always the group available at a certain time of the day, the week, and the season, regardless of the programs. Most viewers watch by the clock and either do not know what they will watch when they turn on the set or follow established routines rather than choose each program as they would choose a book, a movie or an article" (p. 19).

Thus, empirical and theoretical work regarding VCR use still leaves us with many questions. How does VCR use fit into and/or alter existing models and patterns of media behavior, and what are the implications for cultivation research given these conflicting results?

To begin to explore these questions, a three-part research design was employed. Two separate sets of personal interviews were conducted with VCR owners in urban and suburban towns in the greater Boston area, yielding a total of more than 50 completed viewer profiles. To provide an aggregate base for the research, over 500 people (both VCR owners and non-VCR owners) were interviewed through a random digit telephone survey, stratified by exchange. The research was conducted in early 1986, a time when approximately one-third of all American television households had a VCR (*Video Marketing Newsletter*, 1985).

Results

Differences between Heavy and Light Viewers

At the time when this research was conducted, VCR owners were a more upscale group than nonowners; nationally, most had completed college or some form of graduate school, and had incomes over $35,000 ("Video News," 1985). The demographic profile of those in this sample

Table 4.1 Light and Heavy Viewing and VCR Ownership

	VCR owners	*Non-VCR*	*Row total*
Heavy viewers (3 or more hours viewed per day)	35.5% (n=89)	66.9% (n=170)	51.3% (n=259)
Light viewers (0-3 hours viewed per day)	64.5% (n=162)	33.1% (n=84)	48.7% (n=246)
Totals	100.0% (n=251)	100.0% (n=254)	100.0% (n=505)

$p < .001$.
gamma = .43.

was not dissimilar to the national profile. Within the total telephone survey sample (n = 505) about half had VCRs (n = 251). 46.8% of those owning VCRs also subscribed to some kind of cable or pay television service. Among VCR owners in the sample, 51.2% had college degrees, about a third had graduate or professional degrees, and 48.6% reported incomes of $35,000 or more. Almost a third of the VCR owners in the telephone survey sample had two or more VCRs (32.3%, n = 81). Those in the in-depth interview group had similar characteristics.

Research has documented that this type of demographic group tends to be relatively light and consequently relatively selective viewers (Comstock, Chaffee, Katzman, McCombs, & Roberts, 1978; Gerbner, 1985). However, in this sample a little more than one-third of the VCR owners could be considered heavy viewers, according to their self-reports of hours of television viewed on a daily basis, including any programs recorded and played back. Heavy viewers were considered those who reported watching 3 or more hours on weeknights and 4 or more hours on weekends. By contrast, about two-thirds of the non-VCR owning sample could be considered heavy viewers using the same measure. See Table 4.1.

Significant differences were found between the viewing patterns of VCR owners according to their self-reports of hours viewed. On both weekdays and weekends, heavy viewing VCR owners used the VCR to

Table 4.2 Weekday and Weekend Time-Shifting Patterns of Heavy
and Light Viewing VCR Owners

Weekdays	Light viewers	Heavy viewers
Time-shifting		
A lot	18.5%	38.2%
	(n=30)	(n=34)
A little	34.0%	31.5%
	(n=55)	(n=28)
Not at all	47.5%	30.3%
	(n=77)	(n=27)
Totals	100.0%	100.0%
	(n=162)	(n=89)
Weekends		
A lot	21.0%	75.6%
	(n=28)	(n=87)
A little	42.2%	19.1%
	(n=58)	(n=22)
Not at all	36.8%	5.3%
	(n=50)	(n=6)
Totals	100.0%	100.0%
	(n=136)	(n=115)

time shift more frequently than did lighter viewing VCR owners. Especially on the weekends, heavy viewers reported that they were far more likely to use their VCRs to time shift "a lot" than were light viewers. See Table 4.2.

Among VCR owners, heavier viewers appeared to use their VCRs primarily for the purpose of time shifting. Lighter viewing VCR owners, on the other hand, reported using their VCRs primarily to watch movies and other types of tapes (including how-to and other instructional tapes, videocassettes having to do with individualized ethnic communities, etc.), and thus diversifying the content to which they were exposed. Controlling for age, gender, income, education, and cable or pay TV subscription within subgroups did not alter these relationships.

Data from the in-depth interviews supported the results of the telephone survey. "I'm a TV junkie" admitted one heavier-viewing VCR owner. "The best thing about this machine is that it lets me watch more of what I want to." One woman stated that "The best thing about having a VCR is being able to see my soaps. Now I can tape three soap operas every day when I'm at work, and I just watch them all in one or two sittings over the weekend. It's great — I can watch more soaps than ever before!"

Concentration or Diversification?

The data on using a VCR for time shifting frames the larger question of whether VCR use in fact concentrates television viewing around favorite shows or types of shows, or whether it actually enables people to diversify their total viewing. This is an important question for those interested in cultivation analysis, since over-the-air television has been measured and analyzed consistently, revealing a remarkable cohesiveness of message. Are VCR-owning viewers going to use this technology to time shift and watch more of the same television fare, or are they using it to diversify their viewing? The results from this work indicate that VCR use does both, although again there were significant differences between heavy and light television users. When reduced to a dichotomous variable, it became clear that while heavy viewers used their VCRs primarily to time shift, lighter viewers used the technology primarily to view prerecorded videocassettes. See Table 4.3.

Some of the personal interviews with VCR owners further clarified how being attracted to specific types of programming led them to purchase a VCR in the first place. Among the heavier viewers, many respondents stated that a desire to watch more of the programming they most enjoyed — be it sports, news, soap operas, or some other television genre — contributed to a decision to purchase a VCR. An earlier study by Levy (1980) corroborates this finding. Levy noted that VCR owners used their machines to record a relatively small number of existing TV genres, including movies, soap operas, and children's programs. He concluded that ". . . the possibility of 'control over content,' a significant part of the public definition of video, may be an illusion, and that video does little to promote cultural pluralism" (Levy, 1987, p. 467). It must be noted, however, that at the time of this earlier study, VCR penetration nationwide was quite low (VCRs were in fewer than 2% of all American television households) and video rental outlets were not nearly as widespread was they were even 5 years later.

Table 4.3 Differences in Primary Use of VCR between Heavy and Light Viewing VCR Owners

	Light viewers	Heavy viewers
Time-shifting	29.1% (n=47)	62.9% (n=56)
Viewing prerecorded videocassettes	70.9% (n=115)	37.1% (n=33)
Totals	100.0% (n=162)	100.0% (n=89)

However, in the present work many others stated that they used their VCRs primarily to *diversify* their viewing. For the most part, these tended to be lighter viewers. One woman, typical of several light viewers who were parents, said, "I tape and save PBS programs and good movies for my children. Kids are going to watch TV — you can't really stop them — and they might as well be watching good things. The VCR enables my husband and I to ensure that they're watching something other than the endless junk the networks feed to kids."

The majority of those in both the telephone survey and personal interviews who could be considered light viewers stated that the thing they liked best about the VCR was the ability it gave them to view prerecorded cassettes. The largest percentage of light viewing VCR owners in the telephone survey (28.1%) stated that they valued their VCRs most because they could watch prerecorded movies, while another 8.8% cited the ability to view other kinds of prerecorded tapes (including exercise tapes, music videos, and ethnically oriented tapes) as the most valued function.

The in-depth interviews with lighter viewers revealed that many people make a distinction between "watching the VCR" and "watching television." "I'm not a big TV nut," said one man, "but I watch the VCR a lot." Many respondents stated that "watching the VCR" was an activity entailing watching other than taped network or cable television programs, including the viewing of a plethora of prerecorded videocassettes.

Thus, in both the telephone survey and the in-depth interviews, it was clear from their reliance on the time-shifting function of VCRs and from the descriptions of program viewing preferences, that the heavier viewers of television used their VCRs to concentrate their viewing. The lighter viewers, however, used their VCRs primarily to diversify their total media content through their reliance on the VCR to see other than network or cable programming, and through their stated preferences for prerecorded videocassettes.

The data from both the telephone survey and the in-depth interviews revealed that apart from heavy-light viewer distinctions, there were other significant and observable differences in VCR use by subgroup stratification. Most notably, members of particular ethnic groups reported using the VCR to view videocassettes in languages other than English. Respondents from a variety of ethnic and cultural backgrounds (including Indian, Russian, Japanese, Egyptian, Grecian, Mexican, and Filipino), ranging from first generation to third generation immigrants, used the VCR primarily to view films, television programs, language instruction tapes, and sporting events from their or their families' country of origin. While only a relatively small percentage (17.3%) of the total in-person interview sample, the responses of this segment show, again, how the VCR can be used by some to view other than mainstream programs.

Telephone survey and in-depth interview results confirmed that members of these subgroups see the VCR as a way to bypass mainstream American programming, for the most part, and view programming that they feel is more relevant to them. Typifying the responses given was one from a Greek-American woman in her mid-60s who had spent all of her adult life in America, but rents Greek tapes once or twice a week. "I grew up there, and I like to see these things. They remind me of my childhood, my parents, of where my roots are."

Another respondent (a young Egyptian man) said that when he first came to the United States, he would regularly drive a 100-mile round trip to see Egyptian films on a friend's VCR. "American TV wasn't so relevant to me" he said. "I would drive many hours to see something that reminded me of home, and to spend time with others who had come from my country."

It is not known how widespread this type of VCR use is. But what is certain is that VCRs enable people to watch programming other than the relatively stable set of messages comprising network programming.

The VCR and Selectivity

Finally, what of the potential flexibility of the VCR? Respondents were asked to give an indication of their selectivity regarding viewing by stating whether they were more likely to plan their viewing ahead of time, or whether they generally just viewed whatever was on. While it was recognized that some people might consider it more socially desirable to state that they plan their viewing in advance, and that such self-reported responses are of unknown reliability, a carefully worded question that had yielded differential responses in pretesting was asked to assess the relationship of VCR use and planning of viewing. Interestingly, among the VCR owners in the telephone survey, regardless of whether they were heavy or light television viewers, the vast majority (77.2%) reported that they usually planned their television viewing, rather than simply watching whatever was on. Within all educational, income, and age groups, those who owned VCRs were far more likely to say that they planned their viewing than those who did not own VCRs. These relationships were statistically significant ($p < .001$).

Another indication of the potential for increased selectivity that the VCR gives its users was demonstrated by respondents in both the telephone and personal interviews regarding what they valued most about their VCRs. Almost a quarter (24.5%) of the survey respondents and many in the in-depth interviews reported that what they liked most was the flexibility, freedom, and convenience afforded by the VCR technology. Respondents' comments indicated that not only did some actually use their VCRs to control their viewing by actively selecting types of programming or recording certain television programs, but others apparently valued their VCRs for the *feeling* of control that the machines gave them. One man summed it up by saying, "No longer does my TV control me – I control my TV!"

Implications for Cultivation Analysis

The research described here has many implications for cultivation analysis. Contrary to traditional notions of the homogeneous mass audience and running counter to assertions that television viewing is a remarkably undifferentiated activity, all of the VCR-owning television viewers in this sample actively sought to select and control their viewing. But an important distinction was found between the viewing patterns of those who were heavier and lighter television viewers: the heavier viewers used their VCRs to watch more of the same type of programming they enjoyed, while the lighter viewers used the VCR to watch other kinds of content they liked.

If indeed future research, with larger and more diverse samples, bears out this finding that VCR use enables — and perhaps encourages — viewers to watch television selectively, two questions must be considered. First, if heavy viewers are concentrating their viewing, will we see greater evidence for cultivation than before? Not only does the VCR enable the heavy viewers to see a greater proportion of mainstream television programming (and the evidence suggests that this is precisely what they watch), it also gives them the opportunity to view the same programs or messages multiple times. In other work consistent with this hypothesis, Morgan and Rothschild (1983) found greater cultivation among adolescents who had access to cable television, a medium that provides viewers with more of the same programming rather than increasing viewing diversity. Clearly, the potential exists for researchers to find more evidence for cultivation (including mainstreaming and resonance) among VCR users, because the VCR theoretically allows people to become even heavier viewers than ever. Whether or not the VCR will augment the cultivating power of television in these ways is not yet known.

However, it might be argued that those who are already prone to watching television selectively are those who buy VCRs in the first place. As Sears and Freedman (1974) point out, such de facto selective viewing might represent ". . . little more than highly educated persons who . . . also share a common set of . . . social attitudes" (p. 219). This raises the second question. As the ability to watch by the program and not by the clock spreads further through the American (and indeed, world-wide) viewing public, will the greater potential for selectivity to take viewers away from the "centralized system of storytelling" be realized? Will those belonging to demographic groups not previously known for being light or selective viewers change their viewing habits when the widespread presence of the VCR enables them to do so?

The data presented here from the light viewers adds another dimension to these questions. Lighter viewers have always tended to have more diverse media habits, but VCRs might well enable them to move even further from the mainstream. If people are selecting program content containing messages that are consistent with their own opinions, if VCRs allow for the viewing of many types of content, and if it can be demonstrated that this content does indeed contain messages and images other than those shown on network television, then we might predict the cultivation of different perspectives by different groups over the long term. These perspectives might be determined more by social and cultural characteristics than by the simple demographic characteristics that audience researchers and advertisers now say predict audience composition and buying behavior.

This latter possibility challenges cultivation researchers both philosophically and methodologically. We must develop ways of studying VCR owners longitudinally, to see if owning a versatile technology changes or reinforces viewing behavior. Will patterns of VCR use change other media use patterns? Several researchers have suggested that as a "new" technology, the VCR might be subject to so-called novelty effects (Donohue & Henke, 1985; Levy, 1987). Will patterns of video use change over time once the VCR has become an even more familiar presence in American homes for greater amounts of time? What effects might this have on patterns of cultivation analysis?

Levy (1987) raised the very important question of whether people think of VCRs as different from or merely an extension of television, and how then their perceptions about video are similar to or different from their perceptions about "older" media, including film, radio, television, and printed media. It will be interesting to follow up on the results presented here and see if indeed audiences do make a distinction between "watching television" and "watching the VCR," for if the qualitative experience is considered different, there might well be observable differences in use patterns. Audience measurement companies, including A. C. Nielsen and AGB Television Research, have begun to develop ways of ascertaining when a VCR is being used to record programs off the air, and when it is playing back recorded tapes. But the "Peoplemeter" and "fingerprinting" techniques are only in their early stages of development, and more exact measurements will be critical for researchers, as well as for network, video, and advertising officials.

We must begin to develop ways of better surveying prerecorded videocassette use, to see not only what is viewed, but by whom and under what social conditions. This is not only an issue for cultivation researchers in the United States. Researchers studying VCR use in countries other than the United States have found patterns of use that involve more playback of prerecorded videocassettes than time shifting (Boyd, 1987; Cohen, 1987; Boyd & Straubhaar, 1985). But the large number of American television and movie tapes imported by people in other countries (either legally or through an ever-growing black market of pirated cassettes) raises the question for researchers abroad of whether the influx of American programming might give rise to similar types of cultivation patterns that have been observed in the United States.

Finally, cultivation researchers must start the monumental task of ascertaining what the messages in prerecorded videocassette tapes are. We might predict that messages in the majority of prerecorded video-cassettes will be similar to the messages of television, since the majority of rented material in the United States is films, often produced by the same people and systems that produce television. One such content analysis study is already underway to explore whether the proliferation of tapes for children ("kidvid") offers messages that are substantially different from those on network television (Barcus, 1988). But clearly many more such studies need to be conducted to systematically docu-ment the messages of the many segments of the videocassette world.

If VCRs are used by different subgroups to narrowcast and see programming reflective of individual ethnic, religious, cultural, or other values, future researchers must determine not only if video-cassettes present cultural content that is significantly different from mainstream broadcasting, but also must start to determine if VCR use does or does not contribute to the cultivation of individual perspectives. The most important task, however, will be to ascertain if this type of individualized programming could ever occur in sufficient quantities to take viewers away from the American mainstream.

VCR use is neither monolithic nor unidimensional. The data pre-sented in this chapter show that for some people, VCRs enable viewing more of the same content, while for others, they provide more alterna-tives from which to select. These data certainly suggest that VCR use should enhance cultivation research, by making more apparent than ever the differences between groups of heavy and light viewers.

References

Agostino, D., Terry, H., & Johnson, R. (1980). Home video recorders: Rights and ratings. *Journal of Communication 30*, 28-35.

Barcus, F. E. (1988, May). *The availability and costs of children's video.* Paper presented at the International Communication Association convention, New Orleans.

Boyd, D. (1987). Home video diffusion and utilization in Arabian Gulf states. In M. Levy (Ed.), *The VCR age* (pp. 544-555). Newbury Park, CA: Sage.

Boyd, D., & Straubhaar, J. (1985). Developmental impact of the home videocassette recorder on Third World countries. *Journal of Broadcasting and Electronic Media 29*, 5-21.

Bryant, J., & Zillmann, D. (Eds.) (1986). *Perspectives on media effects.* Hillsdale, NJ: Lawrence Erlbaum.

Cohen, A. (1987). Decision making in VCR rental libraries. In M. Levy (Ed.), *The VCR age* (pp. 495-508). Newbury Park, CA: Sage.

Comstock, G., Chaffee, S., Katzman, N., McCombs, M., & Roberts, D. (1978). *Television and human behavior.* New York: Columbia University Press.

Dobrow, J. R. (1987). *The social and cultural implications of VCR use: How VCR use concentrates and diversifies viewing.* Unpublished doctoral dissertation, The Annenberg School of Communications, University of Pennsylvania.

Donohue, T. R., & Henke, L. (1985). *The impact of video cassette recorders on traditional television and cable viewing habit and preferences.* National Association of Broadcasters. Unpublished manuscript.

Gerbner, G. (1985). Mass media discourse: Message system analysis as a component of cultural indicators. In T. A. van Dijk (Ed.), *Discourse and communication: New approaches to the analysis of mass media discourse and communication.* Berlin: Walter de Guyters.

Gerbner, G., & Gross, L. (1976). Living with television: The violence profile. *Journal of Communication, 26*(2), 172-199.

Gerbner, G., Gross, L., Morgan, M., & Signorielli, N. (1980). The 'mainstreaming' of America. *Journal of Communication, 30*(3), 10-29.

Gerbner, G., Gross, L., Morgan, M., & Signorielli, N. (1986). Living with television: The dynamics of the cultivation process. In J. Bryant & D. Zillmann (Eds.), *Perspectives on media effects.* Hillsdale, NJ: Lawrence Erlbaum.

Lardner, J. (1987). *Fast forward: Hollywood, the Japanese, and the VCR wars.* New York: Norton.

Levy, M. (1980). Program playback preferences in VCR households. *Journal of Broadcasting and Electronic Media 24*, 327-336.

Levy, M. (1983). The time-shifting use of home video recorders. *Journal of Broadcasting and Electronic Media 27*, 263-268.

Levy, M. (1987). Some problems of VCR research. In M. Levy (Ed.), *The VCR age* (pp. 461-470). Newbury Park, CA: Sage.

Levy, M. (Ed.). (1987). The VCR age. *American Behavioral Scientist 30*(5). Newbury Park, CA: Sage.

Morgan, M., & Rothschild, N. (1983). Impact of the new television technology. *Youth and Society, 15*(1), 33-50.

Sears, D., & Freedman, J. (1971). Selective exposure to information: A critical review. In W. Schramm & D. Roberts (Eds.), *The process and effects of mass communication*, (rev. ed., pp. 209-234). Urbana: University of Illinois Press.

Technology versus tariffs. (1977, April). *Forbes*, 27-28.

VCR usage on fast forward. (1988, April). *Broadcasting* 114(14).

Video Marketing Newsletter 6(9). (1985, October).

Video News. (1986, February). *Boston Globe.*

Video News. (1985, May). *Boston Globe.*

5

Television's Mean and Dangerous World:

A Continuation of the Cultural Indicators Perspective

NANCY SIGNORIELLI

Almost since the advent of television people have been concerned about its amount of violence (Smythe, 1954). In the 1950s violence appeared in two-thirds to three-quarters of all television plays at a rate of between 6 and 10 incidents per hour in prime time and at rates three or four times as large in children's programming (mostly cartoons). Clark and Blankenberg (1972) found violence in one-third of a sample of movies released between 1930 and 1969, and in half of all movies shown on television. They also found that violence was prevalent in network television news, making up 16% of all news items. These stories were longer than nonviolent items and unrelated to crime statistics.

Dominick (1973) found that two-thirds of all prime-time television programs contained some violence and that 60% of the violence could be categorized as assault, armed robbery, or murder. Unlike real life, violence by strangers was more frequent than violence by those who were known to the victim. Haney and Manzolati (1980) found that television crime and violence emphasize greed and other personal characteristics but rarely address underlying social conditions. In another study, Dominick (1978) noted that television presents violence from the law-enforcement point of view, emphasizes personal violence, ignores social aspects, does not present an adequate picture of the legal process, and does not provide accurate information about crime, criminals, and real-life violence. An analysis of television series with law enforcement or other violent themes broadcast between 1950 and 1976 (Taylor & Dozier, 1983) found that violence was systematically presented within a framework that suggests that people have an unquestioned moral and/or legal right to use violence, including deadly force, to protect the status quo.

Analyses of network dramatic programming have consistently revealed the abundance of violence in story lines. Dating from the studies by Smythe (1954) and Head (1954), violence has been one of the most prevalent themes in programming. Greenberg, Edison, Korzenny, Fernando-Collado & Atkin (1980) analyzed dramatic series during three seasons of programming and found that violence (defined as *physical aggression*) occurred more than 9 times per hour between 8 and 9 P.M., more than 11 times per hour between 9 and 11 P.M., and more than 21 times per hour on Saturday morning children's programs. And, as will be seen in this chapter, violence continues to be one of the most salient and important themes in network dramatic programming.

There have been numerous studies of the consequences of this constant exposure to violence on television. The individualized and mostly psychological approach, including numerous studies on aggression (Bandura, Ross, & Ross, 1963; Bandura, 1968, 1978; Zillmann, 1982), has had a long life and has made numerous contributions to research on media violence. Studies of the social and situational factors in exposure, such as Drabman and Thomas's (1977) investigation of when children, exposed to violence, seek adult assistance when confronted with increasing violent behavior of younger children (visible on a videotape monitor) are relatively rare.

There also have not been many opportunities to examine what happens when television is introduced into a culture. Williams (1986) and her collaborators, however, were able to observe children's behavior during free play and to obtain teacher and peer ratings of aggression in three Canadian communities: one that had television continuously, one with limited opportunities to watch television, and one in which television was just beginning to be available. These researchers found that the children in the community that had recently introduced television were both physically and verbally more aggressive 2 years after the introduction of television than they were before, and more so than the children of the other similar communities who had been exposed to television for some time. Neither age nor amount of viewing or program preference seemed to make much difference.

Cultivation analysis is another approach to the investigation of television and violence (Gerbner, Gross, Jackson-Beech, Jeffries-Fox, & Signorielli, 1978; Gerbner, Gross, Morgan, & Signorielli, 1980, 1982), broadening the scope from looking for aggressive or violent effects to inquiring into the wider consequences of living with a medium in which complex images of violence are deeply and inescapably embedded. This perspective has also found support from investigators other than the Cultural Indicators research team (see, for example, Hawkins & Pingree, 1982).

Doob and Macdonald (1977, 1979) reported that exposure to media violence boosts public estimates of crime and violence, although not equally in all groups. Carlson (1983) found significant relationships between exposure to crime shows and approval of police brutality and bias against civil liberties. Bryant, Corveth, and Brown (1981) and Zillmann and Wakshlag (1985) found that television viewing was related to feelings of anxiety and fear of victimization, although Wober (1978) did not find similar patterns in Great Britain. More recently, however, Gunter and Wober (1983) found that heavy viewers report higher risks than comparable groups of light viewers from lightning, flooding, and terrorist bomb attacks. A large-scale survey by Research and Forecasts (1980) concluded that exposure to violence both in the press and on television relates to expressions of fear. Finally, Haney and Manzolati (1980) found that television tended to cultivate the presumption of guilt rather than innocence of a suspect, the belief that legal rights protect the guilty rather than the innocent, and the belief the police are not restricted by law in their pursuit of suspects.

The Cultural Indicators Perspective

A book on cultivation analysis would not be complete without a discussion of the area of research that is most commonly linked with it — violence and fear. This chapter presents recent findings of the Cultural Indicators project regarding to these measures. It looks at violence in network dramatic programming and continues the examination of the consequences of living with violence-laden programming using data from the NORC General Social Surveys fielded in 1980, 1982, 1983, 1985, and 1986. This chapter examines these data in individual subgroups as well as across the entire data set applying stringent multiple controls.

As past work has consistently exhibited, video mayhem pervades the typical American home and Americans have, for the last 20 years at least, been immersed in a tide of violent representations that is historically unprecedented. Even more significant than the sheer amount of televised violence is its role in the world of television and in the lives of viewers. The conventional media definition reducing that role as only or primarily related to aggression and potential threats to law and order tends to focus attention on only one concern, and to distract attention from more pervasive potential consequences.

Violence is a complex social scenario and its purpose is usually to dominate, control, and terrorize — in short, to make people do things they do not want to do. Symbolic violence, such as that seen on television, demonstrates the same lessons but in an entertaining and painless way. Television tends to confirm and cultivate the traditional distribution of power in the symbolic and real worlds — domination by white males. It tells us who can get away with what against whom, where the safe or dangerous places are, and what one's chances of encountering or falling victim to violence may be. We would thus postulate that the lessons of violence, and especially victimization, are fear, intimidation, and a sense of vulnerability.

The theory can be summed up as follows. The convergence of research indicates that exposure to violence occasionally incites some viewers to commit and/or imitate specific violent actions and that some people may also become desensitized to violence. For most viewers, however, television's mean and dangerous world tends to cultivate a sense of relative danger, mistrust, insecurity, vulnerability, dependence, and — despite its supposedly "entertaining" nature — alienation and gloom. Specifically, this chapter explores the hypothesis that those who watch more television will express greater interpersonal mistrust and perceive the world as a "mean" place as well as endorse statements that reflect alienation and gloom. In addition mainstreaming — the sharing of common outlooks among the heavy viewers in those demographic groups whose light viewers hold more divergent views — should occur.

Methodology

Message System Analysis

The analysis examines data relating to violence isolated in programs and characters in annual week-long samples of prime-time and weekend-daytime (children's) network dramatic programs broadcast between 1967 and 1985.[1] Violence is defined in a simple and straightforward way as the overt expression of physical force (with or without a weapon) against self or other on pain of being hurt or killed, or actually hurting or killing. Idle threats, verbal abuse, or gestures without credible violent consequences are not coded as violence. Any act of violence that fits the definition, regardless of conventional notions about types of violence that may have "serious" effects, is coded. This includes violence that occurs in realistic, serious, fantasy, or humorous contexts. "Accidental" violence and "acts of nature" are recorded because they are always purposeful in fiction, claim victims, and demonstrate power. Dramatic action is never accidental or "natural." There is also considerable research evidence that humor and fantasy are effective forms in which to convey serious lessons (Ellis & Sekera, 1972; Haynes, 1978; Lovas, 1961).

The sample consists of 2,134 programs (1,211 in prime time and 923 during the weekend-daytime hours) and 6,206 major characters (3,868 in prime time and 2,338 on Saturday and Sunday mornings). Coders isolate only those details presented in the particular episode included in the sample. Details of a program's or character's portrayal that may be "well-known" by "fans" would not be coded unless specifically mentioned in the episode. The aggregation of data from all available sample years provides not only a description of images found in network prime-time programs but, because many of the programs in the earlier samples are currently syndicated and broadcast on independent stations, the data base also reflects the images viewers are exposed to now when they watch independent stations.

Each program in the 17 annual samples was independently coded by two pairs of trained monitors in order to provide data for a full reliability analysis. (The final data set consists of a random selection of one of these two codings for each program.) An agreement coefficient (which takes chance agreement into account) was then calculated for each item (see Krippendorff, 1980). All variables included in this analysis have agreement coefficients of at least .60.

Three sets of observations are combined and reported in the Violence Index, a single indicator sensitive to a range of multidimensional program characteristics. These observations measure the extent to which violence occurs at all in the programs sampled, the rate of violent actions per program and per hour, and the involvement of major characters in violence — either as characters who commit violence (hurt or kill others), characters who are victimized (hurt or killed), or both.[2] These measures have achieved high intercoder reliability over the years and meet the statistical and empirical requirements of an index: unidimensionality and internal homogeneity (Signorielli, Gross, & Morgan, 1982).

Cultivation Analysis

The hypotheses under investigation follow up previous research and specify that there should be a relationship between television viewing and expressing views reflecting a "mean world" (interpersonal mistrust) and alienation and gloom. Previous work would suggest the occurrence of mainstreaming among specific subgroups; that is, for certain demographic subgroups, heavy viewers will be more similar than light viewers in espousing these views.

These hypotheses were tested using data from the 1980, 1982, 1983, 1985, and 1986 NORC General Social Surveys that examine the relationships between television viewing and responses to the questions used to calculate two indices: the Mean World Index and the Index of Alienation and Gloom (Anomie Index). Both indices are additive in nature, summing respondents' agreement with statements reflecting interpersonal mistrust (a mean world) and statements reflecting alienation and gloom (anomie).

Alienation and gloom were measured in the 1980, 1982, and 1985 NORC General Social Surveys by three of Srole's (1956) anomie items (TV answer italicized):

1. In spite of what some people say, the lot (situation/condition) of the average man is getting worse, not better. (*agree*, disagree)
2. It's hardly fair to bring a child into the world with the way things look for the future. (*agree*, disagree)
3. Most public officials (people in public office) are not interested in the problems of the average man. (*agree*, disagree)

The reliability of the index of Alienation and Gloom was measured by Cronbach's alpha (a = .56). Only respondents who answered all three items were included in the calculations; those who agreed with two or more of these items were categorized in the "high" alienation and gloom group.

The Mean World Index was made up of the following items, similar to Rosenberg's (1957) "faith in people" scale, asked in the 1980, 1983, and 1986 General Social Surveys (TV answer in italic):

1. Would you say that most of the time people try to be helpful, or that they are mostly *just looking out for themselves*?

2. Do you think that most people would *try to take advantage of you* if they got a chance, or would they try to be fair?

3. Generally speaking, would you say that most people can be trusted or that *you can't be too careful in dealing with people*?

Again, this additive index was made up only of those respondents who answered all three questions, and those who gave the "pessimistic" (underlined) reply to two or more of these questions were included in the "high-scoring" group. The Mean World Index was also reliable; Cronbach's alpha was .67.

Two types of analyses were conducted. First, the relationship between television viewing and these indices was examined by calculating zero-, first-, and sixth- or seventh-order partial correlation coefficients, controlling for sex, age, education, race, income, subjective social class, and political orientation. Second, respondents were divided into two groups—those who had high scores and those who had low scores on either the Mean World or the Alienation and Gloom indices. They were also classified into light (under 2 hours each day), medium (2 to 4 hours each day), and heavy (over 4 hours each day) television viewers[3]. Cross-tabulations of these indices with the reported daily television exposure, independently controlling for the above described control variables, were conducted. Respondents were compared in terms of the cultivation differential (CD)—the percent of heavy viewers minus the percent of light viewers who give a specific response. The degree of the relationship, within each subgroup, was measured using the gamma statistic, with significance level indicated by tau-b or tau-c.

Findings and Discussion

Violence on Television

This analysis shows that the basic structure of themes, characterizations, action, and fate in the world of dramatic television has been remarkably stable for the last 20 years. Children's programs are mostly cartoons (90%) and have been saturated with mostly nonlethal violence. The rate of violent incidents in children's programs is typically more than three times the rate in prime-time; the 19-year cumulative average is 21 violent incidents per hour. Most of this programming (73%) has violence that is at least partly comic or humorous in nature. By comparison, only one in five prime-time programs have violence that is wholly or partly comic or humorous in nature. See Table 5.1.

The analysis also reveals that violence is used in programming to demonstrate who can get away with what against whom, and who should submit to whom. It tells us who matters and who doesn't. Violence as a scenario of social relationships and power is examined by calculating a ratio of violents (those who commit violence) to victims (those who are victimized) in different demographic groups. This calculation yields a risk ratio of relative strengths and vulnerabilities. It shows the calculus of risks in violent encounters: each group's relative chances of ending up victims rather than victors.

In prime-time network programs, for every 10 male characters who commit violence there are 11 who fall victim to it. But for every 10 female perpetrators of violence, there are 16 victims. As television drama goes down the social pecking order (see Table 5.2), it raises the price to be paid for getting involved in violence. Minority and foreign women pay the highest price, no matter how large their role. For every 10 perpetrators, they suffer 22 and 21 victims, respectively. Among the 10 groups most likely to be victimized, only 1 (elderly men) is not female; the only group, however, who is more likely to commit violence than be victimized is formerly married women—for every 10 of these women who are victimized, 11 commit violence. "Bad" men and "bad" women are equally likely to commit violence as be victimized. On the whole, groups of male characters are about equally likely to be victimized as to commit violence.

Table 5.1 Measures of Violence for Prime-Time and Weekend-Daytime Programs

	67-68	69-70	71-72	73-74*	75-76*	77-78	1979	1980	1981	1982	1983	1984	1985	TOTAL
Prime-Time Programs														
SAMPLES (100%)	N	N	N	N	N	N	N	N	N	N	N	N	N	N
Programs analyzed	121	125	122	177	195	131	64	64	65	77	63	65	67	1336
Leading characters analyzed	340	350	386	609	603	401	218	229	216	247	195	221	217	4232
PREVALENCE	%	%	%	%	%	%	%	%	%	%	%	%	%	%
Programs with violence (%P)	75.2	66.4	73.8	67.8	72.3	70.2	70.3	73.4	80.0	63.6	73.0	78.5	79.1	71.9
RATE	N	N	N	N	N	N	N	N	N	N	N	N	N	N
Number of violent acts	549	434	533	919	1058	656	344	336	343	278	280	415	421	6566
Rate per program (R/P)	4.5	3.5	4.4	5.2	5.4	5.0	5.4	5.2	5.3	3.6	4.4	6.4	6.3	4.9
Rate per hour (R/H)	5.2	3.9	4.8	5.3	5.9	5.2	5.7	5.7	5.9	4.6	4.8	6.9	6.8	5.4
ROLES (% LEADING CHARACTERS)	%	%	%	%	%	%	%	%	%	%	%	%	%	%
Involved in violence (%V)	64.4	49.4	53.9	53.7	58.5	53.4	53.7	50.7	50.0	48.2	53.3	63.3	58.5	54.9
Involved in killing (%K)	17.4	9.4	13.5	16.9	13.3	8.5	6.9	4.8	5.6	6.5	9.7	12.7	11.1	11.5
VIOLENCE INDEX:	176.4	140.0	159.4	159.3	166.7	152.5	153.0	150.7	158.0	134.7	154.4	181.1	174.9	158.9

VI = (%P) + 2(R/H) + 2(R/P) + %V + %K

*The figures given for 1973-74 include a spring 1975 sample and those for 1975-76 include a spring 1976 sample.

(Continued on page 94)

Table 5.1 (Continued)

Weekend-Daytime (Children's) Programs

	67-68	69-70	71-72	73-74*	75-76*	77-78	1979	1980	1981	1982	1983	1984	1985	TOTAL
SAMPLES (100%)	N	N	N	N	N	N	N	N	N	N	N	N	N	N
Programs analyzed	62	107	81	114	141	101	62	66	69	44	54	55	53	1009
Leading characters analyzed	115	223	166	378	351	252	163	165	186	120	142	146	149	2556
PREVALENCE	%	%	%	%	%	%	%	%	%	%	%	%	%	%
Programs with violence (%P)	93.5	97.2	88.9	93.9	93.6	94.1	91.9	97.0	91.3	97.7	92.6	98.2	92.5	94.0
RATE	N	N	N	N	N	N	N	N	N	N	N	N	N	N
Number of violent acts	323	694	489	643	807	616	284	407	418	306	350	404	326	6067
Rate per program (R/P)	5.2	6.5	6.0	5.6	5.7	6.1	4.6	6.2	6.1	6.9	6.5	7.3	6.1	6.0
Rate per hour (R/H)	22.3	25.5	16.0	12.6	16.8	19.9	17.2	26.9	30.9	30.3	25.5	27.3	21.3	20.1
ROLES (% LEADING CHARACTERS)	%	%	%	%	%	%	%	%	%	%	%	%	%	%
Involved in violence (%V)	84.3	89.7	73.5	73.8	82.6	81.0	74.8	89.7	83.9	93.3	80.3	89.7	75.8	81.7
Involved in killing (%K)	9.6	2.2	1.2	1.3	1.4	0.0	0.0	1.2	0.0	0.8	0.0	2.1	0.7	1.4
VIOLENCE INDEX:	242.4	253.2	207.7	205.4	222.6	227.1	210.3	254.1	249.2	266.2	236.9	259.2	223.8	229.3

VI = (%P) + 2(R/H) + 2(R/P) + %V + %K

*The figures given for 1973-74 include a spring 1975 sample and those for 1975-76 include a spring 1976 sample.

Table 5.2 Percent of Involved in Violence and Ranking of Violent-Victim Ratios for Major and All Characters in Prime Time (1969-1985)

	All Characters			Major Characters		
	% Involved in Violence	Ratio	Rank	% Involved in Violence	Ratio	Rank
Minority Women	14.1	−2.19	1	29.2	−1.50	2
Foreign Women	33.0	−2.15	2	70.6	−1.83	1
Married Women	18.7	−2.12	3	28.4	−1.35	7
Young Women	23.1	−1.96	4	47.2	−1.41	5
Elderly Women	16.2	−1.82	5	32.4	−1.43	4
Women — marital status unknown	14.9	−1.81	6	28.4	−1.35	7
"Good" Women	24.0	−1.66	7	40.2	−1.29	8.5
Girls	14.5	−1.65	8	36.0	−1.38	6
White Women	19.6	−1.64	9	41.9	−1.20	10
Elderly Men	25.1	−1.53	10	45.8	+1.16	27
Single Women	25.9	−1.50	11.5	49.4	−1.29	8.5
Boys	25.7	−1.50	11.5	50.3	−1.48	3
Middle Aged Women	18.1	−1.48	13	38.9	−1.07	18.5
American Women	18.2	−1.43	14	42.2	−1.06	20
Married Men	34.5	−1.31	15	45.7	−1.19	11
Formerly Married Men	49.2	−1.27	16	54.5	−1.08	17
Foreign Men	33.2	−1.24	17	69.0	+1.17	25.5
Young Men	41.7	−1.21	18	66.1	−1.13	12.5
"Good" Men	35.5	−1.18	19	57.5	−1.10	14.5
White Men	32.0	−1.17	20.5	60.2	−1.07	18.5
American Men	30.7	−1.17	20.5	57.5	−1.09	16
Single Men	44.2	−1.16	22	64.2	−1.10	14.5
Minority Men	32.2	−1.15	23	53.2	−1.13	12.5
Men — unknown marital status	28.6	−1.14	24	65.0	−1.01	22
Middle-Aged Men	30.7	−1.12	25	59.2	−1.05	21
"Bad" Men	73.5	−1.03	26	85.2	+1.05	23
"Bad" Women	49.6	+1.02	27	69.6	+1.12	24
Formerly Married Women	21.1	+1.09	28	35.7	+1.32	28

What Viewers Learn About Violence and the World

It is clear that women, young and old people, and some minorities are the most vulnerable to victimization on television. Research has also shown that symbolic victimization on television and the cultivation of real world fear among women and minorities, even if contrary to the facts, are highly related (Morgan, 1983). Heavy viewers who see that members of their own groups have a higher calculus of risks express a greater sense of apprehension and mistrust in the real world than do viewers who belong to groups that are less victimized on television.

Our earlier work has shown quite consistently that heavy viewers are more likely than comparable groups of light viewers to live in a self-re-inforcing cycle of a mean and gloomy world (Gerbner et al., 1980). This analysis of data from the National Opinion Research Center's (NORC) General Social Surveys fielded during the 1980s, continues to support and expand those earlier findings.

As can be seen in Table 5.3, television viewing is significantly associated with the tendency to agree with the items in the Mean World Index ($r = .14$, $p < .001$). While simultaneous controls for sex, age, income, race, subjective social class, and political views reduce its strength, the relationship remains statistically significant (partial $r = .06$, $p < .001$). The year-by-year analyses show similar patterns, with only one seventh-order partial correlation (the 1986 General Social Survey) failing to reach statistical significance.[4]

Even more revealing than this small overall correlation is the relationship between television viewing and expressing interpersonal mistrust for specific groups of the population. As found in previous analyses, the relationship is strongest for respondents who have had some college education — those who are also least likely to express interpersonal mistrust. (The correlation between education and the Mean World Index is $-.25$, $p < .001$.) The relationship also holds up, under simultaneous controls, for whites and both low- and high-income respondents. Among nonwhites, who tend to score higher on the Mean World Index ($r = .15$, $p < .001$), the significance of the relationship disappears under simultaneous controls, although the correlation is only slightly smaller than it is for white respondents.[5]

The cross-tabular analysis (see Table 5.4) reveals that heavy viewers (those who watch 4 or more hours each day) in almost every group are significantly more likely to express greater interpersonal mistrust than

Table 5.3 Correlational Analysis for Mean World Index

	Overall	Education No College	College	Income Low	Medium	High	Race White	Non White
Simple r	.138***	.070***	.152***	.122***	.084**	.131***	.117***	.094*
Controlling for:								
Sex	.141***	.075***	.155***	.124***	.088**	.135***	.122***	.096*
Age	.148***	.073**	.164***	.130***	.084**	.128***	.131***	.092*
Education	.090***	—	—	.098***	.044	.103***	.069***	.074
Race	.108***	.043*	.122***	.095***	.066*	.109***	—	—
Income	.098***	.042*	.136***	—	—	—	.085***	.075
Political Orientation	.137***	.065**	.152***	.122***	.083*	.131***	.117***	.094*
Subjective Social Class	.122***	.070***	.136***	.121***	.076*	.109***	.097***	.096*
7th Order Partial	.056***	.023	.119***	.076**	.022	.077**	.062***	.057
DF	3084	1953	1127	1147	784	1073	2719	365

*$p < .05$.
**$p < .01$.
***$p < .001$.

SOURCE: The 1980, 1983, and 1986 NORC General Social Surveys.

the light viewers (those who watch under 2 hours each day) in the same demographic groups. This table also illustrates the mainstreaming implications of viewing. For example, combining data from the 1980, 1983, and 1986 General Social Surveys, heavy and light viewers who have not been to college are equally likely to agree with the items in the Mean World Index: 53% of both the heavy and light viewers agree with two or three of these items. Among those who have had some exposure to college however, television viewing makes a considerable difference: 28% of the light viewers compared to 43% of the heavy viewers in this subgroup have a high score on this index. There is thus a 25-percentage-point difference between these two subgroups of light viewers but only a 10 point spread between these two subgroups of heavy viewers.

Table 5.4 Summary of Cultivation Analysis for Mean World Index

	1980, 1983, 1986			1980			1983			1986		
	%L	CD	Gamma	%L	CD	Gamma	%L	CD	Gamma	%L	CD	Gamma
Overall	40	11	.145***	44	8	.115*	37	11	.150***	35	14	.166***
Sex												
Men	41	14	.176***	46	12	.140*	37	16	.193**	37	17	.209**
Women	39	9	.126**	41	8	.109	37	8	.125*	34	12	.140*
Age												
Under 30	46	18	.234***	59	9	.129	42	17	.218*	30	32	.363***
30 to 54	36	15	.183***	37	13	.160*	35	12	.152*	32	21	.255***
55 and older	42	−1	.005	40	2	.024	36	4	.073	46	−10	−.108
Education												
No College	53	0	.018	58	−4	−.030	45	5	.080	50	1	.018
Some College	28	15	.174**	29	19	.212*	29	13	.144	23	16	.214*
Race												
White	37	9	.125***	40	8	.104*	34	10	.130**	32	11	.134**
Nonwhite	71	5	.046	73	4	.071	67	5	−.003	70	3	.053
Income												
Under $10,000	57	4	.077	62	−4	−.005	49	5	.076	54	8	.109
$10,000 to $20,000	42	11	.133*	42	9	.097	44	3	.057	33	15	.154
Over $20,000	32	10	.113*	34	13	.144	26	18	.232**	30	12	.151
Political Orientation												
Conservative	34	18	.221***	38	16	.201*	40	7	.094	26	26	.335***
Moderate	43	24	.071	47	1	.045	41	13	.193	39	4	.030
Liberal	43	13	.171**	47	10	.126	40	21	.265*	39	14	.178
Subjective Social Class												
Lower-Working	51	5	.061	59	0	.023	47	7	.087	45	9	.089
Middle-Upper	31	13	.180***	31	12	.163*	35	17	.194	28	15	.206**

*p < .05.
**p < .01.
***p < .001.
%L is the percent of light viewers (under two hours each day).
CD (cultivation differential) is the percent of heavy viewers (4 or more hours each day) minus the percent of light viewers within each demographic subgroup.
SOURCE: The 1980, 1983, and 1986 NORC General Social Surveys.

Table 5.4 also reveals that nonwhites are so likely to express inter-personal mistrust that television viewing adds little or nothing to that perception: 71% of the light viewers and 76% of the heavy viewers have high scores on this index. Whites, on the other hand, are a little more likely to agree with the items in the Mean World Index if they are heavy viewers of television.

It can be seen that, overall, low-income respondents are consider-ably more likely than the more affluent respondents to have high scores on the Mean World Index. Moreover, light and heavy viewing low-income respondents are about equally likely to express interpersonal mistrust. Among high- and medium-income respondents, however, the heavy viewers are more likely to express interpersonal mistrust than the light viewers. Thus, the more affluent heavy viewers share the percep-tion of a "mean world" with lower income respondents.

Mainstreaming is also found when we examine subjective social class.[6] This analysis revealed that 51% of the light viewing working class respondents and 31% of light viewing middle class respondents had high scores on the Mean World Index — a difference of 20 percent-age points. Among the heavy viewers in these two subgroups, there was a 12 point spread — 56% of the respondents who categorized themselves as working class and 44% of the respondents who categorized them-selves as middle class had high scores on this index.

Similar patterns are found for each of the 3 years included in this analysis for practically each of the above described control variables. Mainstreaming is especially consistent in the subjective social class, education, and income subgroups. It is also interesting to note that in many cases the overall scores on the Mean World Index have decreased between 1980 and 1986. The Cultivation Differentials (CDs), however, have remained relatively stable over time. So, while most groups show less mistrust over time (for whatever reason), television seems to work to counteract that trend.

There were similar, but weaker, patterns in the relationship between amount of viewing and expressing sentiments of gloom and alienation. Table 5.5 reveals that there was a significant relationship between viewing and the Alienation and Gloom Index ($r = .11$, $p < .001$) that withstood simultaneous controls for sex, age, income, race, education, subjective social class, and political orientation, but was substantially reduced (partial $r = .03$, $p < .05$). The year-by-year analysis also revealed similar patterns, although in the 1982 General Social Survey the relationship was not statistically significant when simultaneously

Table 5.5 Correlational Analysis for Index of Alienation and Gloom

	Overall	Education		Income			Race	
		No College	College	Low	Medium	High	White	Non-white
Simple r	.111***	.068***	.044*	.075***	.084**	.063**	.106***	.074*
Controlling for:								
Sex	.110***	.070***	.042*	.077***	.087**	.062*	.106***	.066
Age	.110***	.069***	.045*	.075**	.084**	.062*	.105***	.076*
Education	.052***	—	—	.047*	.044	.022	.041**	.062
Race	.100***	.062***	.024	.068**	.078**	.052*	—	—
Income	.070***	.039*	.130	—	—	—	.068***	.050
Political Orientation	.110***	.065***	.048*	.076**	.083**	.063*	.105***	.075
Subjective Social Class	.092***	.067***	.020	.073**	.078**	.035	.083***	.074*
7th Order Partial	.030*	.039*	.001	.044*	.039	.001	.026	.048
DF	4110	2577	1529	1619	1049	1340	3657	453

*$p < .05$.
**$p < .01$.
***$p < .001$.

SOURCE: The 1980, 1982, and 1985 NORC General Social Surveys.

controlled for the above mentioned demographic variables. When the relationship between television viewing and endorsing statements of alienation is examined within education and income subgroups, the relationship persists for those respondents who, as a group, are more likely to express alienation — those who have not had any exposure to college and those with low income. These relationships, though slight, withstand the implementation of a large number of controls, either singly or simultaneously (see Table 5.5).[7]

The cross-tabular cultivation analysis is presented in Table 5.6. Again, we find that the heavy viewers in most of the subgroups are much more likely to express feelings of gloom and alienation than the light viewers in these subgroups. Moreover, as was true with the Mean World Index, even though respondents were likely to express less gloom in 1985 than they did in 1980, the Cultivation Differentials (CDs) re-

Table 5.6 Summary of Cultivation Analysis for Index of Alienation and Gloom

	1980, 1982, 1985			1980			1982			1985		
	%L	CD	Gamma	%L	CD	Gamma	%L	CD	Gamma	%L	CD	Gamma
Overall	53	12	.163***	57	18	.249***	55	9	.117*	44	12	.160***
Sex												
Men	49	17	.201***	51	30	.392***	56	3	.065	41	15	.178**
Women	56	9	.131***	64	8	.111	55	11	.156**	47	9	.147*
Age												
Under 30	53	10	.142**	56	19	.275**	59	3	.045	40	12	.151
30 to 54	51	18	.212***	55	24	.324***	52	16	.209**	46	12	.141*
55 and older	56	8	.116*	66	7	.139	58	5	.081	42	15	.158*
Education												
No College	66	3	.062	70	6	.102	67	1	.024	58	4	.089
Some College	41	11	.108*	45	27	.262***	44	6	.060	33	5	.059
Race												
White	51	13	.157***	56	19	.257***	54	9	.113**	43	10	.137**
Nonwhite	57	6	.101	72	4	.060	73	-1	.017	54	17	.226
Income												
Under $10,000	67	4	.059	70	10	.153	73	-3	-.023	56	7	.091
$10,000 to $20,000	59	8	.123*	65	13	.215*	55	10	.132	53	3	.040
Over $20,000	43	14	.161***	42	26	.326***	49	3	.048	37	15	.171**
Political Orientation												
Conservative	49	12	.154***	59	18	.241**	50	24	.056	37	16	.200**
Moderate	53	13	.167***	60	15	.210**	52	16	.203**	47	8	.115
Liberal	56	11	.157**	55	17	.235*	64	7	.104	46	12	.162
Subjective Social Class												
Lower-Working	62	7	.096**	70	9	.154*	60	6	.070	55	27	.092
Middle-Upper	45	15	.197***	47	24	.296***	51	11	.146*	35	14	.191**

*p < .05.
**p < .01.
***p < .001.

%L is the percent of light viewers (under two hours each day).
CD (cultivation differential) is the percent of heavy viewers (4 or more hours each day) minus the percent of light viewers within each demographic subgroup.
SOURCE: The 1980, 1982, and 1985 NORC General Social Surveys.

mained stable, indicating that the relationship between viewing and expressing these sentiments is somewhat stable.

Again, there are a number of examples of mainstreaming. For example, light viewing men are somewhat less likely to express feelings of gloom than light viewing women, while about the same percent of men and women who are heavy viewers have a high score on this index. Similarly, among the subjective social class subgroups the heavy viewers are more homogeneous in their likelihood to have high scores on this index while the percent of light viewers in these subgroups who endorse these statements is more dissimilar. Among low-, medium-, and high-income groups the light viewers are more dispersed while the heavy viewers are more similar in their likelihood to endorse these statements. We also find that the patterns exhibited for the education and subjective social class subgroups are quite similar to those found for the Mean World Index. In short, the heavy viewers in these demographic subgroups seem to be more homogeneous and more likely to express gloom and alienation than their light viewing counterparts.

Conclusion

These group differences, and those previously reported for the Index of Perceptions of Danger (see Gerbner et al., 1980), illustrate the interplay of television with demographic and real world factors. In most subgroups those who watch more television tend to express a heightened sense of living in a mean world of danger and mistrust and alienation and gloom. Morgan (1984) also found that heavy viewers tend to feel more lonely, bored, and depressed. Moreover, the cultivation of such anxieties is most pronounced in groups whose light viewers (for example, those who have been to college) are the least likely to be mistrustful and apprehensive.

This unequal sense of danger, vulnerability, and general malaise cultivated by what is called "entertainment" invites not only aggression but also exploitation and repression. Fearful people are more dependent, more easily manipulated and controlled, more susceptible to deceptively simple, strong, tough measures and hard-line postures — both political and religious. They may accept and even welcome repression if it promises to relieve their insecurities and other anxieties. That is the deeper problem of violence-laden television.

Notes

1. Methodological studies have found the solid week sample of network programming as representative of a season's programming as larger randomly drawn samples, and reasonably stable from year to year, at least in basic dimensions employed in this analysis. Analyses of variance conducted on violence-related content data collected over 7 consecutive weeks of prime-time dramatic programming broadcast during the fall of 1976 revealed no significant differences by week for dependent measures such as the number of violent actions, the duration of violence, and the significance of violence. There were significant main-effects for program-related variables including network, type of program, time of broadcast, and so on; but there were no significant interactions with week of broadcast (Signorielli, Gross, & Morgan, 1982).

2. These data sets are called prevalence, rate, and role respectively. Prevalence (%P) is the percent of programs in a particular sample containing any violence. Rate expresses the frequency of violent actions in units of programming and in units of time. The number of violent acts divided by the total number of programs gives the rate per program (R/P) while the rate per hour (R/H) is the number of violent actions divided by the number of program hours in the sample. The latter measures the saturation of violence in time, and compensates for the difference in rates between a long program unit, such as a movie, and a short one, such as a cartoon.

Role is defined as the portrayal of characters as violents (committing violence) or victims (subjected to violence) or both, and yields two measures. They are the percent of violents, victims, or both (%V) and the percent involved in killing, either as killers or as killed, or both (%K). The index is the sum of these five measures with the rates weighted by a factor of two.

The Violence Index is represented as: $VI = \%P + 2R/H + 2R/P + \%V + \%K$.

3. Television viewing is divided into as close to an even three-way split as possible. This division serves to separate those who watch the most television (the heavy viewers) from those who watch the least television (light viewers). Traditional cultivation analysis is set up to focus upon the relative degree of television viewing rather than the exact or specific number of hours a respondent says he or she watches television on an average day.

4. In the 1975 General Social Survey a similar pattern was found (statistically significant sixth-order partial correlation). In the 1978 General Social Survey, the sixth-order partial was not statistically significant but the zero-order and first-order partials were statistically significant.

5. The results for the income-related subgroups are different from those reported in Gerbner et al. (1980), where the relationships held up under the application of simultaneous controls only for the middle-income subgroup. Over the past 10 years, however, income levels have changed considerably (due to inflation and more dual-income families) thus reducing the numbers of respondents in the low- and middle-income groups while increasing the number of respondents in the high-income group. Changing the definition (monetary limits) of low, medium, and high income to take inflation into consideration does not alter the current pattern of findings.

Likewise patterns isolated among nonwhites in the analysis of data from the 1975 and 1978 General Social Surveys are different from those found in the more recent surveys. The earlier analysis revealed a small negative relationship between viewing and the Mean

World Index; the current analysis indicates that the relationship disappears under simultaneous controls.

6. Since very few respondents classify themselves either as belonging to the "upper class" or the "lower class," this analysis examined only two categories of subjective social class — working class (including the small numbers who categorized themselves as belonging to the lower class) and middle class (including the few respondents who categorized themselves as belonging to the upper class).

7. There again is a difference between the findings of this analysis and those reported in Gerbner et al. (1980). In the previous analysis of alienation and gloom items in the 1977 General Social Survey the relationship remained statistically significant for the college-educated subgroup rather than the subgroup who had not been to college (current finding for the 1980s surveys). Examination, however, reveals that proportionately more respondents have had exposure to college in the recent surveys than in the 1977 survey. This may thus account for the difference.

References

Bandura, A. (1968). What TV violence can do to your child. In O. N. Larsen (Ed.), *Violence and the mass media*. New York: Harper & Row (pp. 123-139).

Bandura, A. (1978). A social learning theory of aggression. *Journal of Communication, 28*(3), 12-29.

Bandura, A., Ross, D., & Ross, S.A. (1961). Transmission of aggression through imitation of aggressive models. *Journal of Abnormal and Social Psychology, 63*, 575-582.

Bandura, A., Ross, D., & Ross, S. A. (1963). Imitation of film-mediated aggressive models. *Journal of Abnormal and Social Psychology, 66*(1), 2-11.

Bryant, J., Corveth, R., & Brown, D. (1981). Television viewing and anxiety: An experimental examination. *Journal of Communication, 31*(1), 106-119.

Carlson, J. M. (1983). Crime show viewing by pre-adults: The impact on attitudes toward civil liberties. *Communication Research, 10*(4), 529-552.

Clark, D. G., & Blankenburg, W. B. (1972). Trends in violent content in selected mass media. In G. A. Comstock & E. A. Rubinstein (Eds.), *Television and social behavior, Vol. 1, Media content and control* (pp. 188-243). Washington, DC: U.S. Government Printing Office.

Doob A. N., & Macdonald, G. E. (1977). The news media and perceptions of violence. *Report of the Royal Commission on Violence in the communication industry, Vol. 5, Learning from the media* (pp. 177-226). Toronto, Canada: The Royal Commission.

Doob, A. N., & Macdonald, G. E. (1979). Television viewing and fear of victimization: Is the relationship causal? *Journal of Personality and Social Psychology, 37*(2), 170-179.

Dominick, J. R. (1973). Crime and law enforcement in prime-time television. *Public Opinion Quarterly, 37*(2), 241-250.

Dominick, J. R. (1978). Crime and law enforcement in the mass media. In C. Winick (Ed.), *Deviance and mass media* (pp. 105-128). Beverly Hills, CA: Sage.

Drabman, R. S., & Thomas, M. H. (1977). Children's imitation of aggressive and prosocial behavior when viewing alone and in pairs. *Journal of Communication, 27*(3), 199-205.

Ellis, G. T., & Sekera, F., III. (1972). The effects of aggressive cartoons on the behavior of first grade children. *Journal of Psychology, 81*(1), 7-43.

Gerbner, G., Gross, L., Jackson-Beeck, M., Jeffries-Fox, S., & Signorielli, N. (1978). Cultural indicators: Violence profile no. 9. *Journal of Communication, 28*(3), 176-207.
Gerbner, G., Gross, L., Morgan, M., & Signorielli, N. (1980). The 'mainstreaming' of America: Violence profile no. 11. *Journal of Communication, 30*(3), 10-29.
Gerbner, G., Gross, L., Morgan, M., & Signorielli, N. (1982). Charting the mainstream: Television's contribution to political orientations. *Journal of Communication, 32*(2), 100-127.
Gerbner, G., Gross, L., Morgan, M., & Signorielli, N. (1986). *Television's mean world: Violence profile no. 14-15.* Philadelphia: The Annenberg School of Communications, University of Pennsylvania.
Gerbner, G., Gross, L., Signorielli, N., & Morgan, M. (1979). The demonstration of power: Violence profile no. 10. *Journal of Communication, 29*(3), 177-196.
Greenberg, B. S., Edison, N., Korzenny, F., Fernandez-Collado, C., & Atkin, C. K. (1980). Antisocial and prosocial behaviors on television. In B. S. Greenberg (Ed.), *Life on television: Content analyses of U.S. TV drama* (pp. 99-128). Norwood, NJ: Ablex.
Gunter, B., & Wober, M. (1983). Television viewing and public perceptions of hazards to life. *Journal of Environmental Psychology, 3*, 325-335.
Haney, C., & Manzolati, J. (1980). Television criminology: Network illusions of criminal justice realities. In E. Aronson (Ed.), *Readings about the social animal.* San Francisco: Freeman.
Hawkins, R.P., & Pingree, S. (1982). Television's influence on social reality. In D. Pearl, L. Bouthilet, & J. Lazar (Eds.), *Television and behavior: Ten years of scientific progress and implications for the eighties.* Washington, DC: National Institute of Mental Health.
Haynes, R. B. (1978). Children's perceptions of 'comic' and 'authentic' cartoon violence. *Journal of Broadcasting, 22*(1), 63-70.
Head, S. W. (1954). Content analysis of television drama programs. *Quarterly of Film, Radio, and Television, 9*, 175-194.
Krippendorff, K. (1980). *Content analysis.* Beverly Hills, CA: Sage.
Lovas, O. I. (1961). Effect of exposure to symbolic aggression on aggressive behavior. *Child Development, 32*(1), 37-44.
Morgan, M. (1983). Symbolic victimization and real world fear. *Human Communication Research, 9*2), 146-157.
Morgan, M. (1984). Heavy television viewing and perceived quality of life. *Journalism Quarterly, 61*(3), 499-504, 740.
Research and Forecasts. (1980). *The Figgie report on crime: America afraid.* Willoughby, OH: A-T-O, Inc.
Rosenberg, M. (1957). *Occupations and values.* Glencoe, IL: Free Press.
Signorielli, N., Gross, L., & Morgan, M. (1982). Violence in television programs: Ten years later. In D. Pearl, L. Bouthilet, & J. Lazar (Eds.), *Television and social behavior: Ten years of scientific progress and implications for the eighties* (pp. 158-173). Rockville, MD: National Institute of Mental Health.
Smythe, D. W. (1954). Reality as presented on television. *Public Opinion Quarterly, 18*, 143-156.
Srole, L. (1956). Social integration and certain correlaries: An exploratory study. *American Sociological Review, 21*, 709-712.
Taylor, H., & Dozier, C. (1983). Television violence, African-Americans, and social control: 1950-1976. *Journal of Black Studies, 14*(2), 107-136.

Williams, T. M. (1986). *The impact of television: A natural experiment in three communities.* New York: Academic Press.

Wober, J. M. (1978). Televised violence and paranoid perception: The view from Great Britain. *Public Opinion Quarterly, 42*(3), 315-321.

Zillmann, D. (1982). Television viewing and arousal. In D. Pearl, L. Bouthilet, & J. Lazar (Eds.), *Television and social behavior: Ten years of scientific progress and implications for the eighties* (pp. 53-67). Rockville, MD: National Institute of Mental Health.

Zillmann, D., & Wakshlag, J. (1985). Fear of victimization and the appeal of crime drama. In D. Zillmann & J. Bryant (Eds.), *Selective exposure to communication.* Hillsdale, NJ: Lawrence Erlbaum.

6

Pornography and the Construction
of Gender

ELIZABETH HALL PRESTON

Pornography has held a prominent position in feminist discourse since Brownmiller's (1975) assertion in her pioneering study of rape and male sexual aggression that pornography is at the root of anti-female propaganda. Her argument that pornography promotes the sense that acts of sexual hostility should be tolerated and are also ideologically encouraged has informed much subsequent feminist scholarship and practice.[1] In spite of a substantial body of literature accumulated in the past decade, feminist concerns have not affected noticeably on pornography research in the social sciences. While Brownmiller's perspective resonates throughout much radical feminist scholarship that points to pornography's role in the construction of sexuality and gender stereotypes (and therefore real social inequalities), social science research has instead been narrowly focused on the short-term behavioral and attitudinal effects of pornography.

Studies to date have concentrated primarily on the relationship between pornography and aggression/sexual aggression, focusing on pornography as an agent of change in laboratory studies using a basic stimulus-response model of human behavior. Such research ignores feminist contentions that while isolated incidences of sexual aggression

AUTHOR'S NOTE: The author wishes to thank Michael Morgan for his invaluable assistance throughout all aspects of this research project.

directed against women may be triggered by exposure to pornography, such incidents are dramatic symptoms in a culture that structurally and ideologically creates and re-creates the context in which such events occur.

From a feminist perspective, laboratory research focusing on the relationship between pornography and male sexual aggression is ethically questionable, epistemologically unsound, and theoretically misguided; it ignores the subtle yet potentially far more powerful ways in which pornography may function to maintain the sex-based inequalities of a patriarchal culture. As Fine and Johnson suggest, "feminism as a shaper of theory and research methods meets the research tradition on pornography at the metatheoretical rather than the theoretical level; i.e., it is difficult for feminism to influence research because of the nature of the research itself" (1984, p. 2). Alternative theoretical and methodological approaches have been urged by a number of feminist scholars, but these have been rarely applied to pornography, in spite of the traditions and current practices within the discipline in studying the content of other media.

At the same time, feminist theorists arguing that the impact of pornography extends far beyond the simple and isolated behavioral and attitudinal changes evoked in laboratory studies have ignored alternative theories and methodological strategies widely circulated within the communications discipline. Although empirical methods may strengthen feminist analyses of pornography, feminist research on pornography has been almost exclusively "qualitative." While it has offered important theoretical insights into the mechanisms by which sex-based inequalities and acceptance of myths and stereotypes about male sexual aggression directed against women are reinforced by pornography, feminist research has offered little empirical support for its claims.

The work of George Gerbner and other researchers associated with the Cultural Indicators paradigm offers an important theoretical foundation for understanding the function of the media in the social construction of reality and a research strategy for empirically testing that relationship. Merged with feminist analyses of pornography and the social construction of gender and sexuality, the cultivation model provides a concise and attractive framework for researching the impact of pornography. Within that framework, this study attempts to move away from the narrow orientation of previous research on pornography; it was designed to address the more pervasive role that mass market pornography, as an ever visible and accessible form of mass communication, plays in creating and maintaining aspects of social reality revolving around a number of dimensions, including sex-role, sex-trait, and sexual-behavior stereotyping, and myths about rape.

As in the case of violence, the cultivation framework provides an alternative way of thinking about the effects of pornography. Grounded in the assumption that individuals understand themselves and their world in relation to the symbolic environment and that reality is therefore a social construction, cultivation research is concerned with understanding the cumulative contributions of the broad patterns in the symbolic system we all share. And while most cultivation research in the United States has focused on television, the application of the theories and methods of cultivation analysis to mass-market pornography promises to enhance our understanding of both cultivation and of pornography.

The shift to the cultivation model allows for an exploration of the broad role pornography may play in the maintenance of social structures. As Diamond notes, "admittedly violent pornography and other violent media such as television do provide models for the minority of men who do act out sexual violence against women. But pornography influences reality in much the same way as the idea that 'a woman's place is in the home' does, because both reinforce existing social structures" (Diamond, 1985, p. 48). There may be a tangible difference between pornography and cultural cliches about the appropriate social role for women, but Diamond's point is clear: the primary impact of pornography is the preservation and reinforcing of existing social structures built on sex-based inequalities. Pornography is produced almost exclusively by and for men: the perspective that informs its content reflects the traditional patriarchal structures of our culture.

In mass market pornographic magazines, the focus is almost exclusively on sexually explicit photographs of women: the female body is, in Kuhn's terms, softcore pornography's "singular preoccupation." As she suggests, this "preoccupation with the female body is tied in with the project of defining the 'true' nature of female sexuality. Femaleness and femininity are constructed as a set of bodily attributes reducible to a sexuality which puts itself on display for a masculine spectator" (1985, p. 43).

Within the context of pornography, women are presented exclusively for the attainment of male pleasure: they wait to be possessed by the spectator, no strings attached, no danger of rejection. The images of pornography operate to define women exclusively in terms of a male-defined female sexuality. As a commodity and as a constellation of messages primarily about gender, sexuality, and sexual relationships, pornography may cultivate an acceptance of patriarchal social structures.

This research is based on the premise that pornography is an agent of enculturation, one of many social institutions contributing to our perceptions of social reality. Because the content of pornography is primarily concerned with the representation of women, sexuality, and sexual behavior, it is assumed that it is in those interrelated areas that pornography contributes most heavily in shaping the boundaries of social reality. It is likewise assumed that pornography re-creates a specifically patriarchal pattern of images of women and sexuality. Individuals who are more heavily exposed to pornography may be expected to share a perception of social reality that reflects the patriarchal lessons of pornography more intensely than others who are similar in demographic terms but have had less exposure to pornography.

In sum, it is a fundamental contention of much feminist analysis of pornography that the primary impact of pornography lies in the preservation and perpetuation of sex-based inequalities based in large part on potent sex-role and sex-trait stereotypes (perceptions of certain social roles as more appropriate for men or for women, and personality characteristics as more applicable to one sex than the other) and the continued acceptance of myths about male sexual aggression directed against women. The content of pornography is a vivid source of stereotypes about women (and, to a lesser extent, about men). It is the basic premise of the research presented here that the more exposure people have to the images and themes of pornography, the greater the extent to which they will incorporate the "lessons" of pornography into their perceptions of women. If such is the case, high exposure to pornography should be associated with strong sex-role and sex-trait stereotyping; it should be associated with strong stereotyping about male and female sexuality; and, ultimately, exposure to pornography should be associated with an increased acceptance of myths about rape.

Methodology

The data presented here were collected from several samples over a 6-month period during 1984 and 1985. The samples were drawn from undergraduate students enrolled in eight different communication classes at three state universities in Massachusetts (N=492). Similar questionnaires were used for all samples, although some questions were added and others deleted in the versions given to later samples. The analyses presented here only include those questions that appeared on all surveys.

The pooled sample is 44% (N=218) male and 56% (N=274) female. Virtually all respondents were between the ages of 18 and 23 (95%), and white (93%). Over half identified themselves as Catholic (53%). The remaining respondents identified themselves as Jewish (15%), Protestant (15%), or as having no religious affiliation (11%). Just under half of the respondents (49%) described themselves as either very or somewhat religious, but strength of religious conviction was unrelated to religious affiliation. Most of the respondents came from middle-class families; 28% estimated their parents' income to be between $20,000 and $30,000, 37% between $30,000 and $50,000, and 28% estimated that their parents earned over $50,000 annually.

Questionnaires were administered in classroom settings, with less than half (44%) of the respondents receiving course credit for participating. Prior to receiving the questionnaire, students were informed that a number of items dealt with sex and sexuality, and that several of the questions were quite explicit. Those students willing to participate (two students chose not to) were asked to fill out written consent forms and to complete the questionnaire. In order to assure confidentiality and encourage honest responses in light of the sensitive nature of the questions, the questionnaires were self-administered and respondents were asked to record their answers on optical scanning sheets that were collected separately from the questionnaires and signed consent forms. Students were then debriefed about the nature and purposes of the study and about myths that surround rape in our culture, in an effort to avoid unintentional reinforcement of those myths.

The questionnaire contained series of items designed to be combined into additive indices. For this analysis, four dependent indices were constructed, concerning: (1) sex-role stereotypes, (2) sex-traits, (3) sexuality stereotypes, and (4) rape myths.

Sex-Role Stereotypes

This index measures if respondents would have more confidence in a man or a woman holding each of eight specific jobs (e.g., high school teacher, auto mechanic, mayor), or whether the sex of the individual in the position made no difference. The number of stereotyped responses (in either a male or female direction) were summed. An orthogonal rotation factor analysis of the eight items revealed only one factor, suggesting a high degree of communality, and reliability testing produced an alpha of .793, indicating strong internal consistency.

Sex-Trait Stereotypes

The sex-trait index consists of a series of personal descriptors. Respondents were asked to indicate whether they thought various adjectives (e.g., irrational, aggressive, and indecisive) were more likely to describe a man, a woman, or equally likely to describe either. The specific adjectives were equally divided between traits generally considered to be masculine, feminine, or to apply equally to men and women. Factor analyses suggested the elimination of certain items. The specific traits included in the final sex-trait stereotyping index are "competitive" and "aggressive" (held to be stereotypes generally applied to men) and "irrational," "emotional," "gentle," and "indecisive" (generally considered more characteristic of women). Reliability analysis produced a marginally acceptable alpha of .552.

Sexuality Stereotypes

Five items were used to measure stereotypes relating to sexuality. Respondents indicated whether they felt men, or women (or both, or neither), "are more likely to say 'no' to sex when they don't really mean it," "are more concerned with their partner's satisfaction than their own," and so on. Respondents indicated their agreement or disagreement with the statement, "In general, men have stronger sex drives than women" (based on a 5-point scale). The summed measure reflects the number of stereotyped responses given (alpha = .638).

Rape Myths

This index consists of four items that relate to common myths about rape. Respondents were asked to indicate, on a 5-point scale, whether they agreed or disagreed with statements such as "no woman can be raped against her will," and to choose the appropriate prison term for someone convicted of rape. (Response categories ranged from a low of

1 to 5 years to more than 20 years). Respondents showed little acceptance of the rape myths included in this section, with approximately
90% disagreeing or strongly disagreeing with statements suggesting
that women often actually enjoy being raped (one of the central themes
of much pornography) and that women can't be raped against their will.
Perceptions of an appropriate prison sentence for someone convicted of
rape varied considerably, however. While only 2% selected the lowest
term of 1 to 5 years, 13% felt that 5 to 10 years appropriate, 21%
considered 15 to 20 years to be appropriate, and just under half (45%)
felt that persons convicted of rape should be sentenced to more than 20
years in prison. Factor analysis of the items revealed only one factor,
although the reliability tests yielded a relatively low alpha (.549);
despite the low alpha, the index was analyzed because of its conceptual
importance.

The questionnaire also included a number of demographic questions
including sex, age, ethnic background, parents' income, religious preference and strength of religious convictions, academic grade point
average, and self-rating on a liberal/conservative scale of social and
political outlook. Because of the nature of the study and the desire to
control for potential intervening variables, respondents were also asked
to indicate how often they were currently involved in sexual activity
and how satisfying they found their current sexual experiences.

Finally, exposure to pornography was measured by several series of
questions, which were asked last in an effort to avoid sensitization.
Among numerous other measures of pornography exposure, respondents were asked to indicate how often they read or looked at each of
12 mainstream, soft-core pornographic magazines. This was used as the
primary independent variable of "pornography exposure" in this analysis, and was constructed by summing responses for each of these 12
magazines (where 1 = "never read" and 4 = "read almost every issue";
scores thus range from 12-48).

Although the vast majority of both men (99%) and women (89%)
reported having looked at least one mass market pornographic magazine at some point in their lives, there were large differences in exposure
to pornography according to sex. Not surprisingly, males scored significantly higher on the exposure index (18.5 vs. 15.0, $p < .001$). In
addition, 68% of the women, compared to 40% of the men, responded
that they had never looked at these or similar magazines in a store or at
a newsstand. Likewise, twice as many men as women reported pur-
chasing mass market pornography. On a similar measure, one-third

of the male respondents reported watching upwards of three X-rated films on a VCR over the past two years, as opposed to just 5.5% of the women.

The women who did look at pornography read the least explicit of the mass market magazines: they were more likely to say they have read *Playboy* than any of the other easily available softcore magazines (including, interestingly, *Playgirl*, which is marketed specifically for women).

Findings

Sex-Role Stereotypes

If exposure to mass market pornography cultivates sex-role stereotyping, then individuals more heavily exposed to its content should score higher on the index of sex-role stereotyping than light users. Simple and first-order partial correlations (Table 6.1) clearly show a strong positive relationship between exposure to pornography and scores on the sex-role stereotyping index for college men; the relationship holds across all demographic subgroups, as well as under simultaneous controls. Eighth-order partials suggest that for college men the relationship between pornography and sex-role stereotyping is not spurious: simultaneously controlling for age, income, grade point average, self-designated political orientation, and religious convictions as well as current involvement in and satisfaction with current sexual relations yields a correlation of .24 ($p < .001$).

Among college women, however, there is no apparent relation between exposure to pornography and sex-role stereotyping. This is perhaps not surprising, given women's overall low score on the sex-role stereotyping index and their lower degree of exposure to pornography. It may be that the greater sex-typing among males predisposes them to the implicit messages of pornography. In any case, the low correlations among females could be masking significant subgroup variations, but inspection of the data within all relevant female subgroups (and male subgroups) does not change the results shown in Table 6.1: almost all male subgroups (and almost no female subgroups) show significant associations between pornography exposure and sex-role stereotypes.

Table 6.1 Correlation between Exposure to Pornography and Sex Role Stereotyping

	Males (n=218)	Females (n=274)
Simple *r*	.22***	.04
Controlling for:		
Age	.22***	.04
Income	.20**	.04
Strength of Religious Convictions	.22***	.04
Political/Social Orientation	.25***	.04
Grade Point Average	.22***	.04
Daily Television Viewing	.21***	.02
Current Involvement in Sexual Relations	.21***	.04
Satisfaction with Current Sexual Relations	.22***	.03
All Controls	.24***	.02

*p < .05.
**p < .01.
***p < .001.

Sex-Trait Stereotyping

As with sex-role stereotyping, if exposure to pornography cultivates sex-trait stereotyping then one would expect to find amount of exposure to pornography positively correlated with the scores on an index comprised of elements designed to measure sex-trait stereotyping. Heavy exposure to pornography should be related to a tendency to perceive men as aggressive and competitive, for example, and to see women as more irrational, emotional, gentle, and so forth. This assumption is given further credence by the relatively high correlation between scores on the sex-role and sex-trait stereotyping indices for both men and women. For men, the simple correlation between the indices is .40 ($p < .001$); for women, the correlation is less strong ($r = .28$) but remains highly significant ($p < .001$). In spite of this, however, the relationship was considerably different.

As Table 6.2 suggests, the relationship between pornography exposure and sex-trait stereotyping is very different for males and females.

Table 6.2 Correlation between Exposure to Pornography and Sex Trait Stereotyping

	Males (n=218)	Females (n=274)
Simple r	.07	−.13*
Controlling for:		
Age	.07	−.12*
Income	.05	−.13*
Strength of Religious Convictions	.06	−.13*
Political/Social Orientation	.08	−.13*
Grade Point Average	.07	−.12*
Daily Television Viewing	.05	−.14*
Current Involvement in Sexual Relations	.07	−.11*
Satisfaction with Current Sexual Relations	.07	−.12*
All Controls	.06	−.12*

*$p < .05$.

For men, amount of exposure to pornography shows weak, positive but nonsignificant associations with sex-trait stereotyping. For women, on the other hand, there are significant *negative* correlations between amount of exposure and sex-trait stereotypes. Women who are heavily exposed to pornography, for example, are less likely to see men as more ambitious or competitive, and they are less likely to perceive women as more emotional, more irrational, or more gentle than men.

Analysis of variance of within-group index scores shows significant subgroup variations for females, and some curvilinear patterns. For example, while the overall relationship is similar for both older and younger women, women in the medium exposure group vary noticeably according to age. For younger women, scores on the stereotyping index were highest for those in the medium exposure group; among older women, those in the medium exposure group had the lowest scores on the index.

As in the case of the sex-role stereotypes index, however, the within-group patterns largely mirror the partials shown in Table 6.2. For males, exposure to pornography is unrelated to impressions about sex-traits, and females who read pornography more often tend to be *less* likely to hold narrow stereotypes about sex-traits.

Sexuality Stereotyping

For college males, the relationship between amount of exposure to pornography and stereotyping around dimensions of male and female sexuality is strong (Table 6.3). For males, heavy exposure to pornography is clearly associated with a greater tendency to accept stereotypes about male and female sexuality. Exposure to pornography is correlated with the impression that men have stronger sexual urges than women and that they have less control over their sexuality. Women, on the other hand, are perceived as being less able to admit that they have sexual desires, and more likely to "say 'no' to sex when they don't really mean it." Separate analysis of this last item found that while 35% of male respondents characterized as "low" exposure stated that women were likely to deny wanting to have sex, 62% of both medium- and heavy-exposure respondents suggested that such was the case — a difference of 27 points between low- and high-exposure groups ($p = .004$).

As the correlations on Table 6.3 reveal, the relationship between exposure and stereotyping is again reversed for women, though not significantly. While the relationship is not statistically significant, together with the relationship between exposure and sex-trait stereotyping, it begins to suggest interesting differences between men and women and the overall relationship between exposure to pornography and stereotyping. For women, high exposure to pornography is associated with *less* stereotyping around sexuality than is low exposure, although the relationship is relatively weak.

For women, the relationship remains relatively stable across subgroups, although mediated by involvement in sexual relations. While scores on the stereotyping index are negatively associated with exposure to pornography for women who report being currently involved in sexual relations on a regular basis or from time to time, the relationship is reversed for women who are either involved in sexual activity only once in a while or not at all. For these women, exposure to pornography is associated with relatively higher stereotyping about male and female sexuality, clearly suggesting that direct sexual experience mediates the impact of pornography along those dimensions.

Acceptance of Rape Myths

Overall, exposure to pornography was not related to acceptance of rape myths for either men or women (see Table 6.4). While men were

Table 6.3 Correlation between Exposure to Pornography and Sexuality Stereotyping

	Males (n=218)	Females (n=274)
Simple *r*	.24***	−.09
Controlling for:		
Age	.23***	−.08
Income	.22***	−.09
Strength of Religious Convictions	.24***	−.09
Political/Social Orientation	.24***	−.09
Grade Point Average	.24***	−.09
Daily Television Viewing	.24***	−.10
Current Involvement in Sexual Relations	.23***	−.07
Satisfaction with Current Sexual Relations	.24***	−.09
All Controls	.22***	−.08

*$p < .05$.
**$p < .01$.
***$p < .001$.

significantly ($p < .001$) more accepting than women of myths about rape — the notion that women can't be raped against their will, often derive sexual satisfaction from being raped, and so on — both men and women scored quite low on the index overall. Likewise, within-group comparisons showed no significant differences according to pornography exposure within any male or female subgroup.

Individual item analysis also showed no relation between exposure to pornography and responses to any of the items comprising the index, with one exception. In keeping with the well-publicized findings of Zillmann and Bryant's (1982) research on pornography and callousness toward rape, respondents classified as heavy users of pornography recommended noticeably shorter prison terms as appropriate for someone convicted of rape. For men, the percentage of respondents recommending either of the longest sentences (15 to 20 years and upwards of 20 years) dropped from 67% of light users to 56% of the heavy exposure group ($p = .013$). For women, the relationship was not significant but followed the same trend: 77% of the low exposure group recommended the strongest sentences, versus 70% of the heavy exposure group.

Table 6.4 Correlation between Exposure to Pornography and Acceptance of Rape Myths

	Males (n=218)	Females (n=274)
Simple *r*	−.02	.04
Controlling for:		
Age	−.00	.04
Income	−.01	.04
Strength of Religious Convictions	−.01	.05
Political/Social Orientation	−.03	.04
Grade Point Average	−.02	.04
Daily Television Viewing	−.02	.04
Current Involvement in Sexual Relations	−.03	.03
Satisfaction with Current Sexual Relations	−.00	.04
All Controls	−.01	.04

*p < .05.

NOTE: High score on the index indicates low acceptance of myths about rape.

Overall, however, with the other variables relating to myths about rape taken into consideration, there was no notable relationship between exposure to mass market pornographic magazines and the acceptance of myths about rape. This may have, at least in part, been due to a low acceptance of rape myths in general among those surveyed, perhaps as a result of educational efforts on the various campuses where data were collected.

Discussion

While most research on the impact of pornography has explored potential short-term links between exposure to pornography and acts of sexual aggression directed against women within the limited context of laboratory experimentation, the research presented here begins to investigate the more long-term contribution of pornography to fundamental assumptions about gender and sexuality. It is not meant to replace either the findings of laboratory research or to preclude ethnographic investigation, but to provide quantitative evidence for persuasive claims about the impact of pornography made by feminist scholars over the past decade. For years, feminists have argued that the fundamental impact of pornography lies not in the direct triggering of acts of male sexual aggression, however extreme and tragic those instances might be, but rather in the cultivation and perpetuation of a social order in which those acts are both made inevitable and excused. By bringing together a powerful analysis of pornography firmly grounded in feminist theory and the equally powerful theoretical and methodological framework of cultivation, this research offers empirical evidence for the validity of feminist concerns about pornography.

Before discussing the implications of the findings, there are a number of methodological issues that need to be addressed. First, the samples obviously limit the generalizability of the results. While the use of college undergraduate respondents is commonplace in the social sciences, the convenience of such a sample must be balanced against its limitations. The use of undergraduates in the context of this particular study may in part be justified by their role as regular consumers of pornography, but it must be remembered that the sample is clearly limited and that its homogeneous nature has prevented comparison across more diverse subpopulations. As a result, the findings may represent an underestimation of the overall impact of pornography, given the curtailment of variance associated with a homogeneous sample, especially for the dependent measures.

Although the data indicate a relationship between exposure to mass market pornography and dimensions directly related to its unique content, the nature of that relationship remains a matter of conjecture; cross-sectional data provide no measure of causality. The relationship, however, is assumed to be reciprocal, in line with the premises of cultivation analysis. The number and range of demographic variables used as controls clearly lessens the likelihood of spuriousness, but offers no guarantee: longitudinal data might reveal patterns undetectable with cross-sectional data.

While the relationships between exposure to pornography and intensity of stereotyping across the dimensions most closely associated with the content of pornography vary in size and in statistical significance, certain patterns emerge from the data. For men, exposure to pornography is consistently associated with relatively high stereotyping, particularly around gender-appropriate sex-roles and perceptions of male and female sexuality. Unexpectedly, given the findings of previous research, this stereotyping was not associated with an increased acceptance of myths about rape. This may reflect, however, the success of educational efforts on the campuses where data were collected or the weakness of the measures used to assess acceptance of rape myths.

For women, the findings suggest a different relationship between exposure to pornography and gender stereotyping. While there was virtually no relationship between exposure and sex-role stereotyping for women, the correlations between gender stereotyping and sex-traits (and sexuality, though not significantly), were consistently negative. As the interaction between amount of exposure and current romantic involvement suggests, the relationship may be mediated by a third factor: among women who are sexually active, more exposure to pornography may indicate (and cultivate) a more "liberal" or "open" attitude toward sexuality and gender stereotypes. It may be that for women, stereotyping is less fixed than it is for men, or that, approaching pornography with a different set of assumptions than men, women interpret its content differently. Whatever the explanation, it is clear that at the very least the relationship between exposure to pornography and gender stereotyping is very different for men and women. The data suggest that the impact of pornography is neither monolithic nor uniform. Further research should continue to emphasize and explore gender differences.

Over the past two decades, researchers working within the Cultural Indicators paradigm have attempted to challenge mainstream research on the impact of television, and to document the broader, more pervasive ways in which television works to maintain existing social structures. Researchers have continually refined the methodological strategies and applied them to more and more issues. The research presented here suggests that the cultivation framework can be successfully applied to media other than television, and further documents the ways in which long-term exposure to the media functions in the maintenance of inequitable structures. In so doing, this study provides empirical validation for feminist analyses of pornography, which suggest that exposure to pornography functions to preserve existing sex-based inequalities.

Notes

1. There is, of course, no single "feminist perspective" on pornography. The debate surrounding pornography within the contemporary movement has been heated and bitter, at times threatening to eclipse the issue itself. Nonetheless, there exists a clear and

well-articulated feminist critique of pornography, which, while challenged from a number of positions within the feminist community, provides a powerful analysis of the content and social impact of pornography.

References

Brownmiller, S. (1975). *Against our will: Men, women, and rape.* New York: Simon & Schuster.

Burt, M. R. (1980). Cultural myths and supports for rape. *Journal of Personality and Social Psychology, 38*(2), 217-230.

Diamond, S. (1985). Pornography: Image and reality. In V. Burstyn (Ed.), *Women against censorship.* Vancouver: Douglas and McIntyre.

Fine, M., & Johnson, F. L. (1984, November). *The impact of feminist analyses on research about pornography.* Paper presented at the Speech Communication Association Annual Meeting, Chicago.

Gerbner, G. (1984, September). *Gratuitous violence and exploitative sex: What are the lessons?* Presentation to the Study Committee of the Communications Commission of the National Council of Churches Hearing, New York.

Kuhn, A. (1982). *Women's pictures.* Boston: Routledge & Kegan Paul.

Kuhn, A. (1985). *The power of the image: Essays on representation and sexuality.* Boston: Routledge & Kegan Paul.

Rakow, L. (1985, May). *A paradigm of one's own: Feminist ferment in the field.* Paper presented at the International Communication Association Conference, Honolulu, HI.

Rakow, L. (1986). Feminist approaches to popular culture: Giving patriarchy its due. *Communication, 9*(1), 19-42.

Root, J. (1984). *Pictures of women: Sexuality.* Boston: Pandora.

Treichler, P. A., & Wartella, E. (1986). Interventions: Feminist theory and communication studies. *Communication, 9*(1), 1-18.

Zillmann, D., & Bryant, J. (1982). Pornography, sexual callousness, and the trivialization of rape. *Journal of Communication, 32*(4), 10-21.

Zillmann, D., & Bryant, J. (1984). Effects of massive exposure to pornography. In N. Malamuth & E. Donnerstein (Eds.), *Pornography and sexual aggression.* New York: Academic Press.

7

Television, Religion, and Religious Television:

Purposes and Cross Purposes

STEWART M. HOOVER

In spite of what has been called the substantial ferment in the field of mass communication research, most perspectives seem to share the idea that television, as it is experienced by its viewers, is primarily about meaning. As a central ritual or experience of daily life and leisure, television viewing has come to play an important role in the establishment, maintenance, or change of cultural values, social behaviors, and beliefs.

A wide and diverse literature has addressed these issues. Traditional empiricism in a variety of fields has looked at the role of television in a wide variety of beliefs and behaviors, from political attitudes to antisocial behaviors. In contrast, "cultural studies" and "critical" approaches have addressed the theoretical underpinnings of our assumptions about such effects. These and other approaches have produced debates about whether media effects are direct or indirect, limited or powerful, and about the best way to study them. These controversies may never be settled, but much can be learned from both perspectives about how television relates to the ways in which its viewers live and think about their lives.

A "middle range" of theory about television has been attempted by some researchers, where evidence of television's involvement or effects is analyzed in terms of its "enculturative" significance. The most prominent example of such a middle range of approaches has been the ongoing work in television and enculturation undertaken by those who identify themselves with the "cultural indicators" approach to media studies. George Gerbner and his colleagues (Gerbner, Gross, Morgan, & Signorielli, 1980, 1982, 1986) have pioneered this field, but they already have been joined by others (for example, Hawkins & Pingree, 1980, 1982; Bryant, Carveth, & Brown, 1981) in a quest for evidence of television's cultural power. Much has been learned about television's involvement in beliefs about power relationships and about social attitudes and its involvement in education and attitude formation among children and youth.

Even though this evolving literature has focused on meaning and belief, little of it has addressed the central activity or orientation of specifically *religious* belief. Admittedly, religion is a particular and unique aspect of social attitude and social behavior. There is much controversy over even the definition of the word *religion*. The classic strains of positivist social theory and social research have tended to discount its importance as a dimension of modern life and modern consciousness. Modernity—it has been thought—will proceed apace *away* from the earlier eras where religious belief competed with more rationalistic worldviews for cultural and social ascendency.

Recent experience, however, has illustrated how important it is to come to terms with religion if we are to work toward comprehensive theories or understandings of individuals and society. A resurgence of interest in religion, and a resurgence of self-conscious religiosity as an aspect of public social and political life, has been a major element of recent American experience. Worldwide, fundamentalist religiosity has become important in many places. While we may have thought at one time that the role of religion as a central force in culture was on the wane, replaced by—among other things—rapidly developing and presumably powerful media institutions, it has become clear that religion has *not* gone away. The mass media and religion are, in some ways, both about the same things—values, beliefs, behaviors. We may have to begin thinking about how they coexist, rather than how the former is "replacing" the latter.

A major setting for their coexistence emerged on the American scene beginning in the mid-1970s. As an aspect of the larger revival of neoevangelicalism of that period, large, prominent, and seemingly powerful religious broadcasting establishments (called, generally, *the electronic church*) began to appear. While they were once thought to have been a flash in the pan, a momentary phenomenon, they have become established to the point that recent scandals involving some of their most prominent leaders have made national and international headlines.

What was unique about these ministries? First of all, they seemed to eschew the "traditional" form and content of religious broadcasting. They were on television, placed at times other than Sunday morning, and delivered by the most sophisticated new technologies (cable and satellite television). They mimicked the form of conventional television. There were Christian talk shows, soap operas, dramas, variety shows, game shows, children's programs, and more. Their hosts and guests were, while not quite of commercial quality, at least smoother and more conventional-looking than was the case with the previous stereotype of the "radio preacher." Most important, they claimed (and were believed by the usually skeptical secular media) to have achieved huge audiences of viewers. Claims as high as 100 million were reported — and uncritically published — in major national magazines and newspapers. Their assumed significance was further related not only to the *size* of these audiences, but to their breadth. It was widely thought that, due to their new formats and appeals, a more diverse audience was being reached. Instead of the highly religious, particularist, and marginal audience of religious radio, these programs were beginning to attract an upscale, urban, and middle-class audience.

This development is of concern to us because it appeared, on its face, to be a new wrinkle in the relationship between television and culture. If, as has been said, television is in a way a "new cultural religion" (Gerbner & Connoly, 1978), what do we do with a kind of television that claims to be *real* religion? If we assume for the sake of argument that television (or mass culture in general) now fulfills the role once taken by the church and formal religion in enculturation and socialization, what do we do when religion captures television?

These are large questions, too large to answer fully here. There are some smaller questions, though, that we can address, within the context of the research traditions we have available to us. Cultural approaches to television are, above all else, open to data that relate to qualitative aspects of belief and behavior. There is more to evidence than clear causality. Associations are also important, even though they cannot prove to be fully predictive. What causes religion? What does religion cause? These are nonsensical questions. What religion is associated with and how it interacts with other sources and centers of meaning is a far more profound issue. It is the purpose of this chapter to discuss what we know, and perhaps what we *can* know, about how television and religion relate to one another in contemporary life. We can assume that they are, in many ways, on the same turf. By looking at how television that claims to be "religious" and television that does not, compete and relate to beliefs and behaviors, we can gain insights into their relationships and power in contemporary culture.

The cultivation perspective provides some theoretical formulations, frameworks, and methodologies through which these issues can be addressed. It also provides a rich set of findings with reference to the cultural functioning of conventional television against which we might compare this new "religious" television. We know, for example, that amount of television viewing has been found to be associated with a wide range of beliefs and behaviors. A major development in this tradition has been the formulation of the idea of mainstreaming (Gerbner et al., 1980). That is, many of television's most interesting contributions to belief and behavior are not directly or universally present, but are conditionally so. Television seems to play a type of *demographic* role where it is differentially involved, interacting with other demographic dimensions. It seems to cultivate a common set of values or ideas among its most involved (heavy) viewers including viewers from a wide range of demographic groups that traditionally have been distinct. More educated viewers, for instance, who should vary significantly in belief and behavior from those who are less educated, often do not, if they are *also* heavier viewers of television.

Thus the cultural power of television is revealed in complex associations, not in direct causal relationships (a matter that has understandably led to a good deal of speculation about directionality; see, in particular, Hirsch, 1980).

Very little research on specifically *religious* television has taken this more associational (or "cultural") approach. From the earliest days of religious broadcasting, surveys and other studies have charted the demographic characteristics of the audience, while leaving aside questions of how these programs relate to broader cultural meaning. The one early exception was the field's landmark study, by Parker, Barry, and Smythe (1955), that attempted to address religious radio and television audiences along a number of dimensions, including cultural ones.

More typical was the study done by Johnstone (1972), that charted the demographic characteristics of the audience for religious radio, finding it to be largely made up of older, religious, lower-income, less-educated, and female listeners. More recent studies, such as those of Buddenbaum (1981) and Gaddy and Pritchard (1985) confirmed that the religious television audience is made up of the "already religious" (in spite of the electronic church's claims to be reaching outside this traditional audience — and fueling the controversy *within* religious institutions about these programs' possible negative effect on other kinds of religious behaviors.

An extensive literature is developing in this field, but it continues to be concentrated primarily on questions of content, demographics, and beliefs, with little of it moving to the broader question of how the experience of religious television viewing might relate to that of conventional viewing for the audience. Abelman and Neuendorf (1985, 1987), for example, have found that religious television content addresses a wide range of political, religious, and social issues. Gaddy (in press) has found that viewing of religious television bears a significant relationship to conventional religious behaviors, at least for certain sectors of the audience. A recent controversy has centered around the size and demographic characteristics of the audience, with defenders of the electronic church arguing that it is an entirely new and powerful form of broadcasting, attracting a new, nontraditionally religious audience (and one less marginal and thus more significant politically and socially; see, in particular, Clark & Virts, 1985) while other observers have proposed a note of caution (Hoover, 1987).

The most important recent study, the Annenberg-Gallup Study of Religious Broadcasting (Gerbner, Gross, Hoover, Morgan, & Signorielli, 1984), was also primarily concerned with potential social, political, and religious-institutional effects of religious broadcasting. (For an extensive discussion, see Hadden & Frankl, 1987, and Gerbner et al., 1989).

This study was significant both for the scope of its analysis, and for the quality and depth of the sample of religious viewers it was able to obtain. Working through the viewing-diary archives of the Arbitron Corporation, the researchers were able to obtain a large sample of *confirmed* viewers of religious broadcasting. (Because this type of viewing is a relatively *infrequent* behavior, few actual religious viewers appear in most probability samples of the total audience; for a complete discussion, see Hoover, 1987). Gerbner et al. (1984) were thus able to obtain two large samples of respondents who indicated (in viewing diaries) that they were viewers and nonviewers of religious television.

These data thus provide an unprecedented opportunity to evaluate how religious and conventional television relate to a wide range of beliefs and behaviors, allowing us to evaluate the relative contribution of each to the enculturation of the audience. This was an extension of previous cultivation analyses in that it entailed examination of correlates of exposure to two different types of television viewing along a range of demographic, belief, and behavior dimensions.

Methodology

The sample was drawn from a random selection of viewers who had participated in Arbitron's diary-based ratings sweeps in 1982, in 10 northeastern and 10 southeastern television markets. Respondents were drawn from two "pools," made up of (1) those who had viewed 15 minutes or more of religious television during their week of diary keeping, and (2) those who had not. One thousand three hundred one of each type were selected, and reinterviewed, by telephone, in fall 1983. The interview covered a wide range of religious, social, political, and media beliefs and behaviors, making direct comparisons with previous research possible.

For this study, the sample was analyzed in two modes. First, comparisons were made between the religious-viewing and nonreligious-viewing respondents as separate samples. Second, the two groups were combined into one sample, weighting the religious-viewing subsample so as to represent its actual proportion of the total conventional television audience.

The Annenberg-Gallup data set allows for some basic groundwork on which further research and theory building can and should be done. The following issues were addressed. First, consistent with the methodological approach described by Gerbner (1973), it examines the *content* of religious and conventional television. What religious, social, political, or other dimensions are present? What is the point of view of the content on which we might base an analysis of how it contributes to beliefs and behaviors? Second, it looks at the relationship between *conventional* television and religiosity. We already know, from previous research, how religious television relates to the religious lives of its viewers. If we are to compare these two types of programs however, we must also be able to say something about how conventional television relates to religious belief and behavior. Third, it focuses on the contribution of religious and conventional television to a variety of religious and social beliefs and behaviors and evaluates evidence concerning how these two classes of viewing may compete for a role in cultivating certain beliefs and behaviors. A summary of what has been learned so far follows.

The Content of Religious and Conventional Television

The Annenberg-Gallup Study did not conduct a systematic analysis of the religious content of conventional television. Ongoing content analyses connected as part of the Cultural Indicators project, however, contained at least one religious dimension, that of whether a given program contained any religious content. An analysis of these data revealed that religion has been infrequent as a theme of conventional prime-time television. Out of 1,420 programs analyzed in the years from 1967 to 1979, only 311 had religion present as a theme, and it never appeared as a "major" theme.

Religious programs and people on religious television are, not surprisingly, much more likely to be religious. Beyond that obvious conclusion, the content analysis of religious programs conducted as part of the Annenberg-Gallup Study found relatively little difference between the demographic make-up of religious and conventional television (Gerbner et al., 1984). Table 7.1 presents a comparison among the gender, age, and race distribution on religious and conventional television programs.

The idea that religious television might provide some sort of an alternative to conventional television, at least in terms of its demographics, is not supported by these data. If anything, the power and prominence concentration enjoyed by white males in prime-time drama is also found in religious television.

In an analysis of the representation of family life in the two types of programming, there was an interesting difference. While religious television participants were much more likely to be married (34% vs. 19%), they were a bit less likely to have children (13% vs. 19%) and much less likely to appear to think that family life was important (25% vs. 42%).

In these ways, as well as some others, the overall sense of the relationship between the content of religious and conventional television was a general concordance on those issues where data were avail-

Table 7.1 Social Age, and Race/Ethnic Group of Participants in Religious Television Programs and Major Characters in Prime-Time Dramatic Programs

	Religious Programs (1982)								Prime-Time Dramatic Programs (1969-1981)							
	All		Men			Women			All		Men			Women		
	N	C%	N	C%	(R%)	N	C%	(R%)	N	C%	N	C%	(R%)	N	C%	(R%)
N =	752		498			254			3012		2123			886		
Social Age																
Child-Adols.	28	3.7	17	3.4	(60.7)	11	4.3	(39.3)	187	6.2	127	6.0	(67.9)	60	6.8	(32.1)
Young Adult	99	13.2	54	10.8	(54.5)	45	17.7	(45.5)	644	21.4	395	18.6	(61.3)	249	28.1	(38.7)
Settled Adult	599	79.7	413	82.9	(68.9)	186	73.2	(31.1)	2023	67.1	1484	69.9	(73.4)	539	60.8	(26.6)
Elderly	23	3.1	11	2.2	(47.8)	12	4.7	(52.2)	95	3.2	72	3.4	(75.8)	23	2.6	(24.2)
N =	752		498			254			2794		1972			819		
Race																
White	666	88.6	436	87.6	(65.5)	230	90.6	(34.5)	2507	89.7	1757	88.9	(70.0)	753	91.9	(30.0)
Black	77	10.2	56	11.2	(72.7)	21	8.3	(27.3)	212	7.6	159	8.1	(75.0)	53	6.5	(25.0)
Oriental	6	0.8	3	0.6	(50.0)	3	1.2	(50.0)	28	1.0	23	1.2	(82.1)	5	0.6	(17.9)
Cannot Code	0	0.0	0	0.0	(0.0)	0	0.0	(0.0)	37	1.3	27	1.4	(73.0)	7	0.9	(18.9)
Hispanic	11	1.5	6	1.2	(54.5)	5	2.0	(45.5)	60	2.1	49	2.5	(81.7)	11	1.3	(18.3)
Average																
Chronological Age	41		42			39			36		37			32		

NOTE: Two percentages are given for each category: the percent of men or women who fall within that category (C%) and the percent of each category who are men and the percent who are women (R%).

able for both. The major contrast between religious and conventional content was their topicality. Because of the thematic nature of many religious programs, they differ from prime-time network programs in their greater tendency to deal with social and political issues (Abelman & Neuendorf, 1985).

Religious and Social Beliefs and Behaviors

How, then, do religious and conventional television compare and contrast in terms of their relationship to sociocultural dimensions of their audiences? As noted above, the general demographic outline of the religious audience has been known for some time. In recent years, as the political significance of these programs has become an issue, it has become clear that these programs are also associated with the conservative political values that have always been a part of the evangelical and fundamentalist subcultures (Hoover, 1987).

Table 7.2 contrasts viewers of religious and conventional television on a number of self-explanatory demographic dimensions using Pearson Correlation Coefficients (using unweighted data). The two religiosity variables are constructed from standard belief items. In order to clarify the extent to which involvement in the neoevangelical movement might be important, a special scale of literalism-pentecostalism was constructed out of items on: biblical literalism, having been born again, and agreeing that speaking in tongues is an appropriate behavior. The directionality of these items is toward that of the labeled value. For example, for the Neoevangelicalism scale, a higher value indicates neoevangelicalism. (In addition, sex was coded so that female is the higher value, and for race, nonwhites take the higher value.)

From this table it appears that in basic demographic terms, the audiences for religious television and that for conventional television are reasonably similar. Heavy viewers of either religious or conventional television tend to have less education and lower incomes, to be female and nonwhite; they also tend to be older (but not significantly so for conventional television). It is only on the specifically religious dimensions that large differences appear. Consistent with what we already know about the nature of contemporary religious television, viewers of religious television are much more religious overall than is the general television audience.

Table 7.2 Demographic and Belief Variables Related to Amount of Religious and Conventional Television Viewing

	Religious Television	Conventional Television
Education	−.262*** (2496)	−.251*** (2505)
Income	−.232*** (2233)	−.250*** (2242)
Age	.321*** (2518)	.169 (2602)
Sex	.064*** (2518)	.112*** (2602)
Race	.187*** (2244)	.129*** (2320)
Importance of Religion	.382*** (2503)	.083*** (2521)
Neoevangelicalism Scale	.495*** (1843)	.049* (1964)

*$p < .05$.
**$p < .01$.
***$p < .001$.
(Ns in parentheses)
(unweighted data)

Associations between viewing and the religiosity variables are much stronger for religious than for conventional television, confirming, among other things, the evangelical orientation of the religious audience. Further, associations between conventional television viewing and the religiosity variables are inconsistent, as described below.

Closer investigation of the relationship of both types of viewing to a variety of beliefs and behaviors reveals that the religious audience differs in important ways from the conventional television audience. In particular, key demographic and belief measures reveal differences between the two groups of viewers that are hidden in the overall relationships.

These data allow us to compare associations of both religious and conventional television viewing with beliefs and behaviors on both social and religious levels. Table 7.3 presents Cultivation Differential data for religious and conventional television viewing for questions

Table 7.3 The Contribution of Religious and General Television to Religious and Social Attitudes

	Religious Television:			Conventional Television:		
	Light: (n) %	CD	Gamma	Light: (n) %	CD	Gamma
Bible Reading "frequent"	241 19.0	32.8	.619***	591 36.3	– 3.4	–.026
Have had a "religious experience"	273 21.9	29.3	.578***	596 37.7	– 3.9	–.085*
Prayer "frequent"	714 56.5	27.1	.576***	1104 68.1	4.2	.109**
Attendance "frequent"	556 44.7	21.1	.408***	885 56.0	– 2.6	.053
Giving "high"	489 43.0	16.5	.325***	790 53.3	– 9.5	–.103**
Pornography Laws "favor tougher"	901 76.3	4.6	.137**	1210 78.8	– 1.2	–.034
Premarital Sex "oppose"	339 28.7	31.2	.486***	690 45.6	– 2.8	–.049
Homosexuality "oppose"	795 69.6	19.9	.562***	1179 78.8	2.8	.083
Voting "voted"	924 72.8	4.4	.117*	1305 79.0	–10.7	–.274***

*$p < .05$.
**$p < .01$.
***$p < .001$.
(unweighted data)

about religious beliefs and social attitudes. For Bible reading, the table presents data for those respondents who report reading the Bible "frequently"; for prayer, the percentages are for those who pray "frequently"; for attendance, it is those who attend church or religious services "once a week or more"; for "giving" it presents the figures for those who contribute $180 or more annually to their church or place of worship. The social attitude items present data for respondents who take the most restrictive approach to the social issues. For pornography laws, it is those who favor "tougher" laws. For the two items having to do with sexual attitudes, the figures are for those who think premarital sex and homosexuality are "always wrong." Voting refers to those who voted in the 1980 general election.

For each item, the first column presents the number and percentage of light-viewing respondents who gave the response. The second column presents the Cultivation Differential (the percentage-point difference between the percentage of "light" and "heavy" viewers who chose that response, subtracting "light" from "heavy"). The third column presents the strength and significance of the relationship between viewing and the item under analysis (Gamma). Parallel columns present these data for light and heavy viewers of religious television alongside light and heavy viewers of conventional television. The viewing measures were dichotomized: "heavy" viewers of religious television are those who reported viewing "sometimes" or "frequently" in the Annenberg-Gallup regional survey. "Light" viewers are those who reported no viewing or "infrequent" viewing of religious television. "Heavy" viewers of conventional television are those who reported watching 4 or more hours of conventional television per day on that same survey. "Light" viewers are those who viewed less than 4 hours per day.

A relatively modest 19% of light viewers of religious television report reading the Bible frequently. Viewing religious television and Bible reading reveal a strong relationship, with heavier viewers more likely, by 33 percentage points, to report frequent reading. No such relationship exists for conventional television. In addition, more frequent religious television viewers are more likely to report having had a "religious experience." More frequent conventional viewers are less likely than lighter viewers to have had such experiences.

Praying is a much more frequently reported behavior. When compared with religious television viewing, a very high proportion of the respondents report frequent prayer. Over half of the light viewers and 85% of the heavy viewers reported that they prayed frequently. The association with conventional television viewing was less extreme, though nearly 70% of the light viewers report praying frequently. This relatively larger light-viewing figure for conventional television is probably less a statement on the power of this type of viewing than it is on what it means for a respondent to say he or she is a "light" viewer of *religious* television. Those who eschew religious television in this sample are, on the whole, less religious than the population at large.

The impact of religious television on church attendance was an early source of controversy about the electronic church. Simply put, the claim was made that religious television might be harming conventional churches by attracting people away from attendance at services into a solitary relationship with religious television programming instead. As Table 7.3 shows, there is instead a strong *positive* association between viewing religious programs and church attendance. There is an insignificant negative association between viewing conventional programs and attendance, however. The figures for contributions of $180 or more per year to a local church show a similar pattern to that of attendance. This time, though, there is a significant negative relationship between conventional television and giving.

The picture is one in which viewing conventional and religious television have different relationships with religiosity. Viewing both religious and conventional television seems to be associated with a mainstream American religiosity of the kind often called "civil religion" or "civic piety." Religious television viewing, however, is far more strongly associated with all these behaviors. There is some evidence, further, that conventional television viewing is negatively associated with some aspects of religiosity.

For example, investigation of subgroups reveals a mainstreaming phenomenon in certain cases. Heavy viewers of conventional television in groups such as those over 65, who are the most frequent church attenders, are significantly less likely to attend church regularly (by 10 percentage points) than light viewers who are over 65. It seems to be the case, then, that while religious television is postively and universally associated with religiosity, conventional television viewing is less so.

There is further divergence between viewers of religious and conventional television in regard to social issues. While there is a significant association between religious television viewing and preferring tougher pornography laws, it is a small association; the association with conventional television viewing is essentially zero.

Sexual attitudes have been a highly salient dimension of the rise of the "new right." As can be seen in Table 7.3, religious and conventional television viewers differ in their association with the belief that premarital sex is "always wrong." While heavy viewers of religious programs are much more likely to espouse this view, there is no significant tendency for heavy viewers of conventional television to feel that premarital sex is "always wrong."

The differential contributions of religious and conventional television in this area is most interesting in certain subgroups, where significant differences were found. For example, among female viewers of religious television, heavy viewers are more likely by 30 percentage points (62.9% vs. 33.2%) than light viewers to feel that premarital sex is morally wrong. Among female viewers of conventional television, however, heavy viewers are *less* likely by five percentage points to feel that premarital sex is wrong. Interestingly, the same pattern holds for those nonwhites, evangelical Christians, and heavy viewers of religious broadcasting who are also heavy viewers of conventional television.

Attitudes toward homosexuality are another salient area for the natural constituency of the electronic church revealing similar patterns to those about premarital sex. For viewers of religious television, it is highly salient, with heavy viewers more likely by 20 percentage points to feel homosexuality is always wrong. For viewers of conventional television, there is no significant relationship.

A finding that is more interesting in light of public concern about the political impact of the electronic church relates to reporting having voted in the 1980 presidential election. While conventional television viewing is negatively associated with voting (heavy viewers are 10 percentage points less likely to have voted), religious viewing is *positively* associated with voting (by 4.4 percentage points). Both of these patterns hold across demographic subgroups.

This finding suggests that the much-noted concern about the political implications of religious broadcasting may have some foundation. Heavy viewers of religious television are, indeed, more likely to vote than are light viewers. Interestingly, conventional television viewing seems to mitigate this effect.

Summary and Conclusions

Religious and conventional television are thought to have competing claims in the cultivation of beliefs and behaviors. The evidence would suggest such a role for conventional television in that previous research has found it to be related to a wide range of beliefs and behaviors. But what of religious beliefs and behaviors?

Religion is not a dominant theme in conventional television. In fact one of the major justifications given by the proponents of religious television for its attraction to its audience is its provision of a religious "alternative" to conventional television. Such producers offer a wide variety of programs intended to mimic the entertainment formats of "regular" television. Research has found (Hoover, 1988) that viewers agree with this assessment of its importance and significance.

Most of the analyses here are of simple relationships. In some cases, controls have been consulted where particularly interesting subgroup comparisons exist. In most cases, the patterns seen in overall relationships hold up across subgroups.

These data suggest that conventional television viewing is not particularly associated with conventional religious beliefs and behaviors. This should not be too surprising given the relative paucity of explicitly religious themes in it. In those cases where there are statistically significant associations between television and religiosity, they tend to be small.

To what exent is religious television a significant alternative to conventional television? Its content has been widely heralded to be specifically reflective of the "new-right" social and political agenda, and unlike conventional television, in certain respects. The cultivation of these two types of television are generally consistent with this picture. In the social attitudes examined here, religious television viewing was associated with more conservative attitudes, while conventional television was not, in most areas. Interestingly, religious and conventional television also show a contrasting relationship to voting behavior. Heavy religious viewing seems to go with voting; heavy viewing of conventional television does not.

The contrasts are interesting. The moralistic tone of religious television is not shared by general television in the area of sexual mores. Thus the charge, sometimes heard from conservative religious circles, that conventional television conveys values and beliefs that are troubling to them, seems to have some support from these data. It would also seem to be the case that religious broadcasting could serve as an acceptable alternative for such interests.

The much feared impact of religious television on conventional religiosity, that it might take numbers or income away from conventional churches, has not been supported by these data or elsewhere. It seems that religious television does not neatly fit into the preexisting structures of belief and behavior defining religion for most of its viewers. This should really not be too surprising. Most research on the impact of mass media on social and cultural life tends to move toward limited rather than direct or imitative effects. Mass media should be expected, then, to play a role in contemporary religious life (however

profound) that is interactive and interrelated with other sources of
salience for its viewers and adherents.

Indeed, cultivation theory would propose a role for religious television much like the one observed here. Religious television should be
expected to be one among many cultural inputs out of which its audiences weave meaning and consciousness.

Conventional television, in contrast, does not seem to be associated
with lessened conventional religiosity. This should also not be too
surprising. The majority of Americans are members of the conventional,
prime-time audience, *not* the religious one. Thus the religious implications of conventional television should be of particular interest to us.
Indeed, heavy viewers of conventional television are, by some measures, less religious and less involved in religious behaviors than are
light viewers. Thus the religious role of contemporary television—as
predicted by Gerbner—seems very much to be one of competition. If
television is a kind of religion in contemporary life, we might expect to
find what we did, that its viewers find it less necessary to participate in
conventional religious behaviors.

It is beyond the scope of this work to say more about the issue of
cultural competition between religion and television. It does appear that
there is evidence here that religious and conventional *television* are
presenting competing motivations and saliences to their audiences.
Religious television is centered around a very specific set of contemporary movements, social issues, and institutions. For the subset of
viewers who watch it regularly (and who are also involved in the
broader religious "new-right" revival of which the electronic church is
a part), it acts to cultivate beliefs and behaviors consistent with its
origins and basic commitments. It does *not*, therefore, represent a new
kind of religion born of media technology which can reach outside of
preexisting structures and ideologies. It seems bound to the ideas,
groups, and concepts that have always been at the heart of American
conservative Christianity. It is as marginal as its roots are.

The real competitor for religion, it seems from these data, may well
be conventional television. Through its very ordinariness, it may have
found its place as an enculturator of the most basic and pervasive values
and conceptions in its audiences. This is a task that we think of as the
province of religion in years gone by. It may then be that, while
television (either in its religious or its conventional forms) cannot be
said to have *replaced* religion altogether, these two institutions may find

themselves in an uneasy coexistence. Religion seems to face, in conventional television, a powerful competitor for cultural power.

References

Abelman, R., & Neuendorf, K. (1985). How religious is religious television programming? *Journal of Communication, 1*(35), Winter, 98-110.

Abelman, R., & Neuendorf, K. (1987). Themes and topics in religious television programming. *Review of Religious Research, 2* (29), Winter, 152-174.

Bryant, J., Carveth, R., & Brown, D. (1981). Television viewing and anxiety: An experimental examination. *Journal of Communication, 31*(1), 106-119.

Buddenbaum, J. (1981). Characteristics of media-related needs of the audience of religious TV. *Journalism Quarterly 58*, Summer, 296-272.

Clark, D., & Virts, P. (1985). *The religious television audience: A new development in measuring audience size.* Paper presented at the Society for the Scientific Study of Religion, Savannah, GA.

Gaddy, G. (in press). Religious television and religious behavior. In R. Abelman & S. Hoover (Eds.), *Religious television: Controversies and conclusions.* Norwood, NJ: Ablex.

Gaddy, G., & Pritchard, D. (1985). When watching religious TV is like attending church. *Journal of Communication, 1*(35), Winter, 123-131.

Gerbner, G. (1973). Cultural indicators: The third voice. In G. Gerbner, L. Gross, & W. Melody (Eds.), *Communication technology and social policy* (pp. 555-573). New York: John Wiley.

Gerbner, G., & Connoly, K. (1978). Television as new religion. *New Catholic World,* March/April, 52-56.

Gerbner, G., Gross, L., Hoover, S., Morgan, M., & Signorielli, N. (1984). *Religion and television.* The technical report of the Annenberg-Gallup Study of Religious Broadcasting. New York: Committee on Electronic Church Research.

Gerbner, G., Gross, L., Hoover, S., Morgan, M., & Signorielli, N. (1989). Responses to Star Wars of a different kind: Reflections on the politics of the religion and television research project (pp. 94-98). *Review of Religious Research.*

Gerbner, G., Gross, L., Morgan, M., & Signorielli, N. (1980). The 'mainstreaming' of America: Violence profile no. 11. *Journal of Communication, 30*(3), 10-29.

Gerbner, G., Gross, L., Morgan, M., & Signorielli, N. (1982). Charting the mainstream: Television's contributions to political orientations. *Journal of Communication, 32*(2), 100-127.

Gerbner, G., Gross, L., Morgan, M., & Signorielli, N. (1986). Living with television: The dynamics of the cultivation process. In J. Bryant & D. Zilmann (Eds.), *Perspectives on media effects* (pp. 17-40). Hillsdale, NJ: Lawrence Erlbaum.

Hadden, J., & Frankl, R. (1987). A critical review of the religion and television research report. *Review of Religious Research, 2* (29), December, 111-124.

Hawkins, R., & Pingree, S. (1980). Some processes in the cultivation effect. *Communication Research, 7*(2), 193-226.

Hawkins, R., & Pingree, S. (1982). Television's influence on social reality. In D. Pearl, L. Bouthilet, & J. Lazar (Eds.), *Television and behavior, Vol. II* (pp. 224-247). Rockville, MD: National Institute of Mental Health.

Hirsch, P. (1980). The 'scary world' of the nonviewer and other anomalies: A reanalysis of Gerbner et al.'s findings of cultivation analysis. *Communication Research, 7*(4), 403-456.

Hoover, S. M. (1987). The religious television audience: A matter of significance, or size? *Review of Religious Research, 2*(29), December, 135-151.

Hoover, S. M. (1988). *Mass media religion: The social sources of the electronic church.* London: Sage.

Johnstone, R. (1972). Who listens to religious radio broadcasts anymore? *Journal of Broadcasting, 16*(1), 90-102.

Parker, E., Barry, D., & Smythe, D. (1955). *The television-radio audience and religion.* New York: Harper & Row.

8

Mennonites and Television:

Applications of Cultivation Analysis to a
Religious Subculture

DIANE ZIMMERMAN UMBLE

Introduction

This chapter examines data from a survey on the social, moral, political, and theological views of North American Mennonites. It explores how a relatively cohesive and distinct subculture, which also has a sizable number of nonviewers, is able to maintain its cultural integrity in interaction with the socializing potential of television.

Mennonites are a small religious group springing from the radical wing of the Reformation. At the time of this survey, North American membership stood at about 202,000. The Mennonites have traditionally espoused a biblical theology, a doctrine of peace and nonresistance, and an emphasis on service and simplicity of life style.

In the past, Mennonites have lived in rural areas and been involved in farming or farm-related occupations. Historically they resisted out-side influences, particularly in the areas of dress, social relationships, and adoption of certain technological innovations. For instance among many Mennonites, social dancing, movie attendance, smoking and drinking, and political participation were discouraged. The ownership of television sets was prohibited in some groups (until the late sixties) and discouraged in others. Within the last 30 years, however, many have adopted American middle class dress and life styles, including the ownership of television sets.

What consequences might exposure to the world of television have for Mennonites who hold a contrasting world view? The Mennonite view of the world has been shaped by a long history of nonviolence, nonparticipation in politics, and traditional sex roles. Television, however, presents a world in which violence and aggression are effective (and often the only) ways of solving problems, and in which racial, sexual, and political roles are defined in more varied ways. Furthermore, except for one or two programs (for example, the short-lived network program, *Aaron's Way*, and the film, *Witness*, which focus on Mennonites' Amish cousins[1], American television has been devoid of images of nonviolence and simplicity — images in which Mennonites might see themselves.

The results of a study of a specific subculture's encounter with television can help to shed light on the survival of subcultures and minority points of view in general. Traditional cultures are preserved through the socializing powers of the family, the school, the church, and the community. Cultural change can often be controlled through these institutions. When television enters into a subculture, however, it too can be a powerful force in the socializing process. The investigation of whether a subculture can resist this force is valuable for students of social change as well as those who seek to preserve traditions. In addition, such studies may enhance understanding of cultivation.

In examining this subculture's encounter with television, a counter argument might be posed that only "liberal" Mennonites own televisions, and therefore their liberal attitudes, and not viewing, account for associations. Mennonites as a group, in comparison to the general public, hold overwhelmingly conservative views on various political, social, and sexual practices. While choosing to own a television may signal an openness to information from outside their subculture, ownership is not a de facto indication of more liberal values. Though a significant number of Mennonites were nonviewers, the majority of Mennonites owned television sets in the seventies.

This investigation is guided by two types of studies: (1) studies of Mennonites, and (2) cultivation studies of the general population. The bulk of research on Mennonites has been historical in nature.

A smaller amount of sociological research has been conducted on contemporary Mennonites. Several studies focusing on cultural change in specific Mennonite communities conclude that Mennonites maintain a strong sense of cohesion in the face of cultural change (Appavoo, 1985; Driedger & Kauffman, 1985; Driedger & Peters, 1973; Redekop, 1969; Wiesel, 1973). Urban Mennonites tend to be somewhat more liberal in their social practices, but urbanization does not seem to alter religious beliefs or reduce their sense of group identity or cohesion (Appavoo, 1985; Driedger & Kauffman, 1982; Hardwick, 1974).

Periodic census surveys have been conducted in the Mennonite Church (Gingerich, 1963; Yoder, 1982). The most recent census in 1982 reports that Mennonites are attracting new members and becoming increasingly diverse in terms of race, ethnic origin, residence, occupation, education, marital status, and denominational background. They are leaving the farm, pursuing higher education and technical training, and moving into skilled and professional occupations. In comparison to their non-Mennonite neighbors, however, they remain more likely to be rural and have relative family stability.

Comparable data for other church denominations is not abundant (Campolo, 1971; Glock & Stark, 1968; Kersten, 1963; Lenski, 1961). What comparisons can be made suggest that Mennonites are more restrictive in terms of personal morality (Kersten, 1963; Lenski, 1961), higher in church participation (Kauffman & Harder, 1975), and more communal in their relationships than most other groups (Glock & Stark, 1968). The theme throughout much of the sociological analysis is that Mennonites have maintained a relatively strong sense of self identity in the face of urbanization, diversification, and expanded social contact.

As numerous chapters in this collection have revealed, cultivation theory has steadily evolved over the past 20 years. Cultivation theory is based on the assumption that television provides persistent and pervasive systems of messages that help to define the dominant current of U. S. culture, the mainstream. This theoretical orientation recognizes that the contribution of television is continuous and interactive. The term *cultivation* describes the contribution television viewing makes to viewers' conceptions of social reality. Cultivation theory recognizes that viewing may generate in some and maintain in others a set of orientations that can be traced to cumulative exposure to the world of television (Gerbner, Gross, Morgan, & Signorielli, 1986, p. 24).

Mainstreaming represents one aspect of cultivation. The mainstream is conceived as "a relative commonality of outlooks and values that exposure to features and dynamics of the television world tends to cultivate" (Gerbner et al., 1986, p. 30). Mainstreaming is indicated when heavy viewers in those demographic groups whose light viewers hold divergent views express a commonality of outlooks and values. Differences among light viewers that might arise out of cultural, social, and/or political characteristics are diminished or absent from the responses of heavy viewers with the group. Mainstreaming "represents a homogenization of divergent views and a convergence of disparate viewers" (Gerbner et al, 1986, p. 31).

Many studies of cultivation (see Chapter 1) have focused on the general population and specific social issues such as violence, aging, and sex roles. More recently a cultivation analysis compared viewers of religious and general television (Gerbner, Gross, Hoover, Morgan, & Signorielli, 1984). The study found that viewing of religious programs was strongly associated with measures of religious behavior, conservative perspectives, likelihood of voting, and the cultivation of traditional sexual values. Heavy viewers of general television, on the other hand, were politically moderate and less likely to vote. They were less likely to attend church and participate in church activities. The study suggests that general television may "supply or supplant (or both) some religious satisfactions and thus lessen the importance of religion for its heavy viewers" (p. 10).

The findings of numerous studies suggest that television viewing cultivates a particular world view, one that often affirms conventional values. In addition, findings suggest that television's view of the world may have its strongest observable influence among those viewers who are least likely to share a given perspective.

Methodology

The data used in this analysis came from the 1972 survey of five Mennonite denominations[2] across the United States and Canada (Kauffman & Harder, 1975). The survey included descriptive data on demographics and theological and social orientations as well as a question on television viewing. The respondents were 3,591 Mennonite church members from 174 Canadian and U.S. congregations. They were selected in a two-stage process (a selection of congregations, then a selection of members) from 1,646 congregations with a total of nearly

190,000 members. The written questionnaire was administered by a research visitor to individual respondents in sample congregations during a meeting called for this purpose. The return rate was 70.5%. (Complete details of the methodology are described in the Appendix, Kauffman & Harder, 1975.)

These data are the only extensive collection of information on these five Mennonite groups. Although somewhat dated, these data are valuable because they provide an opportunity to compare a substantial number of nonviewers with those who view television.

Television viewers were defined as light (under 1 hour), medium (1 to 2.9 hours), and heavy viewers (3 or more hours). Light viewers comprise 30.7% of the sample; medium, 37.9%, and heavy, 16.3% of the sample. Those who view no television at all, 15.1%, were analyzed as a separate group. The analyses control for age, sex, residence (urban/rural), income level, and education; race was not included as 99.3% of the sample was white.

Findings

This analysis focuses on two principle distinctions: (1) between those who chose to watch and those who do not watch television at all, and (2) between those who are light viewers of television and those who are heavy viewers.

This sample of Mennonite church members provides a rare opportunity to make comparisons between nonviewers and those who are heavy and light viewers. Nonviewers comprise 15% of the sample. Most nonviewers (88%) do not own television sets. They are most likely to be members of the Mennonite Church or the Brethren in Christ. They tend to be over 50, live in rural areas and have less than a high school education. Nonviewers often fall at the extremes on the attitude measures, holding more restrictive views than their viewing counterparts.

Table 8.1 describes the daily media exposure of Mennonite church members. While most Mennonites' media exposure is 1 to under 3 hours each day, 15% watch no television, and almost 14% say they do not read books. Almost 12% say they never attend movies, while 20% say they attend movies once a month, and 16% attend once a week. Television-set ownership also varies. Almost 14% do not own a television set, 64% own one, and 27% own more than one.

Table 8.1 Daily Media Consumption among Mennonite Church
Members

| | Hours Daily | | | |
	none	under 1	1-2.9	3 or more
Television	15.1	30.7	37.9	16.3
Radio	4.6	43.8	30.1	21.5
Books	13.5	51.1	24.5	10.9
Newspapers and magazines	2.7	63.4	29.0	4.9

Social Practices

In the past, smoking, drinking alcohol, social dancing, attendance
at movies, and gambling were officially discouraged by Mennonite
groups. Television viewing is negatively associated with support for
these prohibitions.

Attitudes toward smoking and drinking reflect some diversity among
Mennonite church members. Overall, 49% say drinking is always wrong
and 63% say smoking is always wrong (see Table 8.2). In both cases,
television viewing at any level is negatively and significantly associated with that attitude for almost all demographic subgroups. More
nonviewers than viewers are likely to say these practices are always
wrong. Furthermore, heavy viewers are less likely than light or nonviewers to say always wrong.

Overall, television viewing at any level is negatively associated with
prohibitions against drinking. When results are examined by gender,
place of residence, and income, they show that television viewing is
significantly associated with the more moderate attitudes for all subgroups. Mennonites with less education are more likely than their more
educated counterparts to say alcohol consumption is always wrong, and
attitudes of both groups are less negative among heavy viewers. Viewing in this case seems to be associated with more moderate attitudes,
but not with homogenization of different perspectives.

For smoking, patterns of association are similar (Table 8.2). Nonviewers are more opposed to smoking than are their viewing counterparts. Viewing is negatively and significantly associated with the attitudes of the elderly and is not associated for younger respondents. All
other subgroup comparisons show across-the-board cultivation in the
direction of moderation of negative attitudes toward smoking.

Table 8.2 Relationship between Amount of Television Viewing and Respondents Who Say Drinking Alcohol and Smoking Are Always Wrong

	Drinking Alcohol				Smoking			
	%N[a]	%L[b]	CD[c]	Gamma	%N	%L	CD	Gamma
OVERALL	66	45	− 3	−0.14***	76	64	− 4	−0.15***
Controlling for:								
AGE								
Teens	60	32	6	−0.11−	69	49	1	−0.10−
Young Adult	40	24	3	0.09−	63	53	0	−0.08−
Middle Age	72	41	17	−0.05−	78	57	13	−0.08−
Older	80	59	− 6	−0.21***	88	73	− 3	−0.22***
SEX								
Male	62	40	− 5	−0.18***	75	60	− 5	−0.20***
Female	71	51	− 6	−0.15***	81	68	− 5	−0.14***
PLACE								
Rural	73	52	− 5	−0.17***	80	68	− 5	−0.18***
Urban	55	39	− 3	−0.11***	72	60	− 4	−0.11**
INCOME								
Low	62	52	− 4	−0.12*	77	71	− 4	−0.18**
Mid	69	42	− 1	−0.15***	77	63	− 5	−0.16***
High	62	40	−11	−0.13**	74	59	− 4	−0.09−
EDUCATION								
Low	76	57	− 3	−0.18***	85	72	− 7	−0.20***
Med	73	50	−10	−0.19***	84	66	− 1	−0.14**
High	42	31	−11	−0.12**	60	55	−12	−0.15***

*$p < .05$.
**$p < .01$.
***$p < .001$.
[a]%N = percent of nonviewers giving response.
[b]%L = percent of light viewers giving response.
[c]CD = Cultivation Differential, percent of heavy viewers giving response minus percent of light viewers giving response.
Viewing: Light = under 1 hour daily
         Medium = over 1 and up to 2.9 hours daily
         Heavy = 3 or more hours daily

Attitudes toward Sexual Practices

Mennonites have a reputation for upholding traditional family values. Their attitudes toward homosexual activity, premarital sex, extramarital sex, and abortion tend to be restrictive. The association of these attitudes with television viewing varies.

A majority of Mennonites (84% overall) oppose premarital sex. Television, however, generally portrays premarital sexual activity in a positive light. Television viewing is negatively and significantly associated with this attitude across all 14 demographic subgroups except the middle aged. Heavy viewers are less likely to say premarital sex is always wrong than their light or nonviewing counterparts (Table 8.3). Among heavy viewers, young adults have more lenient attitudes toward premarital sex than the middle aged or elderly, men have more lenient attitudes than women, and rural dwellers are more lenient than urban dwellers. While attitudes reflect across-the-board relationships, among certain demographic subgroups the level of association is enhanced, possibly related to the salience of the issue.

Attitudes toward extramarital sex present a different picture. Again a majority of Mennonites say extramarital sex is always wrong (86% overall), but in this case, television viewing is not strongly associated with expressing this attitude, although most groups show small negative associations. The subgroups that do show an association include males, urban dwellers, and those with more education. For these three groups, heavy viewers are less likely to say extramarital sex is always wrong than their light or nonviewing counterparts. Television's portrayal of extramarital sex is generally negative, so it is not surprising to find that viewing holds limited association with this attitude among Mennonites who also hold a dim view of extramarital sex.

When it comes to abortion, Mennonites show more diversity. Slightly more than half (57% overall) say abortion is always wrong. Television viewing is negatively and significantly associated with this attitude across all the demographic subgroups except young adults and urban dwellers. Nonviewers are more likely than viewers to say abortion is always wrong than are viewers. Heavy viewing is associated with a moderation in abortion attitudes. Fewer heavy viewers say it is always wrong than do their light-viewing counterparts. Mainstreaming can be observed among young people and the elderly, men and women, and those with little and more education. The gap widens among those with low and high income. Those of high income are more liberal on this issue and are even more so when heavy viewers, though all income groups show less opposition to abortion as viewing increases.

Attitudes toward homosexuality among Mennonites are significantly associated with viewing for half the demographic subgroups (Table 8.3). The vast majority of Mennonites say homosexual activity is always wrong (86% overall). Those who hold the most restrictive

Table 8.3 Relationship between Amount of Television Viewing and Respondents Who Say Always Wrong on Measures of Attitudes toward Sexual Practices

	Premarital Sex				Extramarital Sex				Abortion				Homosexuality			
	%N[a]	%L[b]	CD[c]	Gamma	%N	%L	CD	Gamma	%N	%L	CD	Gamma	%N	%L	CD	Gamma
OVERALL	93	86	−9	−0.26***	88	87	−6	−0.10**	71	57	−7	−0.14***	93	83	1	−0.12**
Controlling for:																
AGE																
Teens	85	80	−15	−0.28***	62	68	−8	−0.03−	63	42	0	−0.12*	90	76	6	−0.07−
Young Adult	80	70	−7	−0.18**	93	88	−2	−0.11−	50	42	7	−0.05−	89	74	4	−0.09−
Middle Age	98	83	5	−0.08−	94	93	1	−0.10−	75	58	−7	−0.15**	98	79	7	−0.02−
Older	98	95	−5	−0.34***	90	87	1	0.01−	85	66	−8	−0.25***	96	90	−1	−0.20**
SEX																
Male	93	84	−14	−0.35***	88	87	−11	−0.21***	65	52	−4	−0.13***	93	83	−2	−0.15**
Female	94	88	−7	−0.25***	90	86	−1	−0.04−	76	63	−11	−0.18***	94	84	1	−0.11*
PLACE																
Rural	95	90	−14	−0.38***	85	86	−6	−0.09−	74	63	−13	−0.21***	95	87	−3	−0.24***
Urban	90	82	−5	−0.15***	92	87	−4	−0.12*	63	52	−2	−0.06−	90	79	4	−0.00−
INCOME																
Low	96	87	−3	−0.33***	88	85	−2	0.11−	73	65	−7	−0.18**	97	86	7	−0.18*
Mid	93	88	−11	−0.26***	92	88	−5	−0.12−	70	59	−6	−0.12**	94	83	1	−0.05−
High	93	81	−10	−0.22***	93	89	−2	−0.08−	63	48	−9	−0.11**	91	81	−1	−0.10−
EDUCATION																
Low	95	96	−16	−0.46***	83	80	−6	−0.07−	78	68	−14	−0.19***	94	91	−3	−0.20**
Medium	95	83	−4	−0.21***	87	92	−3	−0.03−	74	54	−3	−0.13***	96	89	0	−0.12−
High	88	78	−10	−0.21***	96	91	−7	−0.18*	54	49	−9	−0.13***	89	72	−5	−0.13*

*$p < .05$.
**$p < .01$.
***$p < .001$.

[a]%N = percent of nonviewers giving response.
[b]%L = percent of light viewers giving response.
[c]CD = Cultivation Differential, percent of heavy viewers giving response minus percent of light viewers giving response.

Viewing: Light = under 1 hour daily
Medium = over 1 and up to 2.9 hours daily
Heavy = 3 or more hours daily

149

attitudes are the nonviewers. Heavy viewers are slightly less likely to say always wrong than are their light-viewing counterparts.

An index of attitudes toward sexual practices was created (standardized alpha = .569), and multiple regression analysis was performed. Despite clear subgroup variations, the regression analysis reveals an overall negative association between beliefs that such practices are always wrong and television viewing. The beta for viewing ($-.13, p <$ .001) withstands simultaneous controls for age, sex, residence, income, and education.

Religious Activity, Politics, Voting, and War

Mennonites place high importance on participation in church and are regular church attenders. Overall, 70% attend church weekly or more and 46% say church is very important. Yet, television viewing is generally negatively associated with these attitudes (Table 8.4). Nonviewers attend more and say church is more important than viewers. Furthermore, importance and attendance generally decline among medium and heavy viewers.

Mennonites traditionally have spurned political participation. The attitude arose out of their ambivalence toward civil authority bred in their history of persecution by civil authorities. With the coming of World Wars I and II, Mennonites became somewhat more politically active through advocacy for alternative service for those who were conscientious objectors to participation in the military.

Overall, 77% of the sample said church members should vote, and 65% said members could hold public office. But less than half voted in all or most of the recent elections. As can be seen in Table 8.5, television viewing is significantly associated across all demographic subgroups with positive attitudes toward members voting or holding office. Nonviewing Mennonite church members are much less likely to say members should vote or hold public office than are their viewing counterparts. As viewing increases, support for voting increases (except for those of low income for which support decreases).

For example, while 66% of nonviewing young adults support voting, only 38% of their nonviewing elders hold the same views. Viewers among these two groups hold attitudes differing by only 1 or 2%. At all education levels, nonviewers are less likely to support voting than are viewers. Overall, television viewing is associated with approval of political involvement.

Table 8.4 Relationship between Amount of Television Viewing and Respondents Who Say that Church is Very Important and Those Who Attend Worship Weekly or More

	Church is Very Important				Attend Worship Weekly or more			
	%N[a]	%L[b]	CD[c]	Gamma	%N	%L	CD	Gamma
OVERALL	61	47	− 9	−0.18***	82	73	− 15	−0.24***
Controlling for:								
AGE								
Teens	36	22	0	−0.10−	90	79	−10	−0.28**
Young Adult	40	31	1	−0.80−	73	62	−16	−0.22***
Middle Age	81	50	7	−0.15*	86	74	−12	−0.22**
Older	68	58	−13	−0.20***	78	72	−15	−0.20***
SEX								
Male	61	51	−20	−0.25***	86	75	−21	−0.29***
Female	62	43	− 1	−0.12***	80	71	−12	−0.21***
PLACE								
Rural	32	45	− 5	−0.20***	86	75	−10	−0.25***
Urban	58	49	−14	−0.16***	75	71	−21	−0.23***
INCOME								
Low	66	47	− 2	−0.21***	78	66	−19	−0.26***
Mid	59	52	−16	−0.22***	89	74	−17	−0.33***
High	63	45	− 8	−0.12**	81	74	−12	−0.17**
EDUCATION								
Low	59	50	−12	−0.19***	80	74	−14	−0.24***
Medium	60	45	− 8	−0.20***	87	71	−12	−0.26***
High	64	47	− 9	0.07***	81	73	−23	−0.24***

*p < .05.
**p < .01.
***p < .001.
[a]%N = percent of nonviewers giving response.
[b]%L = percent of light viewers giving response.
[c]CD = Cultivation Differential, percent of heavy viewers giving response minus percent of light viewers giving response.
Viewing: Light = under 1 hour daily
        Medium = over 1 and up to 2.9 hours daily
        Heavy = 3 or more hours daily

Differences among viewers and nonviewers occur in terms of actual voting. Nonviewers are less likely to have actually voted than are viewers. The middle aged, the highly educated and urban dwellers are more likely to be voters than are their counterparts within the subgroup.

Table 8.5 Relationship between Amount of Television Viewing and Responses to Measures of Political Attitudes

	Strongly Agree with Antiwar Stance				Agree Members Should Vote				Actually Voted			
	%N[a]	%L[b]	CD[c]	Gamma	%N	%L	CD	Gamma	%N	%L	CD	Gamma
OVERALL	64	44	−11	−0.25***	49	81	2	0.35***	10	26	−7	0.09***
Controlling for:												
AGE												
Teens	54	41	−12	−0.25***	51	77	9	0.43***	0	1	0	0.01–
Young Adult	58	51	−19	−0.21***	66	80	1	0.22**	10	22	−4	0.07–
Middle Age	65	44	−2	−0.19**	50	84	1	0.26***	12	36	−9	0.10*
Older	70	44	−12	−0.29***	38	78	1	0.40***	11	28	5	0.29***
SEX												
Male	69	45	−8	−0.24***	48	81	6	0.40***	12	31	−14	0.06–
Female	60	43	−12	−0.26***	50	80	1	0.32***	9	20	0	0.12***
PLACE												
Rural	66	47	−13	−0.28***	44	74	5	0.36***	7	24	−9	0.10***
Urban	61	41	−10	−0.21***	58	87	1	0.30***	16	28	−24	0.05–
INCOME												
Low	62	41	−10	−0.25***	53	86	−6	0.37***	15	35	−15	0.14**
Mid	67	44	−11	−0.24***	42	83	2	0.38***	8	28	−10	0.09**
High	67	44	−9	−0.24***	53	80	5	0.36***	10	27	2	0.17***
EDUCATION												
Low	63	41	−5	−0.21***	43	72	6	0.35***	7	21	−9	0.10***
Medium	59	41	−15	−0.28***	45	79	4	0.37***	10	29	−5	0.06–
High	69	48	−14	−0.27***	63	89	5	0.46***	16	29	−3	0.14***

*$p < .05$.
**$p < .01$.
***$p < .001$.

[a] %N = percent of nonviewers giving response.
[b] %L = percent of light viewers giving response.
[c] CD = Cultivation Differential, percent of heavy viewers giving response minus percent of light viewers giving response.

Viewing: Light = under 1 hour daily
Medium = over 1 and up to 2.9 hours daily
Heavy = 3 or more hours daily

152

For those groups for which television has significant association, heavy viewing is associated with a lower likelihood of voting.

Some of the largest differences between heavy and light viewers emerged for the question of participation in war. Mennonites have traditionally held the theological position of nonparticipation in military service. Overall, three-quarters agree that Christians should take no part in war. Nonviewers are most likely to support this position (Table 8.5). Heavy viewers are less likely than light viewers to strongly agree; the association is negative and significant for all subgroups. Young adults' attitudes reflect the largest cultivation differentials in regard to these attitudes (19% difference between the responses of light and heavy viewers). Mainstreaming is found among less and more educated (but not middle groups). Overall, Mennonites who are heavy viewers are less likely to support an antiwar stance. Television's stories lend little support to a pacifist perspective.

On the other hand, when faced with a question about the draft and given a choice between selecting noncombatant or alternative service and joining the military, no significant relationship between viewing and choosing some form of alternative service was found. The vast majority of respondents say they would chose some form of alternative service regardless of viewing level.

For generations, the peace position has been a Mennonite distinctive. While the practice of rejecting combatant military service is not associated with viewing, the antiwar attitude appears to erode in association with viewing.

Summary and Conclusions

Data on Mennonite church members have been interpreted from the theoretical perspectives of cultivation and mainstreaming. In general, Mennonite church members tend to be restrictive in their views on questions of social and sexual morality, and nonviewers are usually more restrictive than viewers. The data illustrate that, in most cases, the widest differences are between Mennonites who chose not to watch television and those who do. Television viewing, even in small amounts, is often associated with a more moderate point of view; heavy viewing contributes to already liberalized perspectives.

Overall, television viewing is generally associated with the cultivation of more moderate views in many measures of social practices and sexual conduct. Heavy viewers are much less restrictive than their light or nonviewing counterparts in attitudes toward smoking, drinking, premarital sex, and abortion.

Mainstreaming occurs in some cases. The most common pattern of convergence (among subgroups whose light viewers would otherwise be at the extremes) occurs among the elderly and young adults. Mainstreaming between younger Mennonites and their elders occurs in association with attitudes toward abortion. In many cases among heavy viewers, differences between groups who usually hold divergent views (the elderly and young adults) are not found.

In terms of Mennonite participation in worship and importance of church, heavy viewing is associated with erosion of support for these behaviors. Furthermore, while the traditional attitude that Christians should not participate in war is sharply reduced among heavy viewers, the practice of personally shunning combatant military duty seems to withstand association with heavy viewing.

Mennonites, on a few issues, do demonstrate some resistance to television's impact on their perspectives. The nature of the issue seems to be a factor in the lack of cultivation. Mennonites seem less likely to demonstrate an inclination to violate moral standards in relation to sexual conduct (homosexual activity or extramarital sex, for example). It may be that television acts as a confirmation for their points of view.

In general, however, the pattern is one of across-the-board cultivation, with mainstreaming occurring mainly among the younger and older generations. The assimilating power of television does appear to encroach upon the boundaries established by traditional Mennonite culture. As a result, some of their attitudes have shifted away from traditional Mennonite perspectives.

Notes

1. The Amish and Mennonites have the same roots in the Radical Reformation and hold in common the practices of adult baptism, nonresistance, and an emphasis on community. The Amish were founded in a division of the Swiss Mennonite in the 1690s over differences in the understanding of exclusion—the insistence that members who were excommunicated be socially avoided or shunned. Amish today differ from Mennonites in the extent to which they have refused to incorporate change into religious and social practices.

2. The five denominations represented in the data include: the Mennonite Church (MC), the General Conference Mennonite Church (GC), the Mennonite Brethren (MB),

the Brethren in Christ (BIC), and the Evangelical Mennonite Brethren (EMC). The groups hold essentially the same doctrinal positions, but vary in the degree to which they have incorporated pietistic and evangelistic influences into their practices. The denominations are listed above from the largest to the smallest in size. Computations for the sample as a whole contain weighting factors for the individual denominations to better approximate numbers in the actual population.

References

Appavoo, D. (1985). Ideology, family and group identity in a Mennonite community in southern Ontario. *Mennonite Quarterly Review, 59*, 67-93.

Campolo, A. R. (1971). *A denomination looks at itself.* Valley Forge, PA: Judson.

Driedger, L., & Kauffman, J. H. (1982). Urbanization of Mennonites: Canadian and American comparisons. *Mennonite Quarterly Review, 56*, 269-290.

Driedger, L., & Peters, J. (1973). Ethnic identity: A comparison of Mennonite and other German students. *Mennonite Quarterly Review, 47*, 225-244.

Gerbner, G., Gross, L., Hoover, S., Morgan, M., & Signorielli, N. (1984). *Religion and television: A research report.* Philadelphia: The Annenberg School of Communications, University of Pennsylvania.

Gerbner, G., Gross, L., Morgan, M., & Signorielli, N. (1980). The 'mainstreaming' of America: Violence profile no. 11. *Journal of Communication, 30*(3), 10-29.

Gerbner, G., Gross, L., Morgan, M., & Signorielli, N. (1986). Living with television: The dynamics of the cultivation process. In J. Bryant & D. Zillmann (Eds.), *Perspectives on media effects*, Hillsdale, NJ: Lawrence Erlbaum.

Gingerich, M. (1963). *The Mennonite family census of 1963.* Mennonite Historical and Research Committee, mimeographed report, Elkhart, IN.

Glock, C., & Stark, R. (1968). *American piety: The nature of religious commitment.* Berkeley: University of California Press.

Hardwick, R. S. (1974). *Change and continuity in two Mennonite communities: The effect of urban and rural settings.* Unpublished doctoral dissertation, University of Virginia.

Kauffman, H., & Harder, L. (1975). *Anabaptists: Four centuries later.* Scottdale, PA: Herald.

Kersten, L. K. (1963). *The Lutheran ethic.* Garden City, NY: Doubleday.

Lenski, G. (1961). *The religious factor.* Garden City, NY: Doubleday.

Redekop, C. (1969). *The old colony Mennonites: Dilemmas of ethnic minority life.* Baltimore, MD: Johns Hopkins Press.

Wiesel, B. B. (1973). *From separation to evangelism: A case study of social and cultural change among the Franconia Conference Mennonites, 1945-1970.* Unpublished doctoral dissertation, University of Pennsylvania.

Yoder, M. L. (1982). *The 1982 Mennonite church census: A summary of findings.* Manuscript. Elkhart, IN.

9

The Role of Cultural Diversity in Cultivation Research

RON TAMBORINI
and
JEONGHWA CHOI

Since Gerbner and Gross first reported findings on cultivation analysis (Gerbner & Gross, 1976a, 1976b), several studies using nonnative U.S. populations have provided conflicting evidence concerning the predictions set forth in the cultivation hypothesis (e.g., Doob & Macdonald, 1979; Pingree & Hawkins, 1981; Wober, 1978). These findings have given rise to several questions directly related to the role of cultural diversity in determining cultivation influences. In particular, the extent to which individuals are exposed to cultures other than their own is important in considering issues associated with (1) the underlying processes that lead to the relationships predicted in the cultivation hypothesis, and (2) whether or not we should be concerned with the aggregate television picture (total television viewing) or exposure to the specific content and associated images found in selected aspects of television when investigating cultivation processes. These issues continue to draw the attention of many scholars interested in the relationship between exposure to television and perceptions of social reality.

In a panel on cultivation analysis presented at the annual meeting of the International Communication Association in New Orleans (1988), Gerbner gave some advice to researchers investigating these and other issues they claimed were related to the study of cultivation (see also epilogue, this book). In essence he told them "write your own theory and test its predictions, because the research you are conducting is not a test of cultivation theory." In his advice to these investigators, Gerbner was not suggesting that their research was of no value in providing explanations of the media's impact on social perceptions, but only that it did not provide a test of cultivation. The processes of influence investigated were not those at work in cultivation, and the procedures used to make observations would not produce data that applied to the predictions set forth in cultivation theory. In his presentation, Gerbner provided several basic assumptions that lay the foundation for cultivation theory and the manner in which research investigating it should be conducted. The assumptions presented by Gerbner included several factors that greatly limit the population in which cultivation should be tested and the conditions within which it should apply. Some of these assumptions are important when considering the role of cultural diversity.

The assumptions presented by Gerbner suggest that (1) compared to other media, television is unique in the relatively nonselective use by its viewers and the restricted availability of images presented in its programming, and (2) due to this nonselective use and restricted image availability, television presents a relatively coherent set of images and messages produced for total populations. Although these assumptions were not new, Gerbner's suggestion that there may be international differences along these dimensions shows the importance of issues concerning the processes at work in viewers with varying levels of cultural diversity. For example, the assumption that television is characterized by a relatively coherent set of images may prohibit the applicability of cultivation theory to individuals who are exposed to international television programming. Such limitations become very important when attempting to determine the extent to which cultivation processes occur outside of the United States. It may be that scholars should avoid looking for cultivation influences in these populations, or that they should not expect to find the same type of evidence for cultivation influence in these viewers that they find in the United States.

These issues are vital when attempting to consider or test the cultivation hypothesis in cross-cultural settings. Diversity in cross-cultural experience should play an important role in an understanding of television's impact on social perceptions. This chapter will investigate the manner in which cultural and intercultural backgrounds are related to the processes associated with cultivation influences. This investigation will compare evidence of cultivation influences in research on: (1) foreign residents living in the United States and exposed to U.S. television; (2) residents of foreign nations exposed either to U.S. television transmission or to U.S. television imports; and (3) residents of foreign nations exposed to their native television. By comparing the evidence of cultivation in these different populations, it may be possible to provide greater insight concerning the nature of the underlying processes. Before we can do this, however, we must first look at the issues concerning the relationship of cross-cultural diversity with exposure to total television viewing and cultivation's underlying processes.

Cultural Diversity and the Television Picture

If we accept Gerbner's position that the important factor in television content is the overall television image, then in order to do research on cultivation in cross-cultural settings we must first do content analyses to determine the "coherent set of images and messages produced" by television for a given culture. Then we can test for cultivation in the association between heavy viewing and perceptual convergence by members of that culture. On the other hand, if we assume that the important factor is exposure to specific content from selected television programming, then we can investigate these hypotheses by concentrating on the association between the viewing of specific programs and perceptual tendencies in line with the images portrayed in those particular program types. It is interesting to note that the second approach is not based on the assumption (and necessary condition) that all television programming in a culture portrays one "coherent set of images and messages." Thus, if we accept the proposition that different television genres and television programming from different geographical and ideological sources often portray a variety of coherent images within a given nation or culture, it is still possible to test the proposition on which this approach is based.

When considering the impact of exposure to U.S. program content on cross-cultural viewers (i.e., foreign sojourners viewing U.S. television programming in the United States, or foreign natives viewing imported U.S. television programming content within their own country), it is difficult to assume that the combination of indigenous television programming and U.S. imported programming provide one coherent set of images. For example, it is likely that many foreign sojourners have been exposed to a great deal of program content in their native country that presents distinctly different images than those presented on U.S. television. In addition, such sojourners may be heavy viewers of imported television content from their native culture made available through U.S. distribution outlets (e.g., a Spanish broadcasting channel, or a home video distributor). Since this chapter is directly concerned with both exposure in cross-cultural settings and exposure by residents of foreign nations to their native television, the ability to deal with the type of exposure situation found in both populations necessitates incorporation of an approach that considers specific programs viewed.

Cultural Diversity and the Underlying Processes of Cultivation

In an extensive literature review of television's influence on the construction of social reality, Hawkins and Pingree (1981b, 1982) suggest that research investigating the conditions and processes of cultivation is likely to be more meaningful than simple correlational research based mainly on one-shot survey data, and they identify several areas that need greater consideration. These include differences in information processing abilities or cognitive structure, degree of attention paid to television programs and perceived reality of television program content, real-life experiences, degree of social interaction and integration, and the specific content of television viewed. The importance of several of these areas becomes evident when considering cultivation in the populations of different cultures or in intercultural populations. For example, differences in information processing abilities associated with language proficiency and sociocultural experiences are particularly evident among foreign sojourners in the United States; degree of perceived reality of television program content may be greatly affected by foreigners' familiarity with the environment portrayed in different television programming; real-life experiences may be largely determined by the cultural norms encountered in an individual's native residence or by the length of an individual's stay in his or her new residence; and degree of social interaction and integration is likely to be somewhat limited to members of one's native culture for individuals who have never lived outside their native land or those who have yet to become acculturated in their new environment.

In this chapter, cultivation influences on nonnative U.S. populations are discussed according to the three categories outlined above. In an attempt to provide an understanding of the manner in which cultural diversity is related to these issues, the findings from several investigations are inspected with special attention paid to issues concerning the logical structure of cultivation theory, the way the theory has been tested, and the assumptions on which the theory is based. Finally, suggestions for future research in this area are discussed in relation to these issues.

Cultivation Research Among Nonnative U.S. Populations

Foreign Residents Living in the United States and Exposed to U.S. Television Programs

Despite the recent increase in research on acculturation and various communication-related phenomena among foreign immigrants and so-journers in the United States (e.g., J. Kim, 1980; Y. Kim, 1977a, 1977b, 1978, 1979), relatively few studies have dealt specifically with cultivation in regard to the viewing of U.S. television among cross-cultural populations within the United States. Given that mass media exposure and the resulting impact on perceptions of both host and native cultures have been important variables in the acculturation process among these populations, it is rather surprising to see the paucity of cultivation inquiries in this context. Several acculturation studies have dealt specifically with mass media (e.g., Y. Kim, 1979a); however, these studies have been mainly concerned with areas such as media uses and gratifications, information preference over time, or the potential of interpersonal communication versus various media consumption to influence acculturation.

Although it is interesting to note the similarities between cultivation and acculturation research in their concern with exposure to television and the resulting adoption of cultural norms, it appears that researchers investigating these influences among various cross-cultural populations in the United States have been more interested in macro-level process analysis than in specific micro-level effects research. In fact, one of the problems associated with communication-acculturation research appears to be the lack of specific effect studies.

The cultivation hypothesis seems to suggest an excellent opportunity to add some concrete evidence to areas of research such as communication acculturation. In particular, strong evidence of cultivation among cross-cultural populations would attest to the strong acculturation potential of mass media. Indeed, one of the major dependent measures in acculturation research has been the perceptual-level of communication, a measure that provides an indication of an individual's cognitive structure in perceiving the host society and culture (Y. Kim, 1978).

Recently, two studies using cross-cultural populations living in the United States have brought evidence to bear on the cultivation hypothesis: one among foreign immigrants (Choi & Tamborini, 1988), and the other among foreign students (Tamborini & Choi, 1988). These groups provided a set of unique characteristics and an interesting opportunity to test cultivation processes in a situation where cultural diversity provides some variety in exposure to televised images. The authors suggested that differences in language proficiency, limited understanding of the sociocultural assumptions of a host society, and a lack of direct experience with the life-styles of a host society could result in: (1) social perceptions about the host society that are more easily influenced by the stereotyped portrayal of the society in television drama, and (2) mass media uses quite different from those of native residents. When considering the process issues discussed by Hawkins and Pingree (1982), potential cultivation among these different populations is likely to be enhanced.

The study among foreign immigrants in the United States (Choi & Tamborini, 1988) investigated two major research questions: (1) whether or not the amount of host television viewing was a good predictor for perceptions of crime prevalence in the host society and personal fear of victimization, and (2) whether or not the associations, if significant, differed according to geographical variations in real-life crime statistics. While the former question was designed to investigate the original cultivation hypothesis, the latter was to look at the "resonance effect" conceptualized in later discussion by Gerbner, Gross, Morgan, and Signorielli (1980a; also see Doob & MacDonald, 1979). In short, neither of the hypotheses was supported in data from samples of Korean immigrants in Baltimore, Maryland, and Lansing, Michigan. Specific television viewing measures as well as total television exposure were poor predictors of immigrant perceptions of crime in the United States and of their personal fear of crime victimization. In addition, results from cultivation differential analyses on subgroups were mixed. In some situations (e.g., estimating the percent of violent crimes) stronger cultivation differentials were found for immigrants who had more contact with host society and culture, while in other situations (e.g., estimating chances of being involved in some kind of violence) the opposite was true.

The study among foreign students in the United States (Tamborini & Choi, 1988) incorporated various conceptual and methodological refinements in cultivation research advanced during the early 1980s (e.g., Hughes, 1980; Hirsch, 1980a, 1980b, 1981a, 1981b; O'Keefe & Reid-Nash, 1984; O'Keefe, 1984; Tamborini, Zillmann, & Bryant, 1984; Tyler, 1980, 1984; Tyler & Cook, 1984; Tyler & Rasinski, 1984; Weaver & Wakshlag, 1984). The investigation tested a series of hypotheses among Korean students at a major U.S. mid-western university. Findings from multiple regression analyses generally contradicted or failed to support the predictions set forth by cultivation. This was most evident in the observations that those who watched more crime-related entertainment fare were less afraid of walking alone at night in their neighborhood, and that those more heavily exposed to crime-related news programs tended to perceive Americans as more friendly and more caring about others. The study also suggested that direct experience was more important than television exposure in predicting social perceptions. For example, extensive travel experience in the United States was found to be significantly associated with fear of victimization and urban fear, suggesting that experience with urban environs has a bearing on perceived urban fear among Korean students.

The two studies are important steps in looking at the influence of television exposure on social perceptions among intercultural viewers. Although there may be good explanations for the failure to find strong evidence of cultivation in these culturally diverse individuals, the indication that experience and exposure motivation influence social perceptions, and that amount of contact with a host nation can mediate the relation between television viewing and perception suggests that cultural diversity is an important factor in understanding this relationship.

Residents of Foreign Nations Exposed to U.S. Television Programs

> . . . there is a need to link findings made by systems studies and processes and effect analysis of international mass communication. It is true that findings available in systems analysis and processes and effects analysis

are fundamentally related, despite the differences of research focus and
research technique in past international mass communication research.
                                                          (Hur, 1982, p. 549)

Why do you Americans export programs which make us all think that your
street is running with blood and you have to dodge from doorway to
doorway to avoid being hit by bullets?
                            (a baffled Yugoslav patron, cited from Lee, 1980, p. 67)

Since the classic study by Nordenstreng and Varis (1974) on global
television traffic, the phenomena of "imbalanced" and "one-way flow"
of television programs have been intuitively recognized, thoroughly
documented, and explained with varying interpretative paradigms.
While an extensive review of literature in this area is beyond the
scope of this chapter (for an excellent summary, see Mowlana, 1985),
many critical scholars (e.g., Beltran, 1978; Lee, 1980; Nordenstreng &
Varis, 1974; Nordenstreng & Schiller, 1979; Salinas & Paldan, 1979;
Schiller, 1969, 1976, 1979; Tunstall, 1977) appear to agree with the
claim that foreign media play a significant role in changing the receiving nations' indigenous value system and culture. Media imports such
as international wire news, films, pop music, and particularly television
programs are subjecting the world to a "homogenized American commercial culture" (Lee, 1980).
    Various critical interpretations of global communication flow situa-
tions have been advanced with research on system-level analysis; however, relatively little research has provided concrete evidence to justify
the value-laden claims. Indeed, the plethora of research that has flourished in this area since the early 1970s seems to defy any cohesive
statement on the state of the art in theory and research involving
pertinent areas of the field (e.g., cultural or media imperialism versus
diffusionism; new world information order versus free flow of communication). As indicated by Hur (1982) and Rogers (1982), the only
exception has been a notable trend in the field toward an imbalanced
research emphasis. A heavy concentration on the structural or process
analyses of various global mass communication systems has been
sharply contrasted with a much weaker emphasis on various social and
psychological "effects" variables in international mass communication
research.
    Although there were a limited number of studies investigating the
effects of U.S. media content on national identity (Barnett & McPhail,

1980; Elkin, 1972; Skipper, 1975; Sparks, 1977) and on attitude or value orientations (Beltran, 1978; Granzberg, 1982; Kang & Morgan, 1988; Payne, 1978; Payne & Peake, 1977; Skinner, 1984; Tan, Tan, & Tan, 1987; Tsai, 1970), only a handful of studies have directly investigated cultivation by foreign media content. While the cognitive impact of foreign media appears to have been largely downplayed when compared to the seemingly more immediate and salient attitudinal or behavioral effects, the first-order cultivation of beliefs and conceptions by foreign media should be considered an important facilitating factor for any second-order cultivation of attitudes, value orientations, or behaviors that may be of greater interest (see, Hawkins & Pingree, 1982; Gerbner, Gross, Morgan, & Signorielli, 1986). Pingree and Hawkins (1981, p. 97) sum up the importance of cross-cultural cultivation inquiry as follows:

> One of the most promising approaches to studying the influence of television on culture starts with the hypothesis that information learned from the mass media is incorporated into individuals' conceptions of social reality and presumably guides further learning and behavior. If a careful analysis finds a relationship between television viewing and these conceptions, then we can begin to make a case for television's contribution to our shared values and assumptions.

If one accepts the notion of second-order cultivation, many studies in international mass communication flow may be subsumed under the rubric of cultivation inquiry. Perhaps the first empirical evidence of foreign television's cultivation potential dates back to Brown's (1968) report of a small-sample global survey indicating that American television programs, more often than not, had given foreign viewers a favorable impression of life in the United States. This was chiefly through their portrayal of "harmonious family life, a high standard of living, and a general sense of freedom and equality for and among Americans" (pp. 315-316). Brown also reported that the predominant negative impressions viewers received were violence and "unreality of presentation," with bad taste in terms of "immorality, brashness and excessive emphasis on sex" coming in a very distant third. In a similar vein, Beltran (1978) attempted to synthesize several Latin American research findings. After illustrating a repertoire of images portrayed by Latin American television programs, both local and imported, he classified what he termed the basic images into two main categories: positive and negative stimulations. Among those that might have been fostered by the made-in-USA television programs were: conformism, adventurism, racism, elitism, materialism, aggressiveness, self-defeatism, romanticism, conservatism, and so forth. Beltran went on to call for research that goes beyond the mere identification of explicit and implicit "alien" images to investigate the impact of their exposure.

Following these early descriptive studies, several investigations had limited success in attempts to associate exposure to U.S. television programming with perceptual and attitudinal differences in viewers. In a field experiment among Formosan children, Tsai (1970) hypothesized that the viewers of U.S. television programs on Taiwan television would have a more favorable attitude toward elements of U.S. culture and a less favorable attitude toward their own culture than would their non-viewing counterparts. While some findings suggested an impact of U.S. television programs on specific attitudes toward U.S. culture, little influence was found on the Formosan children's outlook on their culture. In another cross-cultural setting, Sparks (1977) noted that there was little attitudinal change associated with viewing U.S. television news among the Canadian population. In a test of cultural imperialism among Icelandic children, Payne and Peake (1977) reported limited impact from U.S. television viewing on favorable attitudes about the United States. However, a study of Canadian college students (Barnett & McPhail, 1980), which utilized a metric multidimensional scaling method, found a substantial impact of U.S. television program viewing on perceptions of national identity. For example, the more U.S. television viewed by Canadians, the less they perceived of themselves as Canadians and the more they perceived of themselves as Americans. Another study among Korean college students (Kang & Morgan, 1988), however, revealed quite mixed results suggesting that the impact of U.S. programs abroad may be more diverse than the models of cultural imperialism or cultivation research have suggested. For example, heavy Korean viewers of American programs held less traditional values on some topics but *more* traditional (thus less westernized) values on others, and these divergent patterns varied for male and female subgroups.

While these studies were generally concerned with the cognitive and attitudinal impact of made-in-USA television programs viewed across different cultures, a more direct inquiry of the original cultivation hypothesis can be found in other cross-cultural research. In a study among Australian children (Pingree & Hawkins, 1981), U.S. television viewing was associated with both perceptions of violence and interpersonal mistrust in Australian society. The relationships sustained their significance even after simultaneous controls for demographic and other media variables. Pingree and Hawkins (1981) concluded that, as speculated previously by many critical researchers, the effects of television viewing on conceptions of social reality indeed extend beyond the culture that creates the programming. Additional support for cultivation in a cross-cultural setting can be seen in data from two sample surveys among Israeli adolescents (Wiemann, 1984). Wiemann reported that at the time of the surveys about 65% of all television broadcasting in Israel was allocated to imported content (mostly American). Cultivation differential analysis indicated that heavy television viewers demonstrated a strong and consistent tendency to paint a rosier picture of American life even when other factors (age, gender, residence, and ethnic group) were held constant.

Contrary to the findings from these two studies, however, a study by Choi, Straubhaar, and Tamborini (1988) among college students in Korea presented mixed evidence. The presence of a 19-hours-a-day American Armed Forces Television Network (AFKN-TV) in Korea provided an opportunity to investigate a set of hypotheses involving various perceptions about crimes, drug abuse, sexual permissiveness, and affluence in U.S. society. For example, while AFKN-TV crime/adventure show viewing was a relatively good predictor for "mean world" perceptions of U.S. society, several other AFKN-TV viewing measures (i.e., total viewing, information program viewing, entertainment program viewing) showed no association with perceptions of crime in the United States. Furthermore, contrary to cultivation rationales, AFKN-TV crime/adventure viewing was negatively related to the perceived chance of crime victimization in U.S. urban areas. Finally, for non-crime-related perceptions, the study again revealed mixed results. Total amount of AFKN-TV viewing was a good predictor for perceptions of sexual permissiveness and prevalence of drug abuse, but not for perceptions of affluence in U.S. society.

As indicated by these studies, the results of research on U.S. television viewing by residents of foreign nations are somewhat mixed. Several studies show that exposure to U.S. programs is related to perceptions of U.S. life. Of course, it is important to realize that the perceptions dealt with in these studies are perceptions of other cultures and may not apply to the coherent set of images within a culture thought to be important in cultivation theory. However, these effects may be indications of important influence processes in the viewers of some cultural diversity.

Residents of Foreign Nations Exposed to Their Native Television

> Two approaches are available for interpreting this situation. One is that what may be true in America is not true in Britain, for which difference it will be useful to explore the reasons. The second is that the Gerbner thesis has still not been demonstrated convincingly in America, and the effect exists neither there nor in Britain.
>
> (Wober, 1978, p. 320)

While studies reviewed in the previous two sections applied the postulates and methodologies of cultivation theory to the more macro-level concerns of cross-cultural research (e.g., communication-acculturation, media imperialism), several other studies have been concerned with the replicability of cultivation influences in nations other than the United States. As suggested by Wober (1978), "if the effects of heavy violence consumption are as strong as alleged, they should be discernible when sought again in similar culture, and with similar methods" (p. 315). As also indicated by Payne (1978), the replicability of cross-national television effects between "developmentally similar" cultures should be more easily achieved than between cultures with varying degrees of technological sophistication. With other sociocultural variables held fairly constant across similar cultures, conflicting evidence regarding the same issue then may necessitate a need for theoretical reformulation or methodological refinement of the area. In this section studies from such developmentally similar nations (e.g., Great Britain and Canada) are considered in order to explore this issue.

Perhaps the most widely cited research challenging the cultivation hypothesis comes from Canada (Doob & Macdonald, 1979). Results from data collected by door-to-door surveys in four Toronto areas (high- and low-crime areas in both downtown Toronto and the Toronto suburbs) revealed that when controlling for the actual incidence of crime, there was little association between television viewing and fear of crime victimization. While this finding has been addressed by conceptual refinements of cultivation theory such as the "resonance effect" (Gerbner et al., 1980a), questions concerning cultivation influences in this setting remain.

Another challenge to the predictions of cultivation in non-U.S. countries has come from research in Great Britain. Wober (1978) reported results from a national survey on "Attitudes to Broadcasting," which contained two cultivation-related questions. One item dealt with prevalence of violence manifested in terms of one's chances of being a victim of robbery and the other with interpersonal mistrust. No relationship was observed between the summed items and television exposure in viewers of all gender, age, and social class categories. A similar study done in the Portsmouth area (Piepe, Crouch, & Emerson, 1977) also failed to support cultivation in Great Britain.

According to Wober (1986), evidence from abroad indicates that time spent watching television does not relate systematically to perceptions. Instead, there is some indication that another factor, personality, may interact with viewing experiences in determining social perceptions. For example, based on research demonstrating that social anxiety and anomie vary among different social groups and that controls for demographic factors often significantly weaken associations between television viewing and various social perception measures, Wober and Gunter (1982) suggested that both extent of television viewing and anxiety/mistrust are a function of some third variable — such as an underlying personality characteristic. Incorporating Potter's internal-external control dimension (the "fate" factor, manifested in terms of an individual's lack of control of his or her environment or "feelings of powerlessness"), their study showed that while fear of victimization correlated significantly with television viewing initially, the relationship disappeared when the fate factor was partialled out. However, partialling out scores on fear did not substantially reduce the relationship between the fate factor and television viewing. From these findings, Wober and Gunter (1982) concluded that such underlying personality characteristics may be important variables in explaining the relationship between television viewing and perceptions of social reality. The belief that such underlying personality characteristics are important in determining the relationship between television and social perceptions has also been suggested in several other studies from Great Britain (Gunter & Wober, 1983), Canada (Surlin & Tate, 1976), and Europe (Hedinsson & Windahl, 1984).

As can be seen from the studies cited here, serious challenges concerning the generalizability of cultivation theory to nations other than the United States have been advanced by several scholars. The inability of these attempts to replicate cultivation findings raises many questions about the processes at work in the creation of social perceptions. It draws attention to the importance of limited cultural diversity, and points to issues associated with the set of images portrayed by television programming in nations outside the United States.

Discussion

Most of the studies discussed in this chapter were selected because of the issues they raised concerning problems with research on cultivation analysis in non-U.S. populations. Although other studies show mixed support (see the chapter by Morgan, this volume), the studies here demonstrate that many attempts to replicate cultivation findings in non-U.S. samples have failed to find substantial support for the hypothesis. The cultivation potential of native television viewing on residents of foreign nations has yet to be clearly demonstrated, while that of U.S. television viewing on foreign residents living both abroad and in the United States appears to be questionable. While research in these areas is still limited, the failure of many investigations to find strong support for cultivation in non-U.S. viewers leads to a search for explanations. This search could go in several directions. The problems encountered in this research may stem from flaws in the logical structure of cultivation theory, from the way the theory has been tested, or from the assumptions on which the theory is based. In each of these areas, consideration of cultural diversity makes existing issues even more complex.

Questions about the logical structure of cultivation theory have been debated since its inception. As evidenced by Wober's (1978) concerns about what may or may not be true in America and in Britain, these questions extend to research on cultivation in most non-U.S. cultures. Questions about the methodological rigor used in conducting cultivation research have also been debated from the beginning. Issues about the content of televised programming in non-U.S. systems, the use of various television viewing measures, the scope of appropriate dependent measures, and the influence of different spurious and mediating factors become even greater concerns when cultural differences are considered. Although these issues have not been dealt with in this paper, they are apparent in most research in this area and should be noted.

Detailed content analysis on available television programming in a culture is missing in most cross-cultural research. In developmentally similar cultures, replications have relied on an assumed similarity among the television makeups examined, while in dissimilar cultures the presence of U.S. television imports as part of a broadcast schedule have been taken to represent actual viewing of U.S. programs. For example, differences in the degree of violence depicted across two cultures could render any attempt to replicate crime-related cultivation findings meaningless comparisons. As such, the findings from several British studies (e.g., Wober, 1978; Wober & Gunter, 1982) may be criticized in that "the British heavy viewer sees *less* violence than American *light* viewers" (Hawkins & Pingree, 1982, p. 232). In a similar manner, problems with vaguely defined television viewing measures are apparent in several studies discussed. For example, Doob and Macdonald (1979) used the number of programs watched as an index of total television viewing, and a subjective coding process to categorize violent programming. Wiemann's (1984) study, which specifically tested the cultivation of U.S. television imports in Israel, used a median split of total television viewing to distinguish between heavy and light viewers. However, since almost 40% of all broadcasting time on the only Israeli television station was allocated to non-U.S. imports, this broad indicator may not be the best measure to isolate the impact of U.S. television programs.

Regarding the scope of independent variables, there is a growing demand to increase the scope of these measures in cross-cultural cultivation research. Many of the discrepancies illustrated in this research may be due to the use of different dependent variables. Given the importance of possible second-order cultivation of attitudes and values, more frequent replications of cross-cultural research incorporating expanded dependent measures are needed. Finally, the likelihood of spurious and mediating relationships can not be ignored. The nature and size of samples employed in many studies leaves doubt about their generalizability. For example, studies investigating the cultivation potential of AFKN-TV in Korea surveyed college students either in one metropolitan area (Choi, Straubhaar, & Tamborini, 1988) or one private language institute (Kang & Morgan, 1988). Similarly, possible third variable hypotheses (e.g., local crime rate in Doob & Macdonald, 1979; personality characteristics in Wober & Gunter, 1982, & Wober, 1986) and the mediating potential of other situational and experiential variables has not been given the attention that it demands in cross-cultural research.

Although problems associated with the logical structure and methodological rigor of cultivation research are important to note, perhaps the most important issues developed from consideration of cultural diversity stem from questions about the assumptions on which cultivation theory is based. Clearly, difficulties at this level are likely to cause problems with the logical structure of the theory, the methodology used to test the theory, and all other areas of concern. In fact, the assumptions of cultivation theory may be the root of many problems facing cultivation research in non-U.S. cultures. In order to look at these problems, it may be useful to consider the two issues raised at the beginning of this chapter: (1) cultural diversity and the underlying processes of cultivation, and (2) cultural diversity and the television picture.

Cultural Diversity and Nonselective Television Use

The relationship of cultural diversity and the underlying processes of cultivation has important implications for Gerbner's assumption that television is unique in its relatively nonselective use by viewers. Gerbner's nonselectivity assumption seems to imply that selectivity is a constant among heavy viewers. However, it is apparent that cultural diversity can influence the selectivity with which heavy viewers watch television. This problem could be dealt with by arguing that the assumptions of cultivation theory have been violated in situations where diversity results in failure to use television nonselectively. In this case we would not expect cultivation to occur. Unfortunately, the problem does not appear to be with the populations considered as much as it is with the assumption. If cultural diversity is itself a variable, it is likely to have a varying impact on selectivity. As a result, selectivity becomes a variable instead of a constant. Instead of assuming nonselectivity among heavy viewers, it might be more useful to take variations in selectivity into account and see how they might influence the processes of cultivation.

The importance of accounting for cultural diversity's influence on selectivity becomes apparent when attempting to study cultivation in cross-cultural populations. For example, the high acculturation motivation among foreign immigrants or sojourners that increases their willingness to learn about host culture, society, and language may lead to heavier consumption of host media. While viewing television programs, an individual with high motivation may pay closer attention to various aspects of the host culture and the life-styles portrayed in their programming. This may amplify the cultivation potential of television viewing in a fashion resembling that of resonance. In addition, personality traits like communication apprehension or unwillingness to communicate may lead to television viewing by foreign sojourners. It is generally accepted that language deficiency and a lack of understanding the sociocultural assumptions and interpersonal interaction patterns in the host society make interpersonal contact with host members a much more anxiety-provoking experience than watching television. The lack of interpersonal contact as well as the lack of direct experience with the host culture then may lead to a higher degree of perceived reality for various television programs watched. That is, for those foreign sojourners with limited real-life experiences and interpersonal contact, the television world may be considered a magic window with a high degree of informational utility. The "armchair acculturation" through television viewing among the foreign sojourners then may lead to the construction of social reality mainly based on the images presented by television.

The influence of cultural diversity on selectivity is also vital when considering viewers of U.S. television program imports in developing nations. Identifying various reasons for watching programs may provide a helpful clue to isolate any resulting impact from U.S. television program viewing among the indigenous populations. For example, a general aspiration for American culture, living standards, or life-styles may cause both heavy viewing of U.S. television programs (either for more learning or for further reinforcement) and painting a rosier picture of American life. While Wiemann's study (1984) reported findings supportive of the cultivation hypothesis, the study largely ignored the questions concerning who views U.S. television programs and the reasons for this viewing. In order to provide more concrete evidence for the cultivation potential of U.S. television program imports, segmenting the audience according to major motivations for U.S. television program viewing may help further our understanding of the process. Indeed, some indirect evidence of the usefulness of such an approach was demonstrated in research by Choi et al. (1988). In this study, subgroups who were more removed from direct contact with U.S. culture (e.g., no U.S. travel experience and no relatives living in the United States) showed stronger cultivation associations on estimates of the percent of law officials in the United States.

These examples of the manner in which cultural diversity in cross-cultural viewers and viewers of imported television can influence selectivity and cultivation processes are by no means exhaustive. They do, however, demonstrate the importance of considering this variable when attempting to study cultivation in these settings. In addition, they help identify the difficulties that result from problems in assuming the nonselective use of television.

Cultural Diversity and Television Image Coherence

Consideration of the relationship between cultural diversity and the television picture immediately brings to mind Gerbner's assumption that television presents a relatively coherent set of images and messages. Once again, cultural diversity raises questions about the appropriateness of this assumption. Clearly, there is a need for researchers to conduct appropriate content analyses of the television programming available to respondents observed in different investigations. As discussed in the introduction to this chapter, it is difficult to imagine that many viewers with cross-cultural backgrounds or those in intercultural settings would be exposed to a coherent set of images from television. Of course, the expected influence resulting from exposure to a coherent set of television images produced for a population may be limited to individuals who grow up in a single culture.

Limiting cultivation to these individuals seems like a logical solution, but this would exclude us from looking at the influence of television on the perceptions of many viewers. In addition, it may not solve the problem. For example, in the United States it can be argued that *most* U.S. programming portrays a coherent set of images that would be difficult to avoid. At the same time, it can also be argued that the wide variety of native and imported program content available to all U.S. residents through cable transmission and home video rentals makes the assumption of one coherent set of images difficult to accept for many (if not most) individuals within the U.S. culture.

If a different example were used, however, it might be more difficult to build an argument for the availability of wide content variety. Many developing nations with primitive distribution systems or authoritarian control are likely to have more limited program availability. The programming in this type of system should produce a much more coherent set of images than that found in the United States. Viewers exposed to images in this media system should best satisfy the assumptions of cultivation theory. In fact, it may be expected that these settings provide the best environment for conducting a valid test of the predictions set forth by cultivation rationales. Based on this reasoning, it could be decided that viewers of the developing nation should be included and U.S. viewers should be excluded, but this would be unacceptable. The key in this regard may be that the assumption is concerned with a *relatively* coherent set of images. In this case, the argument can be made that both the developing nation and U.S. television present a *relatively* coherent set of images, and that viewers exposed to these images fall within the boundaries set forth in the assumption. At the same time, many cross-cultural viewers such as foreign residents living in the United States and exposed to U.S. television, or residents of foreign nations exposed to U.S. television, are exposed to a relatively incoherent set of images and fall outside of the boundaries set by these assumptions.

Putting aside the fact that many U.S. viewers are exposed to foreign television (e.g., a Spanish broadcasting channel, British television programs featured on public television stations, broadcasts from Canada and Mexico), this argument would seem to solve problems created by considering the relationship between cultural diversity and the television picture. However, by dealing with coherence in relative terms, the problem is solved by treating coherence as a variable factor.

If coherence is a variable, it would seem more useful to take these variations into account and see how they influence the processes of cultivation. It could be suggested that viewers exposed to television with highly coherent images would show greater similarity in perceptions of social life than viewers exposed to television with relatively incoherent images. In this case, we might expect stronger evidence of cultivation to be found in viewers from a developing nation than in U.S. television viewers and less evidence of cultivation in culturally diverse viewers than we would in both U.S. or developing nation viewers. In any case, greater understanding of the processes at work should be provided by accounting for variations in this factor rather than simply assuming it reaches a threshold level. For example, researchers investigating potential cultivation by imported television programming may want to measure differential television exposure to imported and domestic programs by the receiving population. Depending on the degree of intercoherence between the two types of television programming, we may be better able to explain inconsistencies noted in cross-cultural cultivation research.

Summary

The findings reviewed in this paper identify several issues concerning research on cultivation influences in nonnative United States populations. Most of these issues deal with problems stemming from possible violations in the basic assumptions of cultivation research that become difficult to avoid when working with non-U.S. viewers. These violations have repercussions involving the logical structure of cultivation theory, the manner in which the theory is tested, and the usefulness of the theory for providing an understanding of television exposure's influences on social perceptions in culturally diverse viewers.

The issues revolve around the appropriateness of assuming that television presents a relatively coherent set of images, and that its use by viewers is nonselective even when considering non-U.S. viewers in various settings. It can be argued that degree of coherence in the images available through television is likely to vary from relatively high to relatively low depending on the characteristics of the media system and viewers considered. It can also be argued that the degree of nonselectivity in television use will vary depending on the cultural diversity of viewers found in many non-U.S. samples. In order to deal with the problems presented by the violation of these assumptions, selectivity in television use and coherence of television images should be treated as variables instead of assuming that they fall within certain boundaries. Analysis of these variables can be used to determine how they may influence or mediate the cultivation process cross-culturally.

References

Barnett, G. A., & McPhail, T. L. (1980). An examination of the relationship of United States television and Canadian identity. *International Journal of Intercultural Relations, 4,* 219-232.

Beltran, L. R. (1978). TV etchings in the minds of Latin Americans. *Gazette, 24,* 61-85.

Brown, D. R. (1968). The American image as presented abroad by U.S. television. *Journalism Quarterly, 45*(4), 307-316.

Choi, J. H., Straubhaar, J., & Tamborini, R. (1988, May). *American Armed Forces Television in Korea and its shadow viewers: Who views what for what reasons with what impact?* Paper presented to the Intercultural and Developmental Division of ICA, New Orleans.

Choi, J. H., & Tamborini, R. (1988). Communication-acculturation and the cultivation hypothesis: A comparative study between two Korean communities in the U.S. *Howard Journal of Communication, 1*(1), 57-74.

Doob, A. W., & Macdonald, G. E. (1979). Television viewing and fear of victimization: Is the relationship causal? *Journal of Personality and Social Psychology, 37*(2), 170-179.

Elkin, F. (1972). Communications media and identity formation in Canada. In B. Singer (Ed.), *Communications in Canadian society.* Toronto: Capp Clark.

Elliott, W. R., & Rudd, R. L. (1984). *Evaluating dimensions of television program reality: A commonality analysis of perceived superficiality, perceived plausibility, and the degree of personal utility.* Paper presented to the Theory and Methodology Division of the Association for Education in Journalism and Mass Communication Annual Convention, Gainsville, FL.

Gerbner, G., & Gross, L. (1976a). Living with television: The violence profile. *Journal of Communication, 26*(2), 173-199.

Gerbner, G., & Gross, L. (1976b). The scary world of TV's heavy viewer. *Psychology Today,* April, 41-45.

Gerbner, G., Gross, L., Morgan, M., & Signorielli, N. (1980a). The "mainstreaming" of America: Violence profile No. 11. *Journal of Communication, 30*(3), 19-29.

Gerbner, G., Gross, L., Morgan, M., & Signorielli, N. (1980b). Some additional comments on cultivation analysis. *Public Opinion Quarterly, 44*(4), 408-410.

Gerbner, G., Gross, L., Morgan, M., & Signorielli, N. (1986). Living with television: The dynamics of the cultivation process. In J. Bryant & D. Zillmann (Eds.), *Perspectives on media effects* (pp. 17-40). Hillsdale, NJ: Lawrence Erlbaum.

Granzberg, G. (1982). Television as story-teller: The Algonkian Indians of central Canada. *Journal of Communication, 32*(1), 43-52.

Gunter, B., & Wober, M. (1983). Television viewing and public trust. *British Journal of Social Psychology, 22,* 174-176.

Hawkins, R. P., & Pingree, S. (1981a). Uniform content and habitual viewing: Unnecessary assumptions in social reality effects. *Human Communication Research, 7,* 291-301.

Hawkins, R. P., & Pingree, S. (1981b). Using television to construct social reality. *Journal of Broadcasting, 25*(4), 347-364.

Hawkins, R. P., & Pingree, S. (1982). Television's influence on social reality. In D. Pearl, L. Bouthilet, & J. Lazar (Eds.), *Television and behavior: Ten years of scientific progress and implications for the eighties. Vol. 2: Technology report* (pp. 224-247). U.S. Dept of Health and Human Services: National Institute of Mental Health.

Hedinsson, E., & Windahl, S. (1984). Cultivation analysis: A Swedish illustration. In G. Melishek, K. E. Rosengren, & J. Stappers (Eds.), *Cultural indicators: An international symposium* (pp. 389-405). Vienna: Verlag der Osterreichischen Akademie der Wissenschaften.

Hirsch, P. M. (1980a). On Hughes's contribution: The limits of advocacy research. *Public Opinion Quarterly, 44*(4), 411-413.

Hirsch, P. M. (1980b). The "scary world" of the nonviewer and other anomalies: A reanalysis of Gerbner et al.'s finding on cultivation analysis, Part I. *Communication Research, 7,* 403-456.

Hirsch, P. M. (1981a). Distinguishing good speculation from bad theory: Rejoinder to Gerbner et al. *Communication Research, 7,* 403-456.

Hirsch, P. M. (1981b). On not learning from one's own mistakes: A reanalysis of Gerbner et al.'s findings on cultivation analysis, Part II. *Communication Research, 8,* 3-37.

Hughes, M. (1980). The fruits of cultivation analysis: A reexamination of some effects of television watching. *Public Opinion Quarterly, 44,* 287-302.

Hur, K. K. (1982). International mass communication research: A critical review of theory and methods. In M. Burgoon (Ed.), *Communication yearbook* , *Vol. 6*. Beverly Hills, CA: Sage.

Kang, J. K., & Morgan, M. (1988). Culture clash: Impact of U.S. television in Korea. *Journalism Quarterly, 65*(2), 431-438.

Kim, J. K. (1980). Explaining acculturation in a communication framework: An empirical test. *Communication Monographs, 57*, 10-17.

Kim, Y. Y. (1977a). Communication patterns of foreign immigrants in the process of acculturation. *Human Communication Research, 4*(1), 66-77.

Kim, Y. Y. (1977b). Inter-ethnic and intra-ethnic communication: A study of Korean immigrants in Chicago. In N. C. Jain (Ed.), *International and intercultural communication annual, vol. IV*. Falls Church, VA: Speech Communication Association.

Kim, Y. Y. (1978). A communication approach to the acculturation process: A study of Korean immigrants in Chicago. *International Journal of Intercultural Relations*, 197-223.

Kim, Y. Y. (1979). *Mass media and acculturation: Toward development of an interactive theory*. Paper presented at the Annual Convention of the Eastern Communication Association, Philadelphia, PA.

Lee, C. C. (1980). *Media imperialism reconsidered: The homogenizing of television culture*. Beverly Hills, CA: Sage.

Mowlana, H. (1985). International flow of information: A global report and analysis. *Reports and Papers on Mass Communication (No. 99)*. Paris: UNESCO.

Nordenstreng, K., & Schiller, H. I. (1979). *National sovereignty and international communication*. Norwood, NJ: Ablex.

Nordenstreng, K., & Varis, T. (1974). Television traffic—A one-way street? *Reports and Papers on Mass Communication (No. 70)*. Paris: UNESCO.

O'Keefe, G. (1984). Public views on crime: Television exposure and media credibility. In R. Bostrom (Ed.), *Communication yearbook,Vol 8*. New Brunswick, NJ: ICA-Transaction Press.

O'Keefe, G., & Reid-Nash, K. (1984). *TV crime news and real world blues: A panel study of social reality*. Paper presented to the Theory and Methodology Division, Association for Education in Journalism and Mass Communication Annual Convention, Gainsville, FL.

Payne, D. E. (1978). Cross-national diffusion: The effects of Canadian TV on rural Minnesota viewers. *American Sociological Review, 43*, 740-756.

Payne, D. E., & Peake, C. A. (1977). Cultural diffusion: The role of U.S. TV in Iceland. *Journalism Quarterly, 54*, 523-531.

Piepe, A., Crouch, J., & Emerson, M. (1977) Violence and television. *New Society, 41*, 536-538.

Pingree, S., & Hawkins, R. P. (1981). U.S. programs on Australian television: The cultivation effect. *Journal of Communication, 31*(1), 97-105.

Potter, W. J. (1988). Perceived reality in television effects research. *Journal of Broadcasting and Electronic Media, 32*(1), 23-41.

Rogers, E. M. (1982). The empirical and critical schools of communication research. In M. Burgoon (Ed.), *Communication yearbook* , *Vol. 6*. Beverly Hills, CA: Sage.

Salinas, R., & Paldan, L. (1979). Culture in the process of dependent development. In K. Nordenstreng & H. I. Schiller (Eds.), *National sovereignty and international communication*. Norwood, NJ: Ablex.

Schiller, H. I. (1969). *Mass communication and American empire*. New York: Kelly.

Schiller, H. I. (1976). *Communication and cultural domination*. New York: International Arts and Science Press.

Schiller, H. I. (1979). Transnational media and national development. In K. Nordenstreng & H. I. Schiller (Eds.), *National sovereignty and international communication*. Norwood, NJ: Ablex.

Skinner, E. (1984). *Dependency theory: A preliminary analysis of quantitative applications in imported mass media research*. Unpublished doctoral dissertation, Michigan State University.

Skipper, J. (1975). Musical tastes of Canadian and American college students: An examination of the massification and Americanization theses. *Canadian Journal of Sociology, 1*, 49-59.

Sparks, V. M. (1977). TV across the Canadian border: Does it really matter? *Journal of Communication, 27*, 40-47.

Surlin, S. H., & Tate, E. D. (1976). All in the family: Is Archie funny? *Journal of Communication, 26*, 61-68.

Tamborini, R., & Choi, J. H. (In press). *The cultivation of intercultural viewers: A study among foreign students in the U.S.* Manuscript submitted for publication.

Tamborini, R., Zillmann, D., & Bryant, J. (1984). Fear of victimization: Exposure to television and perceptions of crime and fear. In R. Bostrom (Ed.), *Communication yearbook, Vol. 8*. New Brunswick, NJ: ICA-Transaction Press.

Tan, A. S., & Tan, G. K. (1987). American TV in the Philippines: A test of cultural impact. *Journalism Quarterly, 64*(1), 65-72.

Tsai, M. K. (1970). Some effects of American television programs on children in Formosa. *Journal of Broadcasting, 14*, 229-238.

Tunstall, J. (1977). *The media are American*. London: Constable.

Tyler, T. R. (1980). The impact of directly and indirectly experienced events: The origin of crime-related judgements and behavior. *Journal of Personality and Social Psychology, 39*, 13-28.

Tyler, T. R. (1984). Assessing the risk of crime victimization: The integration of personal victimization experiences and socially transmitted information. *Journal of Social Issues, 40*(1), 27-38.

Tyler, T. R., & Cook, F. L. (1984). The mass media and risk judgements: Distinguishing impact on personal and societal level judgements. *Journal of Personality and Social Psychology, 47*(4), 693-708.

Tyler, T. R., & Rasinski, K. (1984). Comparing psychological images of the social perceiver: Role of perceived informativeness, memorability, and affect in mediating the impact of crime victimization. *Journal of Personality and Social Psychology, 46*(2), 308-329.

Wakshlag, J., Vial, V., & Tamborini, R. (1984). Selecting crime drama and apprehension about crime. *Human Communication Research, 10*, 227-242.

Weaver, J., & Wakshlag, J. (1984). *Perceptions of personal vulnerability to crime, criminal victimization experience, and television viewing*. Paper presented at the Annual Meeting of the Broadcast Education Association, Las Vegas.

Wiemann, G. (1984). Images of life in America: The impact of American TV in Israel. *International Journal of Intercultural Relations, 3*, 185-197.

Wober, J. M. (1978). Television violence and paranoid perception: The view from Great Britain. *Public Opinion Quarterly, 42*, 315-321.

Wober, J. M. (1986). The lens of television and the prism of personality. In J. Bryant & D. Zillmann (Eds.), *Perspectives on media effects* (pp. 205-228). Hillsdale, NJ: Lawrence Erlbaum.

Wober, J. M., & Gunter, B. (1982). Television and personal threat: Fact or artifact? A British survey. *British Journal of Social Psychology, 21*, 239-247.

Zillmann, D. (1980). Anatomy of suspense. In P. H. Tannenbaum (Ed.), *The entertainment functions of television* (pp. 133-163). Hillsdale, NJ: Lawrence Erlbaum.

10

Cultivated Viewers and Readers:

A Life-Style Perspective

BO REIMER
and
KARL ERIK ROSENGREN

Introduction[1]

This article will address the question of cultivation from a Swedish perspective, a perspective that somewhat differs from the American one (Gerbner, Gross, Morgan, & Signorielli, 1986). This is due partly to a different societal context, inside which the cultivation process is interpreted. The perspective is theoretically different, in that a *life-style perspective* to the concept of cultivation is applied. Research on life-style and cultivation may be constructively combined in different societal structures and contexts — not only in the Swedish context but also in, for example, an American context.

The article starts with a description of our theoretical framework. Different perspectives on the mass media as the agents of cultivation are discussed, followed by what is to be cultivated, in this case *human values*. An empirical analysis of cultivation in Sweden in the mid-1980s is presented. Finally, arguments are summarized and the implications of this perspective are discussed.

Socialization and Life-styles

Cultivation may be regarded a special case of *socialization*. It is one of the many processes through which, in an intricate interplay with different socialization agents, we become subjects of, and participants in, society. In understanding the process of cultivation it seems reasonable, then, initially to locate the process in this broader context of socialization. There are two good reasons to this strategy. First, the knowledge accumulated from socialization research may, in many ways, be relevant to the cultivation process. Second, starting with the broader perspective of socialization (before moving to the specifics of the cultivation process) makes it easier to analyze the cultivation process as a general — as opposed to a specific — concept, more or less at work in different societal contexts and structures, where socialization is the common denominator.

Traditional socialization research dealt mainly with the question of cultural transmission, the question of how, in order to ensure society's survival, its norms and values were passed on from one generation to another. This original perspective has been increasingly contested, however, on the grounds that it neglects the possibility that individuals "make their own history" and that it holds an "over-socialized conception of man" (Wrong, 1961). Today, we must take into account socialization from two perspectives, from the perspective of society and from the perspective of the individual. These two perspectives are not incompatible, however, and newer socialization research strives to overcome this distinction by trying to integrate them (Johnson-Smaragdi, 1983; McCron, 1976; Rosengren, 1986; Zigler & Seitz, 1978). Socialization is seen as a process, where, in a complex network of relations, individuals as acting subjects interact with other subjects and with socialization agents toward a goal that is not always predetermined.

When discussing socialization, one runs a risk of treating socialization and its agents as timeless and ahistorical. The importance of the different agents, however, does not vary only for different individuals but also over time and between cultures. In order to be analyzed properly, the socialization process must be fixed at specific occasions, in the actual relations where the socialization agents are at work.

The site at which this pattern of relations is located may be termed a person's *life-cycle*. This is the site at which, in a historically specific setting, one's past — one's socioeconomic background and one's earlier encounters and experiences — meets the present. The "meaning" of one's former experience is to be understood at this site, as something that is transformed and molded during one's life span. One has to distinguish between what it means to be socialized into a certain class, a certain sex, and so on, and what these characteristics mean at a specific time. Traditional background characteristics must be interpreted within the perspective of the whole trajectory of an individual acting within the framework of a given social structure.[2]

The Mass Media as Cultivation Agents

In modern societies we have to take into account at least eight main socialization agents. Three of these — family, peer group, and work group — exist in all types of human societies, whereas three others — church, law, and school — exist in most societies. That leaves us two that may be characterized as typically "modern" socialization agents: large organizations representing popular movements and interest groups, and the mass media (Rosengren, 1988).

The focus of this article is on the mass media as agents of socialization, or, in Gerbnerian terms, as agents of cultivation. (The fact that the traditional cultivation analysis approach deals only with television, not with the total mass media output, will be taken up in a moment.) We prefer to regard cultivation as a special case of socialization and welcome the growing tendency in contemporary socialization research toward viewing the socialization process from both an individual and a societal perspective.

In mass communication research, a similar shift in emphasis from the passive object (as in "effects" research) to the active subject (as in uses and gratifications research) has been underway for quite some time (Bryant & Zillmann, 1986; Rosengren, Wenner, & Palmgreen, 1985). Currently the active subject perspective put forward, for instance, in reception theory discourse (Jensen, 1986; Schröder, 1987), seems to be somewhat in favor.

The active subject perspective is not held by Gerbner and his associates. In their view,

most viewers watch by the clock and either do not know what they will watch when they turn on the set or follow established routines . . . and the more they watch, the less selective they can and tend to be. Most regular and heavy viewers watch more of everything (Gerbner et al., 1986, p. 19).

In discussing the above statements, however, it must be remembered that the focus is on American television. No claim is made about its validity for general audiences outside the American context. Obviously the media structure in whatever country or context being studied is of major importance (see Weibull, 1985). For example, the Swedish media structure is different than the American one, leading (among other things) to more heterogeneous television output. Moreover, the Swedish audience combines their television viewing with the use of other media in a manner that hardly can be considered nonselective. (In a Swedish context, where more than 90% of the adult population regularly reads a newspaper, the omission of newspapers from a cultivation discussion would be absurd.)

Table 10.1 presents the relationships between the watching and reading of different types of media content among Swedes.[3] It reveals that the relationships are strongest for the use of the same type of content in different media. Especially strong are the correlations between watching and reading about sports (.79) and between watching and reading about high culture (.63). *Inside* each medium, the relationships between the use of different types of content are, at the most, moderately strong. And between the use of high cultural material and light material, such as entertainment and sports, there are no relationships at all — not even negative ones. There is no question that it would be very wrong to characterize Swedes' media use as "nonselective." We nourish strong suspicions that Swedes are by no means unique in this respect. It may well be that concentrating on television alone, the Gerbner group has come to exaggerate the nonselectivity of American media audiences.

Cultivating Values

Thus far we have left untouched one component of the cultivation process: what it is actually to be cultivated. When it comes to mental characteristics, American studies on cultivation have focused mainly on people's opinions and attitudes. In the Internalized Culture program, however, the decision was taken to focus on even more basic patterns of thoughts and feelings, namely, on people's *values*.

Notwithstanding the inevitable confusion surrounding such a broad and commonly used concept as the concept of values (Hutcheon, 1972; Spates, 1983), some kind of general agreement seems to exist on placing

Table 10.1 Media Use Combinations, Swedish National Study 1986 (Product Moment Correlations)

	Newspaper Reading					TV Watching			
	Local News	Domestic News	High Culture	Sports	Radio/TV	News	High Culture	Entertainment	Sports
Newspaper Reading									
Local News	–								
Domestic News	.45*	–							
High Culture	.17*	.38*	–						
Sports	.06	.02	-.06*	–					
Radio/TV	.17*	.10*	.03	.16*	–				
TV Watching									
News	.30*	.40*	.20*	.08*	.10*	–			
High Culture	.12*	.26*	.63*	-.06	-.01	.33*	–		
Entertainment	.16*	.04	-.12*	.17*	.42*	.27*	.02	–	
Sports	.06	-.01	-.18*	.79*	.14*	.16*	-.01	.16*	–

*Significant at the .01 level.
N = 1,520

values among the most abstract sets of ideas, as more basic and stable than norms, attitudes, or opinions (Levitin, 1970; Meddin, 1975). Values must thus be considered of utmost importance in the guidance of one's life. Rokeach goes as far as to say that ". . . values are determinants of virtually all kinds of behavior that could be called social" (1973, p. 27). A distinction between values and value orientations is often made. According to Meddin, value orientations serve as organizing principles for a number of values and are thus ". . . the most abstract of all units of human outlook" (Meddin, 1975, p. 891).

The Rokeachean and Inglehartian value constructions are used in the Internalized Culture program. Together they seem to capture important aspects of value orientations in contemporary Western societies. The Rokeach Value Survey consists of 18 terminal and 18 instrumental values; we use the terminal values only. Most of them are personal or social, such as "Inner harmony" and "Social recognition." Also included, however, are values referring to states in the external world, such as "A world of beauty" and "National security" (Rokeach, 1973, cf. Montgomery, Drottz, Gärling, Persson, & Wara, 1985). The value scale constructed by Inglehart (1977) taps the dimension of materialist and postmaterialist values, a special case of the more general dimension of instrumental/expressive value orientation (cf. Rosengren, 1986). Underlying this scale is a theory of scarcity and socialization, according to which — due to increasingly prosperous environments in which to live — every new generation has more postmaterialists than the generation preceeding it.[4]

Values, Life-styles, and the Media

In earlier work we have related the value scales of Inglehart and Rokeach to different background characteristics and life-styles (Reimer, 1988, 1989). One regional study also examined the relationship between values and media use (Rosengren & Reimer, 1986). In this chapter, the question of cultivation on a national level is approached empirically. In so doing, we must specify how various components of the cultivation process — values, life-styles, socioeconomic background, and mass media use — theoretically and empirically hang together. It seems reasonable to argue that socioeconomic background influences all other components. In addition, it is also necessary to take the social context surrounding each individual, what we have called a person's life-style, into account. It is within this context that human beings make sense of previous experiences and start the analysis of present ones. The past is "filtered" through the site of one's life-style.

The role of the mass media must also be considered in relation to life-style: a person's media use is connected to — and originates in — life-style.[5] To consider the media use as dependent on one's life-style is not to disregard the influence of the media. Instead, the meaning of media use is illuminated by taking its context into consideration. Furthermore, positioning the viewer/reader as an active subject does not make him or her invincible. On the contrary, active subjects using the media consciously may be more sensitive to a message or a system of messages than a passive viewer/reader would be. Whether this is the case is an open question that very probably does not have *one* single answer.

This perspective on cultivation seems to imply a simple, one-way causality: socioeconomic background brings about a certain life-style. This life-style in turn leads to a specific media use, and this media use cultivates a person's values. The concept of cultivation is problematic, however, in that some components in this complex relationship have to be positioned as determining other components. (The question of time does not help either, since all components are present at any given time.) We should therefore avoid speaking in causal terms. These are structural relations and when we order them the way we do, it is in accordance with the perspective chosen for this research question. They are by no means the only ones at work, however.

Moving to a specific context — in this case Sweden in the mid-1980s — we must initially construct a set of life-styles that may be relevant for our purpose. These life-styles should be internally relatively homogeneous and externally heterogeneous. Some should be relatively "undistinguished" and common, some should be "distinguished" and rare (see Bourdieu, 1984).

One such construction, made with the help of leisure activities and interests (see Reimer, 1989), consists of three undistinguished life-styles directed toward domesticity, popular culture, and nature (or "Natural Life"), and two distinguished life-styles directed toward economy and high culture. "Domesticity" contains a high proportion of married people and people with high levels of income. (Females are also overrepresented.) "Popular Culture" consists to a large extent of young people. "Natural Life," conversely, contains a large proportion of elderly people. "Economy" includes a large proportion of, as well as many people voting for nonsocialist parties. "High Culture" contains a large proportion of females and people from the middle or upper classes. This life-style is also positively correlated with education. As we have constructed them, the three "undistinguished" life-styles each make up roughly 40% of the population, whereas the "distinguished" life-styles are 10% (Economy) and 20% (High Culture) of the population. Theoretically and empirically, it is possible to belong to more than one life-style. The most common combination is belonging to both Natural Life and Domesticity. This is a combination encompassed by some 20% of the population.

The members of these five life-styles are characterized by very different relations toward the mass media. The two life-styles showing the strongest relationships with the media are High Culture and Popular Culture. High Culture is characterized by frequent use of high cultural and news media content, as well as of a high consumption of books. Popular Culture, on the other hand, is encompassed by people reading and watching more entertainment and less high cultural media content than in other life-styles. This group also spends more money on cinema tickets and the rental of video tapes. Natural Life shows similarities to High Culture, although the relationship to high cultural media content is not as strong. The people in the Economy life-style have rather weak relationships to most types of mass media content, except that a large proportion have video tape recorders and personal computers in their homes. Domesticity is related mainly to owning a video tape recorder.

Life-styles and values, we have maintained, are closely related. In the following sections we examine the two value orientations post-materialism and materialism and two values from the Rokeach Value Survey, "A comfortable life" and "Inner harmony."[6]

The research, then, examines differences in values and value orientations among present-day Swedes. First, however, we must acknowledge that the values involved are relatively important to most people and thus to a certain extent shared. We therefore do not expect radical interindividual differences.

Second, we hypothesize that the value differences that *do* exist will be group specific, in the sense that previous experiences leading up to a certain life-style — and the social/cultural context that continuously shapes and reshapes this life-style — will be of utmost importance in accounting for these differences.

Third, media use, although closely related to a person's life-style, will, partly due to an active participation in the media culture, make a contribution of its own in the process of value cultivation.

Cultivation and Value Orientations

We begin to examine the cultivation of materialism and postmaterialism by mass media use in Table 10.2, which describes the relationships between the two value orientations, traditional background characteristics, media use, and life-style. In order to facilitate the study of nonlinear relationships, the table contains the means for each subgroup on the variables materialism and postmaterialism.[7] The table also contains the unstandardized regression coefficients (the *b* values) for each variable, taken from a bivariate regression where the independent variables have been dichotomized. The size of the coefficient may be interpreted as the amount of change in the dependent variable associated with change in the independent variable.[8]

On one hand, the results in Table 10.2 follow the expected pattern for materialist and postmaterialist value orientations in Western societies. Voters for socialist parties are more postmaterialist than voters for nonsocialist parties; older people and people with lower levels of education are materialists to a great extent. On the other hand, as a result of allowing respondents to be both materialists and postmaterialists, older people are also *more postmaterialistic* than young people!

In regard to media use, entertainment is highly related to the materialist value orientations whereas high culture is related to the postmaterialist value orientations. News is related to both value orientations. Natural life and domesticity are both materialistic and postmaterialistic life-styles. High culture is a postmaterialistic life-style, economy is a materialistic life-style, and popular culture is neither a materialistic nor a postmaterialistic life-style (in the sense of having no significant relationship with either of the value orientations).

The largest "effect" for materialism comes from reading (as opposed to not reading) local news; and the variable most related to postmaterialism is gender (women rather than men). The subgroup that scored highest on materialism is Conservative party voters; on postmaterialism, Communist party voters. These are, however, bivariate results and cannot be interpreted in isolation. They are but components in a complex system of relationships and must be treated accordingly.

Table 10.2 Postmaterialist and Materialist Value Orientations, Swedish National Study 1986 (means and *b* values)

	Materialism		Postmaterialism		
	b value	*means*	*b value*	*means*	*N*
GENDER	−.007		.319*		
Male		5.83		5.82	761
Female		5.82		6.14	742
AGE	.281*		.159*		
15-29		5.63		5.87	438
30-49		5.73		5.99	523
50-75		6.08		6.07	542
EDUCATION	−.386*		−.047		
Low		5.97		6.07	734
Medium		5.73		5.87	554
High		5.48		5.94	212
HOUSEHOLD INCOME	−.022		−.154*		
Low		5.82		6.02	566
Medium		5.84		6.03	597
High		5.81		5.87	350
CLASS	−.078		−.198*		
Manual worker		5.86		6.10	798
Farmer		5.85		5.77	60
Office worker		5.80		5.92	387
Junior/Senior Executive		5.74		5.84	147
Employer		5.82		5.82	145
URBANIZATION	−.186*		−.066		
Nonmetropolitan Area		5.87		6.00	1046
Metropolitan Area		5.69		5.93	457
MARITAL STATUS	.139*		.118*		
Single		5.73		5.90	482
Married/Living together		5.87		6.02	1030
PARTY	.172*		−.250*		
Communist Party		5.04		6.36	59
Social Democratic Party		5.87		6.08	606
Agrarian Party		5.95		5.99	119
Liberal Party		5.81		5.94	180
Conservative Party		6.12		5.74	259

(Continued)

Table 10.2 (Continued)

	Materialism		Postmaterialism		
	b value	means	b value	means	N
TV WATCHING					
NEWS	.282*		.137*		
Nothing/Almost nothing		5.34		5.72	38
Not much		5.64		5.90	354
Quite a lot		5.84		6.02	902
Everything/Almost everything		6.07		6.02	252
HIGH CULTURE	−.021		.264*		
Nothing/Almost nothing		5.83		5.83	437
Not much		5.82		5.99	735
Quite a lot		5.79		6.17	298
Everything/Almost everything		5.90		6.32	42
ENTERTAINMENT	.299*		.055		
Nothing/Almost nothing		5.27		5.91	56
Not much		5.66		5.94	509
Quite a lot		5.91		6.00	816
Everything/Almost everything		5.99		6.00	166
SPORTS	.076		−.098		
Nothing/Almost nothing		5.74		6.04	307
Not much		5.81		6.02	456
Quite a lot		5.84		5.95	464
Everything/Almost everything		5.88		5.91	312
NEWSPAPER READING					
LOCAL NEWS	.393*		.196*		
Nothing/Almost nothing		5.21		5.75	40
Not much		5.57		5.84	170
Quite a lot		5.81		5.93	740
Everything/Almost everything		6.02		6.14	514
DOMESTIC NEWS	.231*		.155*		
Nothing/Almost nothing		5.73		6.00	46
Not much		5.64		5.84	279
Quite a lot		5.84		5.99	842
Everything/Almost everything		6.01		6.11	279
HIGH CULTURE	−.092		.177*		
Nothing/Almost nothing		5.84		5.77	371
Not much		5.86		6.05	656
Quite a lot		5.78		6.11	268
Everything/Almost everything		5.71		6.17	83

(Continued)

Table 10.2 (Continued)

| | Materialism | | Postmaterialism | | |
	b value	means	b value	means	N
NEWSPAPER READING (Continued)					
SPORTS	–.007		–.175*		
Nothing/Almost nothing		5.73		6.06	400
Not much		5.92		6.06	386
Quite a lot		5.78		5.87	354
Everything/Almost everything		5.84		5.90	290
RADIO/TV	.048		.086		
Nothing/Almost nothing		5.66		5.83	112
Not much		5.82		5.95	448
Quite a lot		5.79		6.01	540
Everything/Almost everything		5.92		6.00	326
LIFE-STYLES					
DOMESTICITY	.143*		.186*		
Low		5.76		5.89	841
High		5.90		6.08	738
THE NATURAL LIFE	.202*		.318*		
Low		5.75		5.86	971
High		5.95		6.18	608
POPULAR CULTURE	–.100		–.090		
Low		5.86		6.02	979
High		5.76		5.93	600
ECONOMY	.159*		–.256*		
Low		5.81		6.01	1431
High		5.97		5.75	148
HIGH CULTURE	–.087		.312*		
Low		5.84		5.91	1235
High		5.75		6.23	344

*Significant at the .01 level.

In U.S. cultivation analyses the next step would be to control simultaneously for background variables. A problem with such a procedure is, however, that it does not deal with the complex structure through which the flow of influence is always channeled; relevant relationships must initially be specified.[9]

Following our earlier discussion, our specification of models will start with life-styles, with media use as intervening variables, and values as the dependent variables. Other background variables will not be taken into account. As already outlined, their relations to media use will be regarded as mediated through life-styles. The life-styles will be treated as uncorrelated; no correlation between them is higher than .20. In order to keep the models simple, media use will be restricted to the watching of news, entertainment, and high culture on TV. They will also be treated as uncorrelated. All included variables are assumed to have direct effects on the two value orientations. Those life-styles related to media use are also assumed to have indirect effects on materialism and postmaterialism. The models are presented in Figures 10.1 and 10.2. The size of the coefficients may be interpreted as the amount of change in the following dependent variable "explained" by each independent variable when all preceding variables in the model are held constant.

Some of the life-styles (under controls for other life-styles and media use) have direct effects on the two value orientations. This is the case especially for Economy, whose positive effect on materialism and negative effect on postmaterialism cannot be accounted for by the use of the media. Other life-styles, especially Popular Culture, Natural Life, and High Culture, are more entangled with media use in their relations to materialism and postmaterialism. The relationships are not easy to interpret, however. A striking example of an intricate relationship is offered by Popular Culture, whose direct effect on materialism is negative, whereas the indirect effects are partly negative (through news) and partly positive (through entertainment), leading to a negligible total effect. The effects of media use hold up rather well even under control for the life-styles (or for other background variables, for that matter). This is true more for the relationship with materialism than it is for the one with postmaterialism, and especially for watching TV entertainment.

Cultivation and Values

The Rokeach Value Survey, from which the two values, "A comfortable life" and "Inner harmony," are borrowed, is not as widely used internationally as are the Inglehartian value orientation measures. Thus there are not as many comparisons to be made. Furthermore, in similarity to the Inglehart measures, the Rokeach Value Survey is normally conducted using ranks, making comparisons even harder (cf. Reimer, 1985). The analysis is partly of an exploratory nature, although the

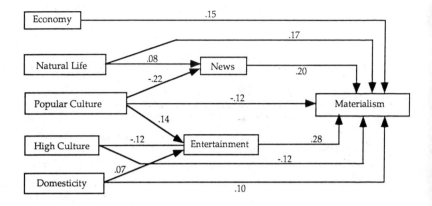

Figure 10.1 Materialism

	Direct Effect	Indirect Effect	Total Effect
TV Watching			
News	.203*	—	.203
Entertainment	.283*	—	.283
Lifestyles			
Economy	.151	—	.151
High Culture	−.117	−.033	−.150
Popular Culture	−.122*	−.004	−.126
The Natural Life	.167*	.016	.183
Domesticity	.102	.020	.122

*Significant at the .01 level.
N = 1,495

selection of these particular values was not made arbitrarily. The importance of the values is expected to vary between groups, and their relations to media use to differ. The means and the regression coefficients for the different groups on the two values may be found in Table 10.3.

Young people and people with less education consider the value of "A comfortable life" to be most important. The value of "Inner harmony" is perceived important by people with more education and by people in the middle or the upper classes.

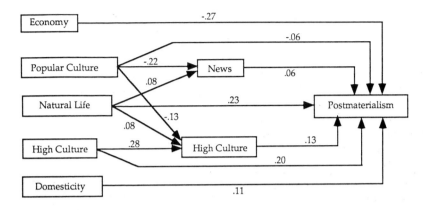

Figure 10.2 Postmaterialism

	Direct Effect	Indirect Effect	Total Effect
TV Watching			
News	.059	—	.059
High Culture	.130*	—	.130
Lifestyles			
Economy	−.269*	—	−.269
High Culture	.201*	.035	.236
Popular Culture	−.061	−.027	−.088
The Natural Life	.232*	.014	.246
Domesticity	.111*	—	.111

*Significant at the .01 level.
N = 1,495

The relationship between the values and media use is rather clear-cut. "Inner harmony" and "A comfortable life" stand in two directly contrasting positions with the media. "A comfortable life" is related to entertainment and other types of light media content; "Inner harmony" is related to high cultural media content and to news.

Turning to the life-styles and their relations to the two values, we initially would expect to find rather distinct relations, in the sense that the members of each life-style would perceive one, but not the other, of the two values as very important. That is not the case, however. The

Table 10.3 Two Important Values, Swedish National Study 1986
(means and *b* values)

	A Comfortable Life		Inner Harmony		
	b value	mean	b value	mean	N
GENDER	−.026		.184*		
Male		4.41		4.19	768
Female		4.39		4.37	760
AGE	−.361*		.187*		
15-29		4.65		4.15	449
30-49		4.38		4.28	528
50-75		4.22		4.39	551
EDUCATION	−.311*		.289*		
Low		4.42		4.23	751
Medium		4.50		4.29	562
High		4.14		4.55	214
HOUSEHOLD INCOME	−.031		.182*		
Low		4.36		4.23	575
Medium		4.45		4.30	606
High		4.38		4.45	354
CLASS	−.169*		.276*		
Manual worker		4.47		4.19	814
Farmer		4.45		4.31	62
Office worker		4.34		4.43	390
Junior/Senior Executive		4.20		4.56	150
Employer		4.11		4.24	146
URBANIZATION	−.096		.110		
Nonmetropolitan Area		4.42		4.26	1055
Metropolitan Area		4.33		4.37	467
MARITAL STATUS	.023		.070		
Single		4.37		4.25	495
Married/Living together		4.40		4.32	1040
PARTY	−.046		.010		
Communist Party		4.25		4.53	60
Social Democratic Party		4.41		4.29	616
Agrarian Party		4.36		4.20	119
Liberal Party		4.34		4.35	182
Conservative Party		4.38		4.34	259

(Continued)

Table 10.3 (Continued)

| | A Comfortable Life | | Inner Harmony | | |
	b value	mean	b value	mean	N
TV WATCHING					
NEWS	−.147*		.141*		
Nothing/Almost nothing		4.50		4.28	40
Not much		4.52		4.20	362
Quite a lot		4.35		4.32	910
Everything/Almost everything		4.43		4.42	260
HIGH CULTURE	−.198*		.270*		
Nothing/Almost nothing		4.52		4.13	444
Not much		4.40		4.32	748
Quite a lot		4.25		4.52	300
Everything/Almost everything		4.23		4.50	44
ENTERTAINMENT	.235*		−.136*		
Nothing/Almost nothing		4.11		4.38	56
Not much		4.27		4.38	514
Quite a lot		4.46		4.25	832
Everything/Almost everything		4.64		4.23	170
SPORTS	.085		−.155*		
Nothing/Almost nothing		4.34		4.44	318
Not much		4.38		4.33	463
Quite a lot		4.39		4.27	463
Everything/Almost everything		4.54		4.15	317
NEWSPAPER READING					
LOCAL NEWS	.008		.029		
Nothing/Almost nothing		4.49		4.59	41
Not much		4.37		4.21	174
Quite a lot		4.39		4.30	747
Everything/Almost everything		4.43		4.34	525
DOMESTIC NEWS	−.144*		.166*		
Nothing/Almost nothing		4.66		4.23	47
Not much		4.49		4.18	287
Quite a lot		4.36		4.33	849
Everything/Almost everything		4.42		4.40	284
HIGH CULTURE	−.232*		.292*		
Nothing/Almost nothing		4.52		4.10	377
Not much		4.43		4.34	666
Quite a lot		4.19		4.53	270
Everything/Almost everything		4.36		4.61	85

(Continued)

Table 10.3 (Continued)

	A Comfortable Life		Inner Harmony		
	b value	mean	b value	mean	N
NEWSPAPER READING (Continued)					
SPORTS	.125*		−.225*		
Nothing/Almost nothing		4.36		4.47	412
Not much		4.33		4.35	388
Quite a lot		4.38		4.26	355
Everything/Almost everything		4.59		4.10	295
RADIO/TV	.152*		.087		
Nothing/Almost nothing		4.15		4.38	112
Not much		4.34		4.36	450
Quite a lot		4.41		4.30	553
Everything/Almost everything		4.53		4.23	331
LIFE-STYLES					
DOMESTICITY	.222*		.169*		
Low		4.30		4.21	854
High		4.52		4.38	752
THE NATURAL LIFE	.077		.235*		
Low		4.37		4.20	990
High		4.45		4.44	616
POPULAR CULTURE	.352*		−.131*		
Low		4.27		4.34	997
High		4.62		4.21	609
ECONOMY	.051		−.147		
Low		4.40		4.31	1456
High		4.45		4.16	150
HIGH CULTURE	−.171*		.336*		
Low		4.44		4.22	1257
High		4.27		4.56	349

*Significant at the .01 level.

members of High Culture, Natural Life, and Popular Culture life-styles hold the expected positions (one of the two values is important), but the other groups take other positions. There is no significant relationship at all between Economy and the two values, and the people in Domesticity on the whole consider *both* values to be very important.

The models of the relationships between the five life-styles, media use, and the two values are somewhat more complicated than the previous two models since all three types of TV content, according to the bivariate analyses, were significantly related to both values. These two models are presented in Figures 10.3 and 10.4.

Figures 10.3 and 10.4 show that — although the direct effects are by far the strongest — the indirect effects play a larger part than they did for the materialist and postmaterialist value orientations. This is true especially for the two life-styles previously described as having the most frequent and active use of the media: High Culture and Popular Culture.

The effects of media use on the two values "A comfortable life" and "Inner harmony" drop under simultaneous control for the life-styles. The two strong positive effects (that of entertainment on "A comfortable life" and that of high culture on "Inner harmony") stay significant, however, suggesting that media use does make an independent contribution to the cultivation of these values.

Conclusion

In this analysis of the possible cultivation of two value orientations and two values, the real interest has not been directed toward these values and value orientations as such. Rather, the values and the value orientations have been used as examples of more general processes. In order to be properly analyzed and understood, however, these processes need to be brought down to specific cases, and therefore, the results of these particular "cultivations" may be of interest in themselves. How are they to be interpreted, then?

It must first be noted that the statistical "effects" of media use on basic values are small. This is to be expected; these values are to a large extent shared, thus the variance to be explained must be small. Also, unlike more specific beliefs and attitudes, these values are deeply rooted in a matrix of social and individual structures. Thus, specific effects from specific media content must be expected to be rather weak. It is still clear, however, that the two key characteristics under study — having a specific life-style and using a specific type of media content — are related to human values.

If we compare the two value orientations of materialism and postmaterialism with the two values, "A comfortable life" and "Inner

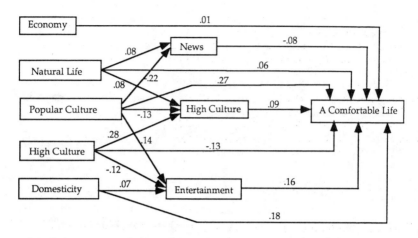

Figure 10.3 A Comfortable Life

	Direct Effect	Indirect Effect	Total Effect
TV Watching			
News	−.079	—	−.079
High Culture	−.091	—	−.091
Entertainment	.163*	—	.163
Lifestyles			
Economy	.010	—	.010
High Culture	−.126	−.043	−.169
Popular Culture	.271*	.052	.323
The Natural Life	.063	−.013	.050
Domesticity	.182*	.012	.194

*Significant at the .01 level.
N = 1,514

harmony," it seems to be the case that media use is more strongly related to the two values than to the two value orientations.[10] Why? First, we have to look at the specific media content. Are these values and value orientations reflected in the media output? Unfortunately, very few content analyses of this kind have been carried out.[11] Second, are the viewers/readers actively searching for content reflecting these values or are values unimportant in these media activities? What happens in

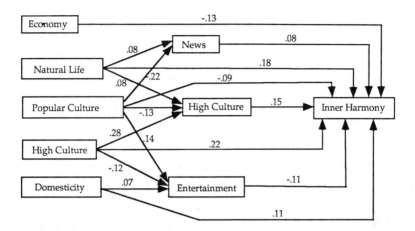

Figure 10.4 Inner Harmony

	Direct Effect	Indirect Effect	Total Effect
TV Watching			
News	.077	—	.077
High Culture	.147*	—	.147
Entertainment	−.112	—	−.112
Lifestyles			
Economy	−.132	—	−.132
High Culture	.221*	.054	.275
Popular Culture	−.087	−.053	−.140
The Natural Life	.178*	.017	.195
Domesticity	.113*	−.008	.105

*Significant at the .01 level.
N = 1,514

these different cases? It is obvious that there are many simultaneous processes underway that have to be taken into account.

Tentative hypotheses may be, first, that specific values, such as "A comfortable life" and "Inner harmony," *are* more related to specific media outputs. Second, values being more specific than whole value orientations means that in specific programs they will be *easier to identify* for viewers. Third, active subjects will, due to different life-styles, and so on, *selectively choose* programs containing said values. Fourth, they will be *cultivated*. Such a cultivation must, however, be regarded as a more or less *conscious cultivation*, carried out by cultivated viewers and readers.[12]

In this article we have argued that our perspective also may be valid within other societal structures than the one under study. If that is so, it is to no small extent due to the inclusion of the concept of life-style in the discussion of cultivation. It is possible by means of this concept to illuminate processes that cannot be reduced to socioeconomic factors and background characteristics. An example only briefly touched on in this chapter is how the apparently simple relationship between media use and the values of "A comfortable life" and "Inner harmony" — a relationship that could be characterized as the typical opposition between refined (high culture and "Inner harmony") and "vulgar" taste (entertainment and "A comfortable life") — broke down in conjunction with different life-styles. Closer analysis would no doubt reveal more "unexpected coalitions" like that one.[13]

The two main points in this chapter have been the argument for a life-style perspective and the demand to regard the viewer/reader as an active participant in the cultivation process. Both points have been based on recent arguments in socialization and communication research, the two fields of research most closely linked to cultivation research. The further implications of such a shift in the perspective applied to cultivation will not be drawn out here. Suffice it now to say that some implications will have to follow such a shift in perspective. But that is only as to be expected. All fields of research change. We hope this change will help us in understanding more of that intricate interplay between individuals and the media called cultivation.

Notes

1. This article has been written as part of the Internalized Culture research program. This program is a continuation of the research program Cultural Indicators: The Swedish Symbol System 1945-1975. Whereas the Cultural Indicators program studied changing values in media over a 30-year period, the aim of the new program is to study the relationship between values and life-styles in Sweden in the 1980s (Reimer 1988, 1989; Rosengren 1985, 1986, 1988; Rosengren & Reimer, 1986). The Internalized Culture program is made possible by a grant from the Bank of Sweden Tercentenary Foundation.

2. American studies dealing with the concept of life-styles tend to do so in ways that theoretically differ from the one proposed here. For overviews, see Peterson, 1983; Zablocki and Kanter, 1976. For empirical studies, see Frank and Greenberg, 1980; Mitchell, 1983. For European perspectives, see Bourdieu, 1984; Featherstone, 1987.

3. Media use was measured on a 4-point scale, ranging from reading or watching "nothing/practically nothing" to "everything/almost everything." The empirical data used stem from a Swedish national study conducted in late 1986. The data were collected with self-response questionnaires and simple random sampling was used. Number of respondents was 1,845; response rate, 68%.

4. According to the Inglehartian theory, materialists put high emphasis on societal goals such as the fight against crime and a stable economy, whereas postmaterialists emphasize freedom of speech and beautiful cities (Inglehart, 1977, 1987, cf. Flanagan, 1987; Harding, Philips, & Fogarty, 1986; Savage, 1985).

5. In one sense media use may actually be seen as a component of life-style, but for heuristic purposes it may be fruitful to separate them. A similar argument could be put forward with respect to the concept of values, of course.

6. Using the Inglehartian value orientations as two separate sets of values is based on the assumption that people's values are too complex and too interrelated to justify an either/or distinction. We regard materialism and postmaterialism as two dimensions (Reimer, 1988). The Rokeachean values are too numerous to facilitate a comprehensive analysis within the space available. Therefore, instead of a more superficial look at all 18 values, we concentrated on a more thorough analysis of the two a priori selected values, "A comfortable life" and "Inner harmony," which could be expected to stand in different relations to different types of media content and media use.

7. Using the 12-item scale by Inglehart, the materialist and postmaterialist value orientations have been measured on 7-point Likert scales. The variables Materialism and Postmaterialism were constructed by taking the means of the separate value items.

8. The independent variables were dichotomized in order to facilitate a comparison. The dichotomizations were made as follows:

Age:	15-49	50-75
Education:	Low/Medium	High
Income:	Low/Medium	High
Class:	Manual worker	Office worker/Executive
Party	Socialist/Communist	Agrarian/Liberal/Conservative
Media Use:	Low	High

9. In Hughes's reanalysis of Gerbner's data, he finds that: "The relationship between sex and television watching is fairly strong before controls, but disappears afterwards, and this disappearance is accounted for by the variable of hours worked per week. . . ," suggesting that women watch TV more than men because they are likely to work fewer hours outside the home than men (Hughes, 1980, p. 291). Although Hughes is correct in claiming that women watch TV because they are at home, it could still be argued that they are at home because they are women (including everything else interrelated to this factor); both TV watching and being at home may be seen as a result of gender positioning.

10. Fourteen out of 18 correlations between media use and the two values "A comfortable life" and "Inner harmony" are significant (Table 11.3). Ten out of 18 correlations between media use and the two value orientations materialism and postmaterialism are significant (Table 11.2).

11. One example of a content analysis on the Rokeachean values has been conducted on American soap operas. "A comfortable life" turned out to be the one value out of Rokeach's 18 terminal values most strongly preeminent in these shows. "Inner harmony" was not a value often reflected in the shows (Schrag & Rosenfeld, 1987). The relationship between the Rokeachean values "freedom" and "equality" in Swedish editorials 1945-1975 has been studied by Block (1984).

12. Palmgreen and Rayburn's Expectancy-Value Model (1985), with its emphasis on the importance of the viewers/readers belief that the gratifications sought will be possible to obtain through a certain media content, is highly relevant in this context.

13. A similar discussion has been carried out by Jarlbro (1988) on the relationship between socioeconomic status and media use with family communication patterns acting as mediator.

References

Block, E. (1984). Freedom, equality, etcetera. Values and valuations in the Swedish domestic political debate, 1945-1975. In G. Melischek, K. E. Rosengren & J. Stappers (Eds.), *Cultural indicators: An international symposium.* (pp. 159-176). Vienna: Akademie der Wissenschaften.

Bourdieu, P. (1984). *Distinction: A social critique of the judgement of taste.* Cambridge, MA: Harvard University Press.

Bryant, J., & Zillmann, D. (1986). (Eds.). *Perspectives on media effects.* Hillsdale, NJ: Lawrence Erlbaum.

Ewen, E., & Ewen, S. (1982). *Channels of desire.* New York: McGraw-Hill.

Featherstone, M. (1987). Lifestyle and consumer culture. *Theory, Culture and Society, 4*(1), 55-70.

Flanagan, S. C. (1987). Controversy: Value change in industrial societies. *American Political Science Review, 81*(4), 1303-1319.

Frank, R. W., & Greenberg, M. G. (1980). *The public's use of television.* Beverly Hills, CA: Sage.

Gerbner, G., Gross, L., Morgan, M., & Signorielli, N. (1986). Living with television: The dynamics of the cultivation process. In J. Bryant & D. Zillmann (Eds.), *Perspectives on media effects* (pp. 17-40). Hillsdale, NJ: Lawrence Erlbaum.

Harding, S., & Philips, D., with Fogarty, M. (1986). *Contrasting values in western Europe.* London: MacMillan.

Hughes, M. (1980). The fruits of cultivation analysis: A reexamination of some effects of television watching. *Public Opinion Quarterly, 44*(3), 287-302.

Hutcheon, P. D. (1972). Value theory: Towards conceptual clarification. *British Journal of Sociology, 23*, 172-187.

Inglehart, R. (1977). *The silent revolution: Changing values and political styles among western publics.* Princeton, NJ: Princeton University Press.

Inglehart, R. (1987). Controversy: Value change in industrial societies. *American Political Science Review, 81*(4), 1289-1303.

Jarlbro, G. (1988). *Familj, massmedier och politik* [With a summary in English]. Stockholm, Sweden: Almqvist & Wiksell International.

Jensen, K. B. (1986). *Making sense of the news.* Århus, Denmark: Århus Universitetsförlag.

Johnsson-Smaragdi, U. (1983). *TV use and social interaction in adolescence: A longitudinal study.* Stockholm, Sweden: Almqvist & Wiksell International.

Levitin, T. (1970). Values. In J. P. Robinson & P. R. Shaver (Eds.), *Measures of social psychological attitudes* (pp. 405-418). Ann Arbor, MI: ISR.

McCron, R. (1976). Changing perspectives in the study of mass media and socialization. In J. D. Halloran (Ed.), *Mass media and socialization* (pp. 13-44). Leeds, England: Kavanagh & Sons.

Meddin, J. (1975). Attitudes, values and related concepts: A system of classification. *Social Science Quarterly, 55*(4), 889-900.

Mitchell, A. (1983). *The nine American lifestyles: Who we are and where we're going.* New York: MacMillan.

Montgomery, H., Drottz, B-M., Gärling, T., Persson, A-L., & Wara, R. (1985). Conceptions about material and immaterial values in a sample of Swedish subjects. In H. Brandstatter & E. Kirschler (Eds.), *Economic psychology: Proceedings of the tenth IAREP annual colloqium* (pp. 427-437). Linz, Austria: Trauner Verlag.

Palmgreen, P. & Rayburn, J. D., II. (1985). An expectancy-value approach to media gratifications. In K. E. Rosengren, L. A. Wenner, & P. Palmgreen (Eds.), *Media gratifications research: Current perspectives* (pp. 61-72). Beverly Hills, CA: Sage.

Peterson, R. (1983). Patterns of cultural choice. A prolegomenon. *American Behavioral Scientist, 26*(4), 422-438.

Reimer, B. (1985). Values and the choice of measurement technique: The rating and ranking of postmaterialism. *Working Paper nr. 8*, Unit of Mass Communication, University of Gothenburg, Sweden.

Reimer, B. (1988). No values–new values? Youth and postmaterialism. *Scandinavian Political Studies, 11*(4), 1-13.

Reimer, B. (1989). Postmodern structures of feeling: Values and life styles in the postmodern age. In J. R. Gibbins (Ed.), *Contemporary political culture.* London: Sage.

Rokeach, M. (1973). *The nature of human values.* New York: Free Press.

Rokeach, M. (Ed.). (1979). *Understanding human values.* New York: Free Press.

Rosengren, K. E. (1985). Culture, media and society. *Massa Communicatie, 13*(3-4), 126-142.

Rosengren, K. E. (1986). Media linkages between culture and other societal systems. In M. L. McLaughlin (Ed.), *Communication yearbook no. 9* (pp. 19-56). Beverly Hills, CA: Sage.

Rosengren, K. E. (1988). *The study of media culture: Ideas, actions and artefacts.* Invited Paper for the S.O.M. Conference "Seeing the Future in the Rear-view Mirror," Veldhoven, the Netherlands.

Rosengren, K. E., & Reimer, B. (1986). The cultivation of values by media. *Lund Research Papers in the Sociology of Communication, 6.*

Rosengren, K. E., Wenner, L. A., & Palmgreen, P. (Eds.). (1985). *Media gratifications research: Current perspectives.* Beverly Hills, CA: Sage.

Savage, J. (1985). Postmaterialism of the left and right: Political conflict in postindustrial society. *Comparative Political Studies, 17*(4), 431-451.

Schrag, R. L., & Rosenfeld, L. B. (1987). Assessing the soap opera frame: Audience perceptions of value structures in soap operas and prime-time serial dramas. *The Southern Speech Communication Journal, 52*, 362-376.

Schröder. K. C. (1987). Convergence of antagonistic traditions? The case of audience research. *European Journal of Communication, 2*(1), 7-31.

Spates, J. L. (1983). The sociology of values. *Annual Review of Sociology, 9*, 27-49.

Weibull, L. (1985). Structural factors in gratifications research. In K. E. Rosengren, L. A. Wenner, & P. Palmgreen (Eds.). *Media gratifications research: Current perspectives* (pp. 123-148). Beverly Hills, CA: Sage.

Wrong, D. (1961). The oversocialized conception of man in modern sociology. *American Sociological Review, 26*(2), 183-193.

Zablocki, B., & Kanter, R. M. (1976). The differentiation of life-styles. *Annual Review of Sociology, 2,* 269-298.

Zigler, E., & Seitz, V. (1978). Changing trends in socialization theory. *American Behavioral Scientist, 21*(5), 731-756.

11

Does Television Cultivate the British?

Late 80s Evidence

J. MALLORY WOBER

One *explains* something that *exists* — but can look for it even
if it doesn't.

Introduction

British research linked to cultivation analysis (Gerbner, Gross, Morgan,
& Signorielli, 1986) began in the mid-1970s (see Wober & Gunter, 1988
for a full account of this work). Briefly, the process started by looking
for a greater perception and fear of a mean and scary world among
heavy rather than among light television viewers. This was not found.

Further studies took the position that content (for which analytic
facilities did not readily exist) should be studied in terms of audience
perceptions of that content. If heavier viewing could be associated with
a particular pattern of perceived content and if it could also be associated with a similar perception of the real world, then interpretations that
television viewing had inculcated certain perceptions or feelings of the
real world could be entertained. As Wober and Gunter (1988) report,
such isomorphism was seldom found; where it was, it tended to be
positive. So, for example, viewers perceived that programming portrayed women as wanting to get on in their careers, and heavier viewers

also thought real women were, and should be, doing this. For comparison purposes, however, this procedure (assessment of audience *perceptions* of content) is a departure from cultivation analysis as studied by Gerbner et al. (1986) (see Chapter 1, this volume).

Beyond this, a fundamental psychological consideration was introduced into cultivation theory (Wober, 1986). Viewing experience among adults may, as a first step, influence attitudes, but it is not likely to form personality. Thus, underlying personality structures such as locus of control or authoritarianism might influence perceptions and attitudes as well as viewing practices and experience. If it could be demonstrated that experience inculcated certain perceptions of screen content (parallel with perceptions and feelings about the real world) and, at the same time, shown that these perceptions and feelings were independent of relevant personality attributes, one could then interpret a plausible effect of heavy viewing. It was also felt that relative immutability of personality structures does not apply so firmly with children; thus it was important to extend cultivation studies among samples of children.

How Much Do Viewers View?

The British have an eager appetite for home screen entertainment. From November 1982 until the close of the decade there have been four channels of terrestrially transmitted television available effectively to the whole nation. Viewing is diversified across a wide range of program types and viewers who see more of a particular type of program in 1 week tend also to see more of that type in another week (Wober, 1988a). The tendency for viewing to be heavy or light, however, across program types is much smaller. Audience viewing data generally reveal that viewing practices are selective, as defined by the tendency to watch certain program types.

Audience data also reveal that programs and program types have widely differing meanings for viewers. While women overall are perceived as stronger characters than men, men are more likely to be seen as strong characters in the adventure and action programs than in soap operas or situation comedies. In general, viewers perceive a morally positive climate that differs somewhat between program types.

VCRs are also widespread and used quite regularly: 62% of individuals aged 12 and over said that they have the use of a VCR at home and the industry's measurement contractor, Audits of Great Britain (AGB), found 4.7 hours of VCR playback (among VCR households) during 1 week (Wober & Kilpatrick, 1988).

Thus British viewers have many opportunities to absorb diverse and generally positive ideas and impressions from broadcast programs. At the same time, it is clear that a substantial proportion of the viewing diet is constructed by the viewer, who watches a wide variety of programming but also has specific and different preferences for certain types of programming.

The stage is thus set to study particular effects attributable to absorbing themes present in programming. A fundamental notion in studying the possibility of cultivation as a homogeneous correspondence of viewers' perceptions and attitudes with the screen's content is that the content consists of units or "molecules" for which specific effects could theoretically be located. If all these molecules of content consist of identical or essentially similar atoms, then it is plausible to expect thematic consequences of the kind described by American cultivation analysts (Gerbner et al., 1986). In Britain, however, it appears that television content and consumption is composed of quite diverse atoms, which provides a reason for a low level of expectancy of cultivation effects.

Viewing and Fear of Crime

A study based on a representative London sample of 448 diarists (Gunter, 1987) established the amount of viewing for each of six program types and collected five measures about the viewers' relationships with crime. First, by direct personal experience, 7% said they had, at some time, been a victim of violent assault (it is not known whether this included both adult and childhood experience). Second, by indirect experience, 26% said they knew a person who had been a victim of violent assault. Two kinds of questions (described below) explored experiences likely to have been mediated by television, which included measures of perception and of affect, or fear. Finally, people also indicated whether or not they felt competent to defend themselves against an attack.

The perception measures explored (1) the likelihood of being assaulted for a person living in each of five locations (Los Angeles, Glasgow, London [West End], farm in the United States, and the

Cotswolds in the English countryside); (2) the likelihood of being a victim in six different contexts (while walking home alone in the dark, in New York, Glasgow, London [West End], local park, and own neighborhood); (3) of being a victim in one's own lifetime; and (4) of having one's home burgled in the next year). The affect measures expressed (1) the respondents' degree of fear of walking alone after dark in Los Angeles, (2) coming home from a local pub, or (3) of being stranded in the English countryside. Nearly 9 in 10 expressed fear of walking home after dark in Los Angeles, nearly half expressed such a sentiment about walking home locally, and just over a quarter said they would be afraid in the English countryside.

Any conclusion about an influence from television would best be supported if a link could be observed between particular kinds of viewing and perceptions or fears. A regression analysis revealed only one link between viewing and perception measures: heavier viewers of news tended to think there was less risk of criminal victimization for people living in Los Angeles. This could conceivably represent an influence of reality sources on misconceptions; but the result, in the absence of any links between crime drama viewing and risk perceptions, is more credibly taken as fortuitous.

In further analysis, total television viewing was significantly related to a greater perceived chance of being victimized oneself, if one was in London's West End or a local park (but not in one's "own area"); viewing soap operas was significantly linked with perceived risk to oneself in New York. Total amount of viewing was linked with greater fear of victimization either in the countryside, walking home from a pub at night, or in Los Angeles. An interpretation was offered that "these findings are not entirely inconsistent with the notion of content specificity as a mediator of television's influence" (Gunter, 1987, p. 87); however, there are at least three good reasons for caution about accepting such a conclusion.

One reason is "psychological"; a precondition of a development of fear may be reasonably considered to exist if there is a relevant perception of risk. Yet perceptions of risk, in this case, were not associated with measured amounts of viewing. It would have to be theorized, then, that risk perceptions are inculcated by various means even among low television viewers, but that viewing transforms such perceptions into feelings of fear. A second reason is that measures of amount of viewing were entered into the regression equations, not only of separate program types, but also of the sum of viewing of all program types. This procedure introduces more internal correlation than is probably desirable and resulting significant relationships become difficult to interpret. A third point is that one measure, amount of viewing sport, is negatively related with fear of walking home at night: heavier viewers are less fearful. This suggests a personality level explanation for some of the findings, namely, that it may be the more aggressive (heavier sport viewing) people who have less fear, while the less aggressive people watch more television and report fear (Wober & Gunter, 1988). The relationship between fear and watching U.S. crime drama was significant, but that of fear with viewing British crime drama (which on face validity should be more likely to inculcate local fears) was not significant. In all, a conservative evaluation of this correlational study may be best advised, without accepting a conclusion, however tentative, that television viewing has cultivated a perception of risk or a fear of victimization by crime.

Since the viewing diet is extremely varied, it may be that a particular strand of viewing might inculcate effects, which may be dissipated or neutralized by other themes in the viewing diet. Certainly, Londoners have established a view that crime is more likely in American cities than locally, but this view is not evidently associated with watching American crime drama (Gunter, 1987, Tables 6.10-6.12) and it could just as well arise from remarks about America made in British drama, jokes made by comedians, and items in the news. More subtly, it has to be asked whether it is true (and if so, why), when British viewers learn of a mass killing in San Diego they take this as something to be expected of Southern California, while news of a mass killing in Hungerford, England, is felt to be atypical. What is believed is clearly deeply rooted and pervasive and it is not easy to show that it is linked with contemporary patterns of television viewing.

If these studies have not convincingly demonstrated a cultivation of fear (linked with viewing the most plausible sectors of television programming), it is possible that adults are more resilient to viewing while children, who are more pliable and still in the process of forming personality and attitudes, may be more affected by what they see. This is certainly believed to be the case by the viewing public. Four surveys were fielded (each with a national sample of over 1,000 adults); the first at the start of a series, called The Power of Television, and on three other occasions during and after the series was aired (Wober, 1985). Four questions were included, one of which asked whether "as far as children's developing personalities are concerned" (I believe that) television in general has a strong/some influence for good/for harm or no overall influence.

Averaged across the four waves, 16% said that television has no influence on children's developing personalities; 41% considered television a good influence on children, and 33% felt it was a bad influence. Audience measurement from an independent source revealed that two thirds of the public had seen at least some part of the series, an average of two programs per viewer. Although it was not possible to integrate this viewing evidence with the opinion data, internally, it could be hypothesized that the programs should have had an effect of increasing belief in the power of television — both directly, by viewing them and accepting their arguments, and by reading articles in the press and discussing the issue with other family members. Nevertheless, the 14% who, at the outset, thought there was *no* influence increased slightly, to 17% who thought similarly after the end of the series. There was also a shift from thinking that it was a good influence (46%, in the first wave, 39% at the last) to believing it was a bad influence on children (31% at the outset, 35% at the last).

In all, the series may have functioned in the way that advertisers say that commercials serve: not to increase total consumption of a commodity, but to alter the shares of brands within the commodity. In this case, the "commodity" (belief in the power of television) has not altered while the "brands" (kinds of opinion — good or bad) have. American cultivation theorists might see, in this case, a shift in the direction of apprehension, corresponding to the reports that television content inculcates fear. However, the series was overtly making an argument, not just about quality but about quantity and in the latter respect it produced no results, suggesting that it is the kind of person who already contemplates television's power who may shift in evaluation while the constituency not acknowledging power is harder to bring into such a belief. In any case, the fact that these were independent samples means that interpretations about changed attitudes must remain speculative.

Studies Among Children

What people believe may have no relation to what actually occurs, however. To explore relationships between children's viewing experiences and their behavior, perceptions and attitudes were examined in three surveys conducted among members of a national children's program appreciation panel. One report (Wober, 1987a) presents results on perceptions and fears and their links, if any, with viewing experience. Panel members were as young as 5, and up to 12 years old. They were asked to "put a tick (check) to show what you think; or if you need help ask your Mum or Dad to put the ticks, to show what you think."

Nine perception items asked (with a 3-point reply scale) whether events "may happen to you, one day" and included, "some of your best things get stolen," "get hurt, if someone else starts a fight, in the street," "come first or second in a sports competition." Four out of five children replied that they were likely to "see a huge spider in the bathtub," and one out of five endorsed each of the two "crime" items, on theft and on being hurt in a fight. Factor analysis revealed four factors: (1) loss or injury (three items, including the two crime ones), (2) achievement, (3) good luck, and (4) "friends and foes." The inquiry about fear was another 3-point scale asking whether, for each of 11 items, the child would be afraid, brave, or not sure which. Two "crime" items included "someone may start a fight and hurt me" and "somebody may steal my favorite toys or things." These two items, with another, loaded together in one "loss and injury" factor. There was another factor combining "dark fears" (ghost story, spider, etc.) and two courage factors.

The final procedure explored links, if any, between perceptions, fears, and patterns of viewing experience (from the appreciation diaries). One validating result was that heavier sport viewing was significantly related with higher scores on the factor that linked bravery in the case of physical experiences including a "ride on Big Dipper at Fun Fair" and "get an injection from a nurse or doctor." It is noteworthy that heavier viewing of adult film and TV miniseries was related to a greater perceived likelihood of achievement, but with less physical and social forms of courage. Physical courage was also related to watching more action adventure series episodes (such as "The A-Team" and "Knight Rider"). Since film viewing may include a range of items from harmless comedies to violence-containing westerns or other thrillers, it is not possible to interpret that link; but if any reinforcement is to be inferred from these results it is that claimed physical courage (though not social courage) is associated with crime thriller viewing.

The core of this children's study was, however, the examination of links between patterns of viewing and the measures of likelihood of loss and of bravery or fear related to such events. In a regression equation, social courage was linked with greater perception of likelihood of loss and of bravery in the face of it. None of the viewing measures, except amount of viewing of adult soap opera episodes, was related with the perception of likelihood of loss. Those who saw more soap operas were less likely to perceive a chance of loss. However, soap opera viewing was not related with any claim that one might be fearful, or brave. Two viewing measures were linked with bravery in the face of victimization: greater viewing of adult film and TV drama were associated with greater anticipated bravery (contrary to the negative association of this measure with physical and social courage), and those who watched more documentaries and shows in the "general information" category were less likely to claim confidence in the face of loss.

These results are noteworthy for at least three reasons. First, there is no consistent pattern of association between gross amount of television viewing and perceptual and emotional measures: different kinds of viewing link in different ways, if at all, with nonviewing measures. Second, there is no sign of a cultivation of fear by the program categories usually theorized to bring this about—films and crime drama. Third, a limited number of cogent associations suggest that the measures have some degree of validity, so that the absence of signs of association—let alone of consistent cultivation of fear—has some reinforcement as a "clearance" of the television system from the blame with which it may otherwise be associated.

In another study, the same panel completed a simple questionnaire entitled WHAT I AM LIKE, 14 weeks before receiving the instruments discussed above. One side of the paper listed 16 self-descriptive phrases for which the children were asked to choose a reply from YES, that's me, or WELL, I'm a bit like this, to NO, I'm not like this. Factor analysis revealed five clear groupings, the first of which is unmistakably a measure of aggression (argue a lot, get cheeky to grown ups, sometimes start fights, get cross and break things, and like to tease other kids). The data (Wober, Reardon, & Fazal, 1987) showed that at the level of multiple partial correlations (eliminating effects of age, sex, and class) there were five significant relationships from a matrix of 55 correlations between 11 program types and 5 personality measures.

Children watching more adult soap opera disclosed lower achievement orientation (keep tidy, help grown-ups, try hard) and those watching more information programs, whether made for children or for adults, showed lower aggressiveness. Going beyond this, regression equations repeated the association between viewing more (children's) information programs and lower aggressiveness and (for boys only) an association between watching more adult films and nonseries drama and aggression. This result is consistent with the crime and bravery study where it was found that watching more adult films was linked with a greater degree of claimed bravery.

The personality study also listed 14 television characters and asked whether children would like to be like each character when they grew up. Four aspirational factors emerged. Women formed a single factor (including characters from different program genres) while males grouped into three factors (deviant characters in fiction, fantasy characters, and actuality). Regression analyses showed that personality and demographic attributes associated with aspirations in very logically predictable ways (girls wanted to be like the female characters; young children wanted to be like fantasy characters such as Tom, Jerry, or Mr. T.). Several viewing measures were also associated with aspirations. Viewing soap operas and children's cartoons was linked with wanting to be like some of the soap opera characters, while wanting to be like the fantasy characters was associated with more frequent viewing of action adventure but less frequent viewing of news.

Finding negative relationships is a telling sign that considerable caution is needed before interpreting positive associations as program effects. Whatever it is that brings about low news viewing may also bring about fantasy aspirations, unless one considers that fantasy aspirations are a normal feature in young children and their suppression is attributed to the realism that comes with later increased news viewing. It is worth noting that amount of viewing of news and information made for adults or for children was not associated with any desire to become like the well-known newscasters.

In all, these two studies of children offer limited support for the idea that viewing experiences may reinforce certain developing strands of attitude and personality. At the same time, it is clear that such relationships are few rather than many, and that they involve different parts of the viewing diet, some in positive but others in negative relationships.

Thus far the whole concern of this research and the tradition that gives us its perspective is to assess the possibility that television has one or another kind of harmful influence. Yet earlier on it was shown that, while people believe television has power, it is more often thought to be constructive than otherwise. A further study using the children's panel looked at possible implications of the world seen on the screen and the development of ideas of what the children would like to do in their working careers (Wober, 1988b).

Fourteen occupational activities were listed and children were asked to answer two questions: (1) whether or how often each kind of activity was seen on television (yes, often; once or twice; no, never) and (2) "when you grow up, do you want to do any of these things as a job?" (Yes!; maybe; no). First, both girls and boys agreed about how often they saw each activity done by girls and done by boys. Next, those activities most often seen as done by boys were in inverse rank order to the frequency with which they were seen as done by girls. In short, there was distinct sex role stereotyping in perceived content: what children saw as boys' work was not girls' work and vice versa.

The order of preference of the things boys wanted to do corresponded well with the order of prominence of what was seen, on screen, as work done by boys and men. The same pattern of recognizable reflection in aspirations of screen perceptions occurred among girls. These parallels were not taken, however, as convincing evidence that television viewing reinforces, let alone constructs, children's future ambitions. It may simply be that television reflects society as it is and as it is likely to be, and that children develop preferences and ambitions based on intrinsic motives (for excitement, security, and so on) together with direct observation through families, friends, school, and the real world, of who does what and of their own options.

A more rigorous test of television's possible contribution was sought. Is it that the more that children watch television, the more likely they are to say they see an occupation and the more likely they are to want to do that activity in the future? Using this more rigorous requirement, it was found that, for girls, heavier viewing (it so happens, of adventure action series) corresponds both with saying they see girls working a computer and in charge of people in an office, and with saying they want to do and be such things themselves. There was also a "matching pair" of correlations, among girls, linking viewing of general informational programming, seeing women do police work, and wanting to do this themselves. For boys, there were three pairs of parallel correlations between viewing and occupational measures, all concerning typing: the more they viewed, the less likely they were to say that they saw boys typing and the less likely they were to say they wanted to do typing in a future job. Boys revealed only one positive pair of correlations (within the matrix of 140 viewing by activity cells): greater viewing of drama made for children was linked with seeing boys and men more often in veterinary work, and with wanting to do this oneself.

There were many single correlations between amount of viewing and perception of an on screen activity or between viewing and own aspiration; but there were only nine matching pairs out of the 280 opportunities for them to occur. There is one further pattern of correlation that is important to distinguish, analytically: when the correlation between viewing and perception of screen content is positive (the more one views, the more one sees some phenomenon) and when the correlation between viewing and aspiration is negative (the more one views, the less one wants to do some activity). This pattern occurs in two places, for girls: the more girls see news, the more they say they see people working fire engines, but the less they want to do this themselves; and the more they see general information programs the more they see women working sewing machines, but the less they want to do such a thing themselves.

In all, among children it is not easy to show that the amount of viewing is related to occupational aspirations in many or in deep rooted ways. The general stereotype (that certain activities apply more commonly to boys, others to girls) appears to exist and to correspond with viewing experience, but within this broader stereotype there are only a few cases where television appears to reinforce certain perceptions and aspirations, or to weaken others. The direction, moreover, in which such influences are possibly detectable is currently considered a positive one, where girls look more favorably on computer work and leadership roles and away from machine operation.

Recent Studies of Perceptions Among Adults

The available fieldwork facilities in Britain changed in the mid-1980s. The single-regional appreciation measurement panels were replaced with a larger nationwide panel and the established procedure of coding viewing into numbers of each of seven types of programs was replaced with a simple three-fold estimate of gross estimate of viewing. Panelists were asked, at recruitment, how many hours a week they viewed, on average; those who replied from 0-17 were designated as light, those who reported 32 or more hours were labeled heavy and the rest were intermediate. Three studies offer some bearing on the question of cultivation effects.

In one study viewers were presented with eight statements concerning the portrayal of violence and were asked to what extent they agreed or disagreed with each one. Four of the items presented positive issues about the portrayal of violence (violent programs have been kept to late hours, proportion of violent programs has been small, violence shown has been necessary for the plots, and there has been enough information in the program journals to inform viewers about violence). Replies differed considerably from people with different viewing habits: the percent who agreed that the positive statements were true from among heavy, medium, and light viewers were, on average, 54%, 48%, and 43% respectively. A similar gradient (43%, 42%, and 35%) was observed with average percentages of agreement with two negative items about violence, and two evaluatively neutral items (there have been many violent films/series) were equally affirmed (23%) at each viewing level. These findings suggest that evaluative statements, whether they are positive or negative, are more easily affirmed by heavy than by light viewers and that the overall level of opinion, regardless of amount of viewing, is that favorable aspects of the perceived portrayal and scheduling of violence outweigh unfavorable perceptions.

The outcome of this study suggest reasons why, in the British television system, harmful cultivation consequences may have been minimized. These reasons, described in the four "positive" items described above, concern ways of scheduling and warning viewers about what they may see; to be forewarned is to be forearmed, which is one way of minimizing unexpected or undesired effects.

More recently, these survey facilities have been used to examine conceptions of the identity of 40 nations, selected to encompass a range of "third-world" and "non-third-world" identities (Wober, 1987b). The list of countries was split into those with less or more "third-world identity" and the extent of "third-world identity" was plotted against the amount each of the countries was seen on television. For the 20 countries with medium to strong "third-world identity," the more they were said to have been seen on television the greater their "third-world identity" score. In the opposite direction, for the 20 countries with medium to very low "third-world identity" the more that people said they had seen these countries the more they considered them to be "non-third-world." Thus television viewing may have reinforced stereotypes.

We must next establish whether the two stereotypes of country identity are objectively valid. There was no index of real GNP or other economic measure in this study, but a measure was used to ascertain if countries were perceived as having improving or declining standards of living. Cultivation would be reflected in inculcating a perception (of identity) together with a reason (perceived alteration in standard of living). Three measures (40 countries rated for "third-world identity", change in standard of living, effect of events on the United Kingdom) were significantly correlated. The amount each country was seen on television over the last 6 months only related to the perceived effects of events in that country on the United Kingdom. Thus seeing more of a country on TV did not relate with perception of a change in its standard of living.

A final reference to an unpublished study is relevant and of use. Following considerable attention to the results of an attitude item reported in a monograph (Gunter & Wober, 1988) in which 6% of a nationwide sample agreed that they "sometimes feel quite violent" after seeing crime thriller programs, another survey was performed to explore this area further. After being asked this same question (on this occasion only 3% agreed), respondents were asked if they had done any of seven kinds of action: three behaviors to contain or assuage "negative arousal" and four aggressive behaviors (hit a person, or an object such as a door or an animal, or shout abuse). The first and most convincing outcome was that reports of containment behavior were clearly more common than those of aggression. Further, there was no significant relationship between viewing patterns and acknowledgments of aggressive behavior (when the four items were combined into a single scale), other than that heavier viewers of music and arts items, and of sports items, were likely to have scored higher on the harms scale. Viewing of sports was negatively related to scores on the containment scale, as was viewing of soap operas. Viewing crime thriller episodes was not significantly or independently correlated with reported aggressive actions, but it was related with affirmation of what was called a "theatrical conception of violence," namely that, "TV showing the pain, injury, and suffering of violence should be shown — but mostly as dramas; watching television stops me from doing other more interesting things; I sometimes wish that violence in programs like 'The Sweeney' or 'Miami Vice' was more realistic; and sometimes I can feel quite violent after watching crime thriller programs" (Gunter & Wober, 1988). Viewing crime thrillers was negatively associated with support for a 4-item scale of statements expressing the idea that television is a harmful influence in various ways.

It is clear that television viewing is functioning in a heterogeneous fashion. It would be extravagant to interpret these results to suggest that television cultivates either aggressive or containment behavior; for some parts of the viewing experience correspond to some extent with one behavior pattern and, in another way, with a quite different viewing behavior pattern. In all, the prudent interpretation of these results may be that certain viewing experiences may reinforce certain attitudes. Viewing crime thrillers certainly is not linked with a more anxious perception that television causes harm; on the contrary, watching more crime thrillers goes with an attitude that television is less responsible for harm. As for behavior, it is possible to offer an interpretation that some viewing experiences inhibit adaptive behavior (for which there is no plausible mechanism that can be put forward).

Discussion

The cultivation theory tradition in America has perhaps been best known for its studies of the portrayal of violence and conceptions of fear. In Britain in the second half of the 1980s, two studies of adults examined violence and related perceptions, attitudes, and reported forms of behavior. In interpreting these two studies it is important to note that the links observed between viewing and attitude or behavior measures have been few and diverse. There has not been compelling and directional logic in these patterns, and it is proposed that it is more plausible to offer a selective viewing than a television-effects explanation of these associations. One reason is that program variety, both in terms of availability and of viewing experience, is considerable so that no particular theme of content can readily dominate a viewer's experience.

One study examines data from a children's panel and explores measures of viewing experience and fear of crime; another examines viewing patterns and measures of aggressiveness and other aspects of personality. The fear study did not find associations between viewing of crime fiction and a greater degree of fear; on the contrary, both this survey and the one examining personality reported that watching more adult movies (not all of which, by any means, involve violence) was linked with attitudes of bravery and with acknowledgments of more aggressive behavior. Among children it is less plausible to suggest that established forms of personality determine viewing patterns, for the young person is in a more malleable condition. Thus it is proposed that some of children's viewing experiences may reinforce certain developing strands of attitude and of personality.

Part of the personality study included measures of aspirations to grow up to resemble familiar role models on television while another children's study looked at occupational aspirations. There was evidence of certain kinds of imitational character aspirations, but few cases where it could be said that viewing helps to construct occupational targets. In the latter study a rigorous procedure has been adopted, first proposed with regard to an examination of adult viewing of soap operas (Wober, 1983). This first looks for a correlation between viewing certain material and reports that certain contents are more often observed; then, if such a correlation exists, more attention is paid to the possibility of a cultivation process if a correlation is also found between the viewing measure and some external, real life attitude. This may be a personal aspiration, or a role perception, a belief, a behavior report, or whatever. Using this "matching correlation" procedure a few cases were found in which it could be said that viewing may have reinforced some occupational aspirations, while even fewer cases occurred in which it may be said that viewing had dissuaded children from expressing particular aspirations. If any generalization can be made from these rather sparse and weak relationships it is that processes regarded as positive (such as girls wanting to do computer and managerial work) may be reinforced.

Two other studies both present a picture of weak but positive links between viewing measures and viewers' perceptions and attitudes. In one study, four repeated waves of the same questions among independent samples showed little or no change in the proportion of people believing television has no influence, during a time when two-thirds of the public had seen at least some part of a major series on television, proclaiming the power of television. In fact a tiny increase occurred of those who held that television has no influence. A small shift occurred however, among the majority who agreed that television does have an influence, in the direction of believing that the power is positive rather than negative.

The overall indications of these studies are of weak and patchy associations. Among children there are further indications of cultivation possibilities, where viewing may reinforce developing strands of aspiration and of personality. In the field of crime, any links are not in the direction of reinforcing fear, but of its opposite, aggression. In the areas of personal character and of occupation, the links are generally positive.

A major increase in amount of television programming is now underway in Britain, with two satellite enterprises adding over a dozen new channels to the existing four. While some newcomers are to be family-type, mixed-content channels others will be streamed by genre. This competition, with weakened public service regulation, may press existing channels to reduce their diversity. Viewing patterns that have been established within public service arrangements, involving considerable diversity, may then change as people seek preferred genre channels and miss unsought material now encountered in diverse schedules. Regulation by market forces will thereby create in Great Britain a television culture more like that in the United States in which less diverse viewing diets foster the conditions in which cultivation processes are reported.

Another outcome may be that the sophisticated regular research services, which have been used to produce the studies in this chapter, would be closed or restricted. A period in which there is likely to be the greatest scope for cultivation research may well be unfulfilled unless there are unforeseen positive developments. Nineteen hundred eighty-nine is therefore a year of challenge, in many ways, in Britain, not just to new entrepreneurs, but to "social structural engineers," who inherit a system that the above accounts show has worked well, and to researchers, who seek to continue to serve the above two groups, and society in general.

References

Gerbner, G., Gross, L., Morgan, M., & Signorielli, N. (1986). Living with television: The dynamics of the cultivation process. In J. Bryant & D. Zillmann (Eds.), *Perspectives on media effects*. Hillsdale, NJ: Lawrence Erlbaum.

Gunter, B. (1987). *Television and the fear of crime*. London: Libbey.

Gunter, B., & Wober, J. M. (1988). *Violence on television: What the viewers think*. London: Libbey.

Wober, J. M. (1983 May). A twisted yarn: Some psychological aspects of viewing soap operas. Paper presented at the annual conference of the International Communication Association, Dallas.

Wober, J. M. (1985, September). *The power of television? No effects on attitudes from a series proclaiming television's influence*. London: Independent Broadcasting Authority Research Department, Research Paper.

Wober, J. M. (1986). The lens of television and the prism of personality. In J. Bryant & D. Zillmann (Eds.), *Perspectives on media effects* (pp. 205-231). Hillsdale, NJ: Lawrence Erlbaum.

Wober, J. M. (1987a, March). *British children, their television viewing and confidence in the face of crime.* London: Independent Broadcasting Authority Research Department, Research Paper.

Wober, J. M. (1987b, October). *TV and the third world: A British view.* London: Independent Broadcasting Authority Research Department, Research Paper.

Wober, J. M. (1988a). *The use and abuse of television: A social psychological analysis of the changing screen.* Hillsdale, NJ: Lawrence Erlbaum.

Wober, J. M. (1988b). *TV and what to be.* London: Independent Broadcasting Authority Research Department, Research Paper.

Wober, J. M., & Gunter, B. (1988). *Television and social control.* Farnborough: Gower.

Wober, J. M. & Kilpatrick, E. (1988, March). *The costs of choice–A calculus of programme want, variety and waste.* London: Independent Broadcasting Authority Research Department, Research Paper.

Wober, J. M, Reardon, G., & Fazal, S. (1987, February). *Personality, character aspirations and patterns of viewing among children.* London: Independent Broadcasting Authority Research Department, Research Paper.

12

International Cultivation Analysis[1]

MICHAEL MORGAN

The theory and methods of cultivation analysis were developed primarily in the context of the political, cultural, and media systems of the United States. As the essays in this book vividly demonstrate, the original concept of cultivation has been refined and elaborated in numerous ways. One of the most important developments has been the extension of the approach to other countries and cultures.

The "final frontier" of international cultivation analysis brings with it significant opportunities, challenges, and problems. Cultivation analysis raises questions that are ideally suited to cross-cultural comparative research (Gerbner, 1977). Are any contributions of television to viewers' conceptions of social reality relatively "global"? How do relationships between television exposure and conceptions vary according to diverse policies, structures, cultures, and audiences? How do the correlates and consequences of U.S. and local programming vary from culture to culture?

This chapter will discuss some conceptual and methodological issues, problems, and challenges in international cultivation analysis, review some previous cross-cultural cultivation studies, and present new findings from Asia (South Korea and the People's Republic of China) and Latin America (Argentina).

Cultivation means that the dominant modes of cultural production tend to generate messages and representations that nourish and sustain the dominant ideologies, world views, perspectives, and practices of the institutions and cultural contexts from which they arise (Gerbner,

Gross, Morgan, & Signorielli, 1986). It does *not* simply mean that television viewing universally fosters fear, apprehension, sex-role stereotypes, aspirations, or other related conceptions, although these have been most studied.

A message is a socially and historically determined expression of concrete conditions and social relationships. Messages imply propositions, assumptions, and points of view that are understandable only in terms of the social relationships and ideological contexts within which they are produced. Yet, messages also reconstitute those relationships and contexts. They thus function recursively, sustaining and giving meaning to the structures and practices that produce them.

The symbolic environment of any culture reveals social and institutional dynamics, and because it expresses social patterns it also cultivates them. Cultivation is then the process within which interaction through messages shapes and sustains the terms on which the messages are premised (Gerbner, 1958, 1969; Morgan, in press). The task of cultivation analysis is to determine the extent to and ways in which a given message system makes an independent contribution to conceptions of social reality that are congruent with the most stable and recurrent values and images expressed in those messages.

The *production* of messages thus takes on special significance, since the resulting social patterns imply cultural and political power – the right to create the messages that cultivate collective consciousness. With *mass* communication we have the mass production of messages, the cultural manifestation of the industrial revolution. Mass-produced messages bear and help perpetuate the assumptions and cultural ideologies of the organizations (not necessarily of the individuals) that produce them.

This of course sounds somewhat similar to the notion of agenda setting, but it is cast on a deeper and more fundamental level. It is not so much the specific, day-to-day agenda of public issue salience that culture (and cultural media) set, as it is the more hidden and pervasive boundary conditions for social discourse, wherein the cultural ground rules for what exists, what is important, what is right, and so on, are made so blatant and repetitive as to become invisible.

All of this implies that cultivation is highly culture specific. If a particular message system (and culture) contains a great deal of (for example) violence, then the media system of that society should cultivate corresponding conceptions; if it does not, then it should not. The fact that U.S. television is dominated by (and cultivates) a particular set of images of violence, sex roles, occupations, aging, health, social power, minorities, and so on, does not mean that other countries' television systems, which may or may not disseminate similar images, cultivate similar views.

International Implications

Over the past few decades, television has transformed the sociocultural landscape of most countries around the world. In almost every corner of the globe, it has become an integral part of daily life for young and old, rich and poor, male and female, and urban and rural populations to a degree not matched by any cultural institution since preindustrial religion. At the same time, many countries in all "three worlds" are becoming ever more interdependent while trying to uphold their own traditions, interests, values, and cultural identities. The emergence of television as the mainstream of national and transnational common cultural environments is likely to have deep and significant implications for such nationalistic efforts in many countries.

International cultivation analysis is conceptually and politically linked with arguments and debates concerning cultural imperialism. There is no question that the U.S. media industries export more of their "product" and to more places than does any other country (Varis, 1984). Often, these programs present values, life-styles, and ideologies that are contrary to those of the host culture and that are in conflict with those presented in the host country's programming.

In structure, policies, and programming, no two television systems of the world are alike; each country's system reflects the unique historical, political, social, economic, and cultural contexts within which it has developed. Given the enormous range of variations in susceptibility to cultivation even within the United States, there is no reason to assume that cultivation patterns will be identical or invariant across cultures.

Moreover, structural differences among systems may be exacerbated by differences in how much of the programming is imported, and by the degree of cultural inconsistency between domestic and imported programs. While many countries broadcast large amounts of U.S. programming, the messages, values, and dramatic conventions of U.S. programs may be only mildly or very sharply distinct from local programming and traditional culture. While no two cultures are identical, U.S. programs may "fit" better or worse in different cultural contexts. Thus,

U.S. programs may seem *much* more "alien" in Asian and Latin American countries than in Western European countries or in countries such as Australia. All this has implications for the extent to which a given television system presents a relatively cohesive set of images (as in the United States), which in turn relates to what television might be expected to cultivate in different countries. Clearly, cultivation hypotheses (and methods) need to deal with situations in which viewers get conflicting messages from domestic and imported programs, and to take local culture into account in every aspect of the research.

A conference on "Cultural Indicators for the Comparative Study of Culture" was held in Vienna in 1982 (Melischek, Rosengren, & Stappers, 1984). That meeting demonstrated the complex theoretical, methodological, and analytical problems inherent in any attempt not only to develop quantitative indicators of "culture" but also in applying such indicators cross-culturally. In a television program, a kiss is *not* "just a kiss" everywhere in the world, or even for all people and groups within a single culture.

On one level, then, international cultivation analysis faces the formidable challenges of any cross-cultural comparative research effort. Using identical, standardized instruments in different locales is a great temptation, as it allows for easy empirical comparisons. Yet the *meanings* of cultivation items vary so much in different social and cultural contexts as to make simple comparisons treacherously deceptive.

Consider a "simple" issue such as sex-role stereotypes. In the United States, television continues to present relatively traditional images of males and females; males are greatly overrepresented, and females are generally shown in a narrower range of roles, most often revolving around romance, home, and family, or in lower status occupations. Heavy television viewers are more likely to endorse such traditional notions as, "By nature, women are happiest when making a home and caring for the family" (Morgan, 1982).

This issue "makes sense" in the context of the United States, where the question of sex roles has a certain level of public salience, given social and political pressures for and against change. The question of sex-role stereotypes is an "issue continuum" along which people can (and do) take positions. But what about in China, where male-female equality is legally mandated, or in Korea, where female subservience is deeply embedded in the culture? And what about a country such as Argentina, vastly different from Korea, but also one in which the male-female power balance has historically and culturally been tipped toward males?

While acknowledging but not going into the complexities of cross-cultural variations in notions about sex roles, and without analyzing differences in the media structures, systems, and messages in the different countries, this chapter simply compares, for four samples of adolescents, empirical associations between amount of television viewing and relatively parallel attitudes about sex roles. Suffice it to say that the four countries considered here have extremely diverse media systems (although all except China feature substantial amounts of U.S. programs) and extremely varied cultural histories. Given such sharp differences, the analyses attempt to determine whether the correlates of heavy viewing are relatively consistent or relatively diverse across different cultures.

Previous International Replications

The early 1980s saw a flurry of attempts to replicate cultivation in other countries, mostly in Western Europe (e.g., The Netherlands, Sweden, England, Germany, and elsewhere), and in Australia (Bonfadelli, 1983; Bouwman, 1984; Hedinsson & Windahl, 1984; Pingree & Hawkins, 1981; Wober, 1984). More recently, the broader questions of cultivation analysis have begun to be examined in countries whose cultural, political, and historical contexts are far more different than the United States, especially in Asia and Latin America.

The number of studies that have explored cultivation patterns in countries other than the United States has now grown to the point where it is not possible to review all of them in this chapter. This section, then, does not attempt to provide an exhaustive and comprehensive overview of existing international cultivation research; rather, the goal is to present some highlights from this growing body of research.

Pingree and Hawkins (1981) analyzed questionnaire and viewing diary data for 1,085 Australian students (from the 2nd, 5th, 8th, and 11th grades). They found that amount of exposure to U.S. programs (especially crime and adventure programs, and with other things held constant) was significantly related to students' scores on "Mean World" and "Violence in Society" indices concerning conceptions of Australia, but *not* of the United States. This finding runs counter to the usual assumption that media effects will be greater in the absence of direct information. Viewing Australian programs was unrelated to conceptions, but those who watched more U.S. programs were more likely to see Australia as dangerous and mean.

On the other hand, Weimann's (1984) study of 461 high school and college students in Israel found that heavy viewers had an idealized, "rosier" image of life in the United States, in terms of wealth, standard of living, material possessions. These patterns held up under controls. Weimann argues that these images may contribute to Israeli emigration to the United States.

In England, Wober (1978) found little support for cultivation in terms of images of violence. But there was apparently little violence in British programming, and U.S. programs only took up about 15% of British screen time. In contrast, at the time of Pingree and Hawkins' (1981) study, U.S. programs constituted 50% to 70% of Australian screen time (and about half of their sample watched only U.S. programs); and in Israel, Weimann notes that 60-65% of programming is imported, mostly from the United States. (For further discussion of Wober's research, see Gerbner, Gross, Morgan, & Signorielli, 1979; Neville, 1980; Wober, 1979, 1984; Wober & Gunter, 1988; Wober, this volume). More recently, Piepe, Charlton, Brown, Morey, and Yerrell (in press) found clear evidence of political mainstreaming in Britain that was highly congruent with patterns reported from the U.S. (cf. Gerbner, Gross, Morgan, & Signorielli, 1982).

Complex and comprehensive cultivation replications were undertaken in the Netherlands (Bouwman, 1984) and in Sweden (Hedinsson & Windahl, 1984). Bouwman conducted telephone interviews with 607 respondents, and asked them a typical battery of questions dealing with perceptions of violence, victimization, and mistrust. Despite numerous associations between viewing and attitudes (and some strong examples of mainstreaming), Bouwman characterized the findings as "very weak" and as a "disappointing quest for cultivation." On one hand, this may reflect a "half empty/half full" difference in interpretation. But it may also reflect some important differences in the Dutch context. Message system analysis showed a good deal of congruence between U.S. and Dutch prime-time television along standard violence measures (Bouwman & Signorielli, 1985; Bouwman & Stappers, 1984); while much programming is imported (mainly from the United States), U.S. imports are mainly comedies and love stories, and not crime dramas. Furthermore, both light and heavy viewers see about equal amounts of fictional entertainment, but heavy viewers see more "informational" programs. Thus, overall, cultivation is neither "confirmed nor weakened" by the Dutch results, at least in terms of violence.

In Sweden, which imports a great deal of U.S. programming but presents much less violence, Hedinsson and Windahl (1984) explored some cultivation patterns within two waves of 5th and 9th graders (N = about 1,000) of the Media Panel Research Program (see Rosengren & Windahl, 1978). Beyond images of violence, they also analyzed respondents' conceptions of the size of different occupational groups, the number of people living in the United States, and occupational aspirations. After controls, amount of viewing was related to four out of five dependent variables among 9th graders; the analysis of complex linear structural equation models (unfortunately, only cross-sectional data are reported) also revealed some consistent associations between attitudes and amount of exposure. Hedinsson and Windahl argue for including uses and gratifications measures (especially "involvement") in cultivation studies.

More recently, cultivation analyses have begun to investigate the contributions of domestic and imported television in countries with increasingly different cultural backgrounds from the United States. In the Philippines, where 60% of programs come from the United States, Tan, Tan, and Tan (1987) administered questionnaires to 225 seniors from three high schools, along with a version of the Rokeach Value Survey. In contrast to both Filipino tradition and dominant response patterns, heavy viewers of U.S. TV were more likely to rate "Pleasure" (allegedly frequently appearing on U.S. TV) as an important value, and to de-emphasize "Salvation" and "Wisdom." Amount of exposure to U.S. TV also predicted intention to visit the United States, other things held constant.

Kang and Morgan (1988) analyzed the contribution of exposure to U.S. programs to the attitudes of 226 college students in Korea. (For a comparison of cultivation patterns among college students in Korea and Taiwan, see Daddario, Kang, Morgan, & Wu, 1988.) U.S. television presents some sharp deviations from traditional Korean values concerning "proper" roles of men and women, of family values, and of respect for parents and elders. In general, exposure to U.S. TV is associated with more "liberal" perspectives among females; females who watch more are less likely to endorse traditional notions of filial piety, less likely to want a traditional "match-making" marriage, more likely to wear jeans and like rock n' roll music, and more likely to see Confucianism as old-fashioned and irrelevant.

In contrast, greater viewing of U.S. TV among Korean male students goes with more hostility toward the United States and greater protectiveness toward Korean culture. This suggests a possible outcome rarely considered — that U.S. TV may have a "backlash" effect, engendering opposition to an imported culture and raising nationalistic cultural consciousness, at least among some politicized college students.

At any rate, it should be clear that hypodermic models of cultural imperialism are not overwhelmingly supported by international studies of cultivation. Just as U.S. research shows systematic variations in susceptibility to cultivation in different subgroups, so too are cultivation patterns highly varied both across and within different countries.

It is also clear that most attempts to explore cultivation in other countries have focused largely, if not entirely, on violence. No doubt this reflects the amount of attention given to those aspects of cultivation research dealing with violence in the United States. In contrast, the rest of this chapter presents the results of some cross-cultural comparative cultivation analyses of sex-role stereotypes among adolescents in the United States, Argentina, South Korea, and the People's Republic of China.

Methods and Measures

The process of collecting cultivation data in other countries can be an extraordinary challenge. Given language, cultural, and other differences, it is essential that survey instruments be pretested in the actual target country. The overall political and historical context of each country plays a major role in all aspects of the research. For example, it was important and necessary in Argentina to include questions pertaining to concepts and practices of "democracy"; it may have been desirable to include similar questions in China, but it was politically impossible to do so.

Moreover, while all of the surveys reported here were designed to deal with issues relevant to cultivation in each country, they were *not* designed as part of a single, integrated, comparative research effort. Thus, there are many differences between the questionnaires, as they were designed for different purposes in each country. The Argentine study deals primarily with political value orientations and mainstreaming, the Chinese mainly with attitudes toward different countries and the role of television in the context of everyday Chinese family life, the Korean mainly with the influence of westernizing forces, and the United States mainly with new communications technologies in the home. There is enough overlap among them to allow for some comparative analysis, but it must be stressed that the various survey instruments were not designed to be, strictly speaking, precisely comparable across countries. Moreover, the fact that the surveys were presented in four very different languages (English, Spanish, Korean, and Chinese) means that there are likely to be subtle and ineffable variations in meanings among the different groups studied.

The Argentine data come from adolescents attending 10 different schools representing a broad variety of socioeconomic contexts, from Buenos Aires and from San Juan province. The data were collected in early-middle 1987; the process of collecting these data took over a year and involved many procedural, practical, and political problems (see Vivoni-Remus, Morgan, & Gorlier [in press], for an account of this process).[2] Despite carefully detailed sampling plans, originally calling for a total of 2,000 students with equal numbers from two each of four different types of high schools (upper-class private, middle-class parochial, middle-class public, and lower-class public), the final result was less than ideal. The sample is less than half the size desired (N = 966) and is heavily dominated by females (almost 70% of the sample). Still, it includes students from 10 very different schools and represents considerable sociodemographic diversity, as indicated by parents' education and occupations.

While many problems collecting the Chinese or Korean data were not encountered, they too have their limitations. The Chinese data come from a single school. We made inquiries to numerous high schools in different parts of the country; one, in Shanghai, agreed to have its students fill out the questionnaires. Of course, no single school could be broadly representative of Chinese adolescents (there are reportedly over 500 middle schools in Shanghai alone). Also, it was not possible to pretest the instrument with students *in China*. But to our knowledge there exists no other data set of this size concerning the uses and functions of television in the lives of adolescents in China. The sample (N = 1,120) is evenly split between males and females and between 10th, 11th, and 12th graders.

The Korean data come from four different schools in metropolitan Seoul, evenly split between males and females and 8th and 11th graders

(N = 1,169). The survey was pretested extensively in Korea (and revised accordingly) prior to data collection. The Korean and Chinese data were collected by classroom teachers, who had been given extensive instructions on how to administer the questionnaires, but had no personal experience in cultivation research.

For comparison purposes, data will be presented from a two-wave study of U.S. adolescents who live in a rural-suburban community in southeastern Massachusetts. The first wave (N = 910), collected in April 1985, includes 7th through 12th graders; the second wave (N = 642), collected in May 1988, includes 9th through 12th graders.

The U.S. and Argentine questionnaires measure television viewing in the same way. Respondents provided estimates of their amount of viewing "on a typical school day between the time you get home and dinner," and "between dinner and the time you go to bed" as well as separate measures of viewing on Saturdays and Sundays. Given the relatively short Korean broadcast day, the afternoon vs. evening difference was not considered relevant, and weekday viewing was taken as a whole (as in most traditional cultivation analyses), in addition to Saturday and Sunday viewing estimates. Finally, as it had been explained that the Chinese adolescents watch very little during the school week, they were asked for an estimate of their total weekly (weekday) viewing, along with separate estimates of Saturday and Sunday viewing.

Table 12.1 shows the mean viewing data for each of the samples. Note that the Chinese adolescents watch by far the least; 53.4% claim to watch *not at all* during the entire school week. In contrast, few students in Korea (10.4%), Argentina (2.4%), and the United States (1.6%) claim not to watch at all on a "typical" school day. The fact that afternoon viewing is greater than night-time ("after dinner") viewing among Argentine adolescents is explained by the fact that they typically eat dinner much later than U.S. adolescents. Total self-reported viewing by Korean students is less than in either the United States or Argentina, but Korean adolescents report more viewing on weekends than respondents in any of the other countries.

The dependent measures of sex-role stereotypes come from items used in previous cultivation studies (Gross & Jeffries-Fox, 1978; Morgan, 1982). The first wave of the U.S. sample and the Argentine sample was presented with the following statements:

Table 12.1 Amount of Viewing among Adolescents in Three Countries

	After School Before Dinner	After Dinner Before Bed	Saturday	Sunday	Total
U.S. (1985) (alpha = .75)	1.74	2.25	3.27	2.60	25.85
U.S. (1988) (alpha = .77)	1.22	1.88	2.34	2.30	20.19
Argentina (alpha = .69)	2.39	1.73	3.13	3.37	27.07
China (alpha = .60)	1.36 (per week)		2.05	1.69	5.10
Korea	1.61 (per day)		3.78	4.62	16.45

NOTE: Alphas based on afternoon, evening, and weekend viewing; for China, alpha based on weekly and weekend viewing.

> By nature, women are happiest raising children and caring for the home.
> It's better if men are out working and women stay home and take care of the family.

These were followed by 4-point Likert-type response scales (in Argentina, from "strongly agree" to "strongly disagree"; in the United States, the categories were "YES!," "yes," "no," and "NO!"). A third statement differed slightly between the U.S. and Argentine questionnaires. The Argentine version also included the statement, "Men have more drive to be ambitious and successful than women," with the same response categories as above; the U.S. version asked "Who has more drive to be ambitious and successful?" and the choices given were "men," "women" and "both just as likely." Interestingly, the set of three items produced the same reliability estimates in both Argentina and the United States (Cronbach's alpha = .64).

The Chinese survey included a statement more appropriate to the Chinese context: "Women should do most of the household chores, like cooking, cleaning, and washing the dishes." This was followed by a

5-point scale from "strongly agree" to "strongly disagree" with "not sure" as the midpoint.

The Korean survey features three relevant dependent items: (1) a variation of the Chinese question, that "Husbands should help out with household chores, like cooking, cleaning, and washing the dishes"; (2) the same question as used in the U.S. and Argentine surveys, that "It's better if men are out working and women stay home and take care of the family"; and (3) an extension of this question, to the effect that "It's fine if my mother works outside the home like my father does." As in the Chinese survey, 5-point scales (from "strongly agree" to "strongly disagree") were used.

Results

Although the exact questions and response categories were not used in all four countries, we can discern some strong and clear overall differences among adolescents in the United States, Argentina, Korea, and China. For example, while 33.2% of the U.S. adolescents in 1985 agreed that "By nature, women are happiest at home raising children and caring for the family", and only 20.0% agreed in 1988, 58.8% of Argentine adolescents agreed. And only 19.8% of U.S. adolescents in 1985 agreed that "It's better if men are out working and women stay home and take care of the family," while about half of the students in both Argentina (48.4%) and Korea (50.0%) agreed. In contrast, 42.3% of the Chinese students strongly disagreed with the notion that women should do most household chores, while only 46.0% of the Korean students found it acceptable for their mothers to work outside the home like their fathers.

Thus, the U.S. and the Chinese adolescents tend to be relatively less likely to endorse "traditional" sex-typed perspectives, and the Argentine and Korean students tend to support more stereotyped views of sex-roles. (This greater apparent sexism among Argentine youth is in fact reduced, not enhanced, by the overrepresentation of females in the Argentine sample; on all three items, Argentine females are significantly and substantially more likely to give the nonsexist response.)

How does amount of television viewing relate to these conceptions? In the following analyses, within-group bivariate associations are presented to highlight the differences and similarities in both baselines and cultivation differentials within and across subgroups and countries. Of

course, cultivation analyses should always include multiple simultaneous controls, to increase confidence that even within-group results
are not spurious. For the data presented here, such controls produce no
substantive changes in the results; although some relationships become
larger and others become smaller, the overall patterns are not particularly affected by the simultaneous application of relevant and available
controls. In order to best illuminate differences across subgroups and
countries, and in the interests of space, these analyses present only the
"simple" results obtained within key subgroups in each country.

For comparison purposes, and to set a sort of benchmark, we begin
with the data from the U.S. adolescents. Table 12.2 presents the results
for the first wave (1985), which included three dependent attitudes, and
the second wave (1988), which included only one. In general, U.S.
adolescents show only moderate support for sexist positions, with a
substantial decrease over time. Males, younger students, and those
whose fathers are less educated are more likely to believe that women
are happiest at home raising children, that it's better if men are out
working and women are taking care of the family, and so on.

Overall, heavy television viewers are more likely to give the sexist
answers to these questions. Television viewing is not particularly related to the likelihood of saying that men are born with more drive to
be ambitious and successful, although relatively few U.S. students
endorse that view in any case. Taking both waves together, there is some
tendency for stronger relationships to emerge among females and older
students.

There are numerous examples of mainstreaming (convergence)
among U.S. adolescents. For example, on the first question on Table
12.2, a 13-point difference among light viewers of the different educational groups is reduced to zero among heavy viewers. On this same
question in the second wave, a 12-point difference among younger and
older light viewers is only 2 points among heavy viewers. On the whole,
these data suggest that at least some U.S. students are becoming less
enamored of traditional notions about sex-roles, but that television
viewing may function to sustain these stereotypes, and that between-
group differences in the size and direction of television's contribution
tend to reflect the kinds of convergences that reflect mainstreaming.

The data for Argentine adolescents in Table 12.3 show a much greater
tendency to endorse more sex-typed responses. In contrast to U.S.
adolescents, a much higher proportion of the Argentine students give
the sexist responses at all viewing levels. As in the United States, the

Table 12.2 Television and Sex-Role Attitudes of U.S. Sample

	Percent who Agree: Women are Happiest at Home Raising Children (1985)					Percent who Agree: It's Better if Men Work and Women Stay Home (1985)					Percent who Say: Men Have More Drive To Be Ambitious & Successful (1985)					Percent who Agree: Women are Happiest at Home Raising Children (1988)				
	LTV	MTV	HTV	CD	Gamma	LTV	MTV	HTV	CD	Gamma	LTV	MTV	HTV	CD	Gamma	LTV	MTV	HTV	CD	Gamma
Overall (890)	30	29	40	+10	.16**	19	18	23	+4	.09	11	9	15	+4	.11	17	17	27	+10	.21**
SEX:																				
Males (433)	42	39	50	+ 8	.11	35	26	31	−4	−.04	17	15	18	+1	.03	20	24	28	+ 8	.12
Females (449)	20	19	28	+ 8	.15*	6	9	12	+3	.27*	7	4	11	+4	.17	15	11	26	+ 9	.20*
AGE:																				
Younger (361)	39	31	44	+ 5	.13	21	16	27	+6	.17*	18	10	14	−4	.05	24	22	26	+ 2	.06
Older (514)	27	27	35	+ 8	.12*	18	18	17	−1	−.01	9	9	15	+6	.18*	12	13	28	+16	.32**
FATHER'S EDUC:																				
Low (464)	33	28	39	+ 6	.11	17	20	25	+8	.17*	12	13	14	+2	.07	20	19	32	+12	.24**
High (386)	26	28	39	+13	.19*	19	14	17	−2	−.04	12	7	15	+3	.09	10	15	20	+10	.21*

*p < .05.
**p < .01.
LTV = Light TV; 1985: under 2 hours/day, 1988: 1 hour a day or less
MTV = Medium TV; 1985: over 2 and under 3 hours/day, 1988: over 1 and under 2.5 hours/day
HTV = Heavy TV; 1985: over 3 hours/day, 1988: over 2.5 hours/day
CD = Cultivation Differential; percent of heavy viewers minus percent of light viewers giving response
Age (1985): Younger = 7th - 9th grade, Older = 10th - 12 grade
Age (1988): Younger = 9th - 10th grade, Older = 11th - 12th grade
Father's Education: Low = High School Graduate, High = Some College or more
1988: N = 633; median splits used on all control variables

Table 12.3 Television and Sex-Role Attitudes of Argentine Sample

	Percent who Agree: Women are Happiest at Home Raising Children					Percent who Agree: It's Better if Men Work and Women Stay Home					Percent who Say: Men Have More Drive To Be Ambitious and Successful				
	LTV	MTV	HTV	CD	Gamma	LTV	MTV	HTV	CD	Gamma	LTV	MTV	HTV	CD	Gamma
Overall (840)	50	57	66	+16	.22***	39	47	56	+17	.23***	17	17	22	+ 5	.12*
SEX:															
Males (275)	55	66	69	+14	.20*	49	62	70	+21	.30***	28	33	38	+10	.15*
Females (560)	46	53	64	+18	.23***	33	41	49	+16	.22***	11	11	14	+ 3	.12
AGE:															
Younger (414)	52	60	67	+15	.20**	50	57	57	+ 7	.08	20	22	21	+ 1	.01
Older (336)	45	55	61	+16	.22**	27	38	53	+26	.34***	15	13	20	+ 5	.10
FATHER'S EDUC:															
Low (411)	57	61	67	+10	.18*	52	58	65	+13	.17**	16	22	27	+11	.21*
High (372)	45	50	59	+14	.19*	30	31	39	+ 9	.11	17	14	16	– 1	.06

*p < .05.
**p < .01.
***p < .001.
LTV = Light TV, under 15 hours/week
MTV = Medium TV, over 15 and under 25 hours/week
HTV = Heavy TV, over 25 hours/week
Age: Younger = 8th - 10th grade, Older = 11th - 12th grade
Father's Education: Low = less than High School, High = High School or more

question concerning who has more "drive to be ambitious and success-ful" shows weaker relationships with viewing. Even so, amount of television viewing is substantially and significantly related to Argentine adolescents' responses in most cases. The data show some remarkably large cultivation differentials (e.g., on the second question, there is a 21-point cultivation differential between light and heavy viewing males and a 26-point difference between light and heavy viewing older students).

Despite the number of across-the-board associations among Argentine adolescents, some between-group comparisons also reveal main-streaming. For example, a 23-point difference between older and younger light viewers on the second question is only 6 points among counterpart heavy viewers. But despite some strong examples of main-streaming, the dominant pattern is that the more time Argentine adolescents spend watching television, the more they tend to express more traditional and stereotyped attitudes about sex roles.

As noted above, the Chinese adolescents are much less likely to endorse stereotypes about sex roles. In fact, so few tend to agree that "Women should do most household chores" that it was necessary to tabulate responses in terms of the percent who "strongly disagree" with that view. The data in Table 12.4 show that television viewing is only moderately to weakly associated with this view, but that, on the whole, Chinese adolescents who watch more television are *less* likely to *disagree* with the sex-typed view; that is, they are less opposed to the notion that household chores are the domain of the woman. This association is stronger among females, younger students, and those whose fathers are less educated. And there is mainstreaming as well; a 14-point difference between younger and older light viewers is reduced to only one point between their heavy viewing counterpart.

The Korean students tend to hold fairly stereotyped views about sex roles, but the relationships with television viewing and these attitudes are not as strong as among the Argentine students (see Table 12.5). Comparing the question used in both Korean and Argentina samples (that it's better if men are out working and women stay home and take care of the family), as shown in Tables 12.3 and 12.5, we see that in most subgroups the Korean light viewers are more sexist than the Argentine light viewers, but also that the Korean heavy viewers are *less* sexist then the Argentine heavy viewers.

As in the United States, Argentina, and China, the data for the Korean students also show instances of mainstreaming, with generally stronger

Table 12.4 Television and Sex-Role Attitudes of Chinese Sample

| | Percent who Strongly Disagree: Women Should Do Most Household Chores | | | | |
	LTV	MTV	HTV	CD	Gamma
Overall (1108)	44	41	39	− 5	−.09*
SEX					
Males (542)	20	26	16	− 4	−.04
Females (566)	67	63	58	− 9	−.16*
AGE:					
Younger (372)	51	50	40	−11	−.16*
Middle (379)	45	41	37	− 8	−.13*
Older (355)	37	35	41	+ 4	.02
FATHER'S EDUCATION:					
Low (377)	44	49	33	−11	−.13*
High (725)	45	37	42	− 3	−.08

*p < .05.
LTV = Light TV, under 3.5 hours/week
MTV = Medium TV, over 3.5 and under 6 hours/week
HTV = Heavy TV, over 6 hours/week
Age: Younger = 10th grade, Middle = 11th grade, Older = 12th grade
Father's Education: Low = High School Graduate, High = Some College or more

associations found among subgroups least likely to support the more sexist positions (females, older students, and those whose fathers attained higher educational levels), and there are many examples of convergence among counterpart subgroups. For example, on the second question on Table 12.5, a 10-point difference between light viewers whose fathers have more and less education is only 1 point among heavy viewers; a 31-point difference between light viewing males and females on the first question is reduced to 21 points among heavy viewers; and a 28-point difference between male and female light viewers shows only a 15-point difference between heavy viewers on the third question. In sum, adolescents in the four countries examined here show sharp differences in their views about sex roles but, in general, those who spend more time watching television tend to support traditional sex-typed divisions of labor and to hold more stereotyped views about the roles, duties, and functions of males and females. The data from all four

Table 12.5 Television and Sex-Role Attitudes of Korean Sample

	Percent who Agree: Husbands should Help with Household Chores					Percent who Agree: It's Better if Men Work and Women Stay Home					Percent who Say: It's Okay if my Mother Works Like my Father				
	LTV	MTV	HTV	CD	Gamma	LTV	MTV	HTV	CD	Gamma	LTV	MTV	HTV	CD	Gamma
Overall (1169)	76	69	66	−10	−.16***	46	49	53	+ 7	.10*	53	46	41	−12	−.16***
SEX:															
Males (585)	59	60	55	− 4	−.06	64	63	66	+ 2	.04	37	39	33	− 4	−.06
Females (575)	90	84	76	−14	−.35***	32	28	42	+10	.17**	65	58	48	−17	−.26***
AGE:															
Younger (582)	65	67	64	− 1	.04	54	52	56	+ 2	.04	46	41	36	−10	−.14*
Older (578)	80	70	72	− 8	−.17**	43	47	47	+ 4	.07	55	51	54	− 1	−.03
FATHER'S EDUC:															
Low (659)	75	70	67	− 8	−.13*	48	51	53	+ 5	.08	53	48	43	−10	−.14*
High (467)	80	66	66	−14	−.17*	38	48	54	+16	.20**	55	46	40	−15	−.18**

*p < .05.
**p < .01.
***p < .001.
LTV = Light TV, under 1 hour/day
MTV = Medium TV, over 1 and under 2 hours/day
HTV = Heavy TV, over 2 hours/day
Age: Younger = 8th grade, Older = 11th grade
Father's Education: Low = High School, High = more than High School

countries also show marked convergences between heavy and light viewing counterpart subgroups, which more often than not reveal mainstreaming.

Conclusion

It must be stressed that the analyses in this chapter omit a very important requirement of cultivation analysis. The results presented here are not based on systematic message system analyses in the different countries. A great deal about the portrayal of men and women on U.S. television is known, but knowledge of gender images in the other countries is limited. In Korea, women appear almost as frequently as do men, but they are generally shown in subordinate roles, both within the family and in the larger society (Kang, 1988). Argentina broadcasts many *telenovelas* that, like U.S. soap operas, often show women in relatively strong positions, but Argentina also presents a great deal of U.S. programming. We know nothing about the gender images portrayed on Chinese television (which, on the whole, presents relatively little fictional entertainment anyway, but a great deal of sports, news, documentaries, self-help programs, etc.; see Lull & Sun, 1987).

While it is very difficult to conduct meaningful cultivation analysis in the absence of reliable, comprehensive message system data, it must be kept in mind that message system analysis is an extremely expensive and time-consuming undertaking; without substantial funds, it just cannot be done. Surveys are relatively less expensive to administer, especially in high school settings; the absence of message data should not prevent cultivation researchers from taking advantage of special data collection opportunities. Message patterns cannot be inferred backward from cultivation patterns, but to the extent that television's representations are likely to be congruent with a country's official cultural policy, certain tentative assumptions can be cautiously made. Even in the United States, important conclusions about television's contribution to political orientations have been reached without reference to *specific* aspect of television content (e.g., Gerbner et al., 1982).

Moreover, for certain types of research questions, message data (while always desirable) are less essential. Specifically, the Argentine and Chinese data were collected primarily to test hypotheses about mainstreaming—that is, the differences in attitudes that may derive from a variety of social and demographic influences will be lessened among heavy viewers, regardless of the direction of television's contribution. The reasoning here is that people who spend great amounts of time watching television are likely to be exposed to a more centralized, consistent, standardized ideology and world view; hence, they should be more like each other than they are like the members of their groups who watch less. Indeed, the many examples of mainstreaming found here do suggest that such background factors as age, sex, and father's education can be less predictive of heavy viewers' attitudes. Television viewing cultivates more consistent, homogeneous conceptions of sex roles within each of the countries examined (see Morgan, 1986).

The results strongly attest to the value of studying cultivation (and mainstreaming) in other countries. In countries as different as Argentina, Korea, and China, adolescents who watch more television generally tend to believe that women are happiest at home raising children, that household chores should be done by women, and so on. The size and baselines vary greatly, but television viewing is also associated with an erosion of the impact of background factors on these attitudes.

The most promising and difficult international cultivation effort is now underway; what began primarily as a U.S.-Soviet collaborative study has evolved into a global research project comparing television policies, content, and effects in more than 25 different countries. This work is attempting to utilize all three "prongs" of the Cultural Indicators paradigm (institutional process analysis, message system analysis, and cultivation analysis), using essentially identical instruments in all countries.

During the week of December 5-11, 1987, all news, public affairs, and entertainment programs were recorded on all major national networks in Argentina, Belgium, Brazil, Canada, The People's Republic of China, Denmark, Finland, France, The Federal Republic of Germany, Great Britain, Hungary, India, Israel, Italy, Jordan, Kenya, South Korea, Malaysia, Mexico, Nigeria, Pakistan, Singapore, Taiwan, Turkey, the Soviet Union, the United States, and Venezuela. As of late 1988, many of these countries were nearing completion or had completed the message system analyses, and plans were in progress for the design and implementation of the cultivation surveys in each country.

The results of this unprecedented, massive effort will provide invaluable, global-level evidence about the relationships between institutional policies and structures, message systems, and audience conceptions in many different cultural contexts. This project will be, surely, a major advance in cultivation analysis.

Notes

1. I would like to thank some of the many people who were involved in the design and execution of the data collection efforts drawn on in this chapter. For the two waves of the U.S. study: Alison Alexander, David Carr, Laurel Hellerstein, Amy Loomis, Elizabeth Preston, M. Sallyanne Ryan, James Shanahan, and Elizabeth Tessier; for Argentina: Juan Carlos Gorlier, C. Alfredo Vivoni-Remus, Ricardo Etchegary, Maria Grossi, Laura Musa, and the Foundation for Change in Democracy, Buenos Aires; and for China, Jong Geun Kang and Changan Gao. The Korean data were collected by Jong Geun Kang, and I greatly appreciate his making them available for these analyses. Much support was provided by the University of Massachusetts in the production of research materials and data analysis resources. I would also like to thank the school officials in all four countries—and most of all, the students—for their cooperation.

2. The Argentine questionnaire was pretested and revised numerous times over a 6-month period. We had invaluable assistance from various groups and organizations in Argentina, including the Ministry of Education, yet we faced significant problems in collecting the data; one must not assume that strikes will not occur in Argentina. First, teachers' strikes closed some schools for long periods; then, strikes by transportation workers meant that neither students nor we could even get to some schools to administer the questionnaires.

We had, naively, wanted respondents to sign their names on the questionnaires. This would have enabled us to match their questionnaires with parallel ones we distributed to their mothers and also to go back at a later date, to collect more data from the same students, for panel analyses. In many years of conducting cultivation surveys among U.S. adolescents, this had never been a problem. Yet, in Argentina, entire classrooms of students refused to fill out the questionnaires. Reassurances of academic legitimacy and the confidentiality of data were of no use. This was, certainly, understandable given the recency of the "Dirty War" in which tens of thousands of (mostly young) Argentines "disappeared" because of their real or presumed beliefs and actions. In the middle of data collection, the procedures were changed, and the questionnaires became anonymous; thereafter, students were more willing to respond, but we had lost the possibility of conducting a longitudinal analysis.

References

Bonfadelli, H. (1983). Der einfluss des fernsehens auf die konstruktion der sozialen realitat: Befunde aus der Schweiz zur kultivierungshypothese. *Rundfunk und Fernsehen, 31*(3-4), 415-430.

Bouwman, H. (1984). Cultivation analysis: The Dutch case. In G. Melischek, K. E. Rosengren, & J. Stappers (Eds.), *Cultural indicators: An international symposium* (pp. 407-422). Vienna: Verlag der Osterreichischen Akademie der Wissenschaften.

Bouwman, H., & Signorielli, N. (1985). A comparison of American and Dutch programming. *Gazette, 35*, 93-108.

Bouwman, H., & Stappers, J. (1984). The Dutch violence profile: A replication of Gerbner's message system analysis. In G. Melischek, K. E. Rosengren, & J. Stappers

(Eds.), *Cultural indicators: An international symposium* (pp. 113-128). Vienna: Verlag der Osterreichischen Akademie der Wissenschaften.

Daddario, G., Kang J. G., Morgan, M., & Wu, Y. K. (1988). Les programmes Americains de television et les transformations culturelles en Corée et à Taiwan (U.S. TV programs and cultural transformations in Korea and Taiwan). *Tiers-Monde, 3*, 65-74.

Gerbner, G. (1958). On content analysis and critical research in mass communication. *AV Communication Review, 6*(2), 85-108.

Gerbner, G. (1969). Toward 'cultural indicators': The analysis of mass mediated message systems. *AV Communication Review, 17*(2), 137-148.

Gerbner, G. (1977). Comparative cultural indicators. In G. Gerbner (Ed.), *Mass media policies in changing cultures* (pp. 199-205). New York: John Wiley.

Gerbner, G., Gross, L., Morgan, M., & Signorielli, N.(1979). On Wober's "Televised violence and paranoid perception: The view from Great Britain." *Public Opinion Quarterly, 43*(1), 123-124.

Gerbner, G., Gross, L., Morgan, M., & Signorielli, N. (1982). Charting the mainstream: Television's contribution to political orientations. *Journal of Communication, 32*(2), 100-127.

Gerbner, G., Gross, L., Morgan, M., & Signorielli, N. (1986). Living with television: The dynamics of the cultivation process. In J. Bryant & D. Zillmann (Eds.), *Perspectives on media effects* (pp. 17-40). Hillsdale, NJ: Lawrence Erlbaum.

Gross, L., & Jeffries-Fox, S. (1978). What do you want to be when you grow up, little girl? In G. Tuchman, A. K. Daniels, & J. Benet (Eds.), *Hearth and home: Images of women in the mass media* (pp. 240-265). New York: Oxford University Press.

Hedinsson, E., & Windahl, S. (1984). Cultivation analysis: A Swedish illustration. In G. Melischek, K. E. Rosengren, & J. Stappers (Eds.), *Cultural indicators: An international symposium* (pp. 389-406). Vienna: Verlag der Osterreichischen Akademie der Wissenschaften.

Kang, J. G. (1988). *Cultural indicators: The Korean cultural outlook profile.* Unpublished doctoral dissertation, University of Massachusetts, Amherst.

Kang, J. G., & Morgan, M. (1988). Culture clash: U.S. television programs in Korea. *Journalism Quarterly, 65*(2), 431-438.

Lull, J., & Sun, S. (1987, May). *Urban families' uses of television in the 'modernization' of the People's Republic of China.* Paper presented to the International Communication Association, Montreal.

Melischek, G., Rosengren, K. E., & Stappers, J. (Eds.). (1984). *Cultural indicators: An international symposium.* Vienna: Verlag der Osterreichischen Akademie der Wissenschaften.

Morgan, M. (1982). Television and adolescents' sex-role stereotypes: A longitudinal study. *Journal of Personality and Social Psychology, 43*(5), 947-955.

Morgan, M. (1986). Television and the erosion of regional diversity. *Journal of Broadcasting and Electronic Media, 30*(2), 123-139.

Morgan, M. (in press). Cultivation analysis. In E. Barnouw (Ed.), *The international encyclopedia of communication.* New York: Oxford University Press.

Neville, T. J. (1980). More on Wober's 'Televised violence...' *Public Opinion Quarterly, 44*(1), 116-117.

Piepe, A. P, Charlton, P., Brown, F., Morey, J., & Yerrell, P. (in press). Political mainstreaming in England: Hegemoney or pluralism. *Journal of Communication.*

Pingree, S., & Hawkins, R. (1981). U.S. programs on Australian television: The cultivation effect. *Journal of Communication, 31*(1), 97-105.

Rosengren, K. E., & Windahl, S. (1978). *Media panel: A presentation of a program.* Mimeograph, University of Lund, Sweden.

Tan, A. S., Tan, G. K, & Tan, A. S. (1987). American television in the Philippines: A test of cultural impact. *Journalism Quarterly, 63*(3), 537-541.

Varis, T. (1984). The international flow of television programs. *Journal of Communication, 34*(1), 143-152.

Vivoni-Remus, C. A., Morgan, M., & Gorlier, J.C. (in press.) Problems in conducting survey research on the effects of television in Argentina: A case study. In U. Narula & W. B. Pearce (Eds.), *Practical problems in field research.* Hillsdale, NJ: Lawrence Erlbaum.

Weimann, G. (1984). Images of life in America: The impact of American T.V. in Israel. *International Journal of Intercultural Relations, 8,* 185-197.

Wober, J. M. (1978). Televised violence and paranoid perception: The view from Great Britain. *Public Opinion Quarterly, 42*(3), 315-321.

Wober, J. M. (1979). Televised violence and viewers' perceptions of reality: A reply to criticisms of some British research. *Public Opinion Quarterly, 43*(2), 271-273.

Wober, J. M. (1984). Prophecy and prophylaxis: Predicted harms and their absence in a regulated television system. In G. Melischek, K. E. Rosengren, & J. Stappers (Eds.), *Cultural indicators: An international symposium* (pp. 423-440). Vienna: Verlag der Osterreichischen Akademie der Wissenschaften.

Wober, J. M., & Gunter, B. (1988). *Television and social control.* New York: St. Martin's Press.

Epilogue:

Advancing on the Path of Righteousness (Maybe)

GEORGE GERBNER

Research rarely advances in a straight line. As I reflect on the journey cultivation analysis has taken so far, and suggest some guideposts for "advances" on its path, I must confess that I have also learned from the "deviations."

Cultivation is what a culture does. That is not simple causation, though culture is the basic medium in which humans live and learn. Cultivation rarely brings change except between generations and regions or among styles of life of which it is more or less a part. Cultivation is not the sole (or even frequent) determinant of specific actions, although it may tip a delicate balance, mark the mainstream of common consciousness, and signal a sea change in the cultural environment. Strictly speaking, cultivation means the specific independent (though not isolated) contribution that a particularly consistent and compelling symbolic stream makes to the complex process of socialization and enculturation.

Leading up to that special meaning, and to some desiderata for its study, I recall the original impetus and continuing concerns that gave rise to the development, definitions, and distinctions of the concept of cultivation. They stemmed from dissatisfaction with the narrowly conceived tactical emphasis of post–World War II communications research, incapable of addressing broader problems of culture. They continued with a concern over developments that challenged conceptions of democracy in communications. The two merged in long-term research under many different auspices but shared a common interest in addressing broader problems relevant to general acculturation and public policy.

The path of that research, I argue, should follow certain specific directions and touch on certain specific considerations. Other chapters in this volume may imply or demonstrate different conclusions. That internal dialogue cannot help but add the right note to this volume: "Advances" refers to the hypotheses we are advancing and not to final destinations. Nevertheless, in research, as in life, good hypotheses, euphemistically called theories, are the only testable guides to action and, therefore, more reliable than certainties. I believe in magic. Unlocking incredible riches through music and dance, conjuring up visions of the unseen through art, creating worlds of imagination and fact through poetry, songs, and stories — that is the essential magic of human life.

Storytelling is my shorthand for that magic. It is what makes humans out of members of the species Homo sapiens. We are the only creatures I know of who live in a world much wider than the threats and gratifications of the immediate environment. It is a world erected through the stories we tell. These are stories called art, science, religion, law, statecraft, and many other things that have been excessively differentiated as if they all had totally different functions. They add up to a historically evolving, organically interrelated, seamless symbolic web called culture.

I was struck with (and have often quoted) the statement attributed to Scottish patriot Andrew Fletcher who said that if he were permitted to write all the ballads, he need not care who makes the laws of a nation. Ballads, songs, tales, gestures, and images make up the unique design of the human environment. All animals "behave" but only humans *act* in a world of towering symbolic constructions.

Culture is a system of messages and images that regulates and reproduces social relations. It introduces us into roles of gender, age, class, vocation; gives us models of conformity and targets for rebellion; provides the range of personalities, temperaments, mentalities said to be our "characteristics"; helps us rise to selfless acts of courage and sacrifice; and makes us accept (and perpetrate) repression and slaughter of unknown people assigned to the appropriate categories of barbarians and enemies.

Culture is a symbolic organization that cultivates our conceptions of existence, priorities, values, and relationships. We derive from it notions of what is; what is important; what is good, bad, or endowed with other qualities; and what is related to what. Its stories tell us how things work, what things are, and what we can or should do about them. Culture provides the overall framework in which we imagine what we do not encounter directly, and interpret what we do encounter directly. It is the context in which experience becomes consciousness. Culture, then, is a system of stories and other artifacts — increasingly mass-produced — that mediates between existence and consciousness of existence, and thereby contributes to both.

The decisive transformation in the quality of human life was the industrial revolution. That was — and is — largely a cultural transformation. Printing begins the industrialization of storytelling. It makes possible the formation of the literate, press-based publics thought to be necessary for self-government. Freedom of expression and of selection is the key requirement for government reasonably representative of competing and conflicting interests. Democratic theory is thus based on the freedom of choice that print and other selectively used media make possible. That may be one reason why liberal and even some radical scholars cling to traditional notions of selective use and exposure even when new developments in telecommunications erode these processes and short-circuit conventional theories of democracy — and of research.

The mass production of messages exposes large and diverse groups to distant sources of stories produced to the specifications of industrial organizations for commodity and political markets. I wrote in 1958 that in the "quest for the *system* behind the facts and forms of mass communication, the media analyst regards content as expressive of social relationships and institutional dynamics, and as formative of social patterns." And: ". . . mass media content bears the imprint of concrete circumstances of its creation. This includes such things as the external outlook and internal dynamics of the producing industry; its relationship to competitors; its control over resources, facilities of production and distribution, the position of its decision makers in the industrial structure; their relationships to audiences, markets, advertising sponsors."

The analysis of mass-produced message systems then has three main objectives. First it yields clues about the outlook and de facto policies of social systems and industrial organizations in the cultural field. It scans the record of industrial behavior in culture. Second, it investigates that record as a system expressive of human potentials, social relations, and values. Neglecting full analysis of that system ("content analysis"), as behaviorally oriented communications researchers often do, limiting their search to measurable consequences of their uses ("effects"), ignores the richest revelations of what a particular culture considers important, relevant, and right, simply because it is not easily observed in action. The third objective, however, is to set the stage for eliciting action indicative of such consequences as can be observed. This objective is based on the belief that implicit in large and aggregated systems of messages are assumptions, contexts, and points of view indicative of cultural contributions to much of what we think and do. That is the task of cultivation analysis.

Trying to distinguish the study of communications as a basic cultural inquiry apart from the dominant research paradigm of persuasion and other forms of tactical manipulation, I stressed in 1966

> the limitations the primarily tactical approach imposes on theory. Some of these limitations are inherent in approaching communications from a point of view which, as an historical phenomenon, is itself rooted in the manipulative pressures of modern society. A recent formulation . . . characteristically defined the study of communications as "the study of ways of arranging stimuli to produce desired responses by the organism." This conception not only fails to define communication but defines it out of existence. It blurs the distinction between communication and other types of social interaction. The researcher might as well study pushing, pulling, shoving, or feeding, or any tactics intending to "produce desired responses." It becomes irrelevant whether or not the transaction involves communication. What really happens as a consequence of "arranging stimuli" is also secondary. The basic question is: did the tactic "produce desired responses," or did it not? . . . Another theoretical difficulty is that the approach can, at best, yield a long and unwieldy list of "do's and don'ts" which must then be related to an almost infinite range of situations and objectives . . .
>
> Underlying the confusion of the study of communications with that of assorted tactics has been the excessive concern with usually short-term, private, and personal effects, conceived as behavior change — such as the adoption of a new practice, the gaining of a vote, the sale of a new product. This preoccupation has obscured not only the concept of communication as a special type of social interaction, but also the meaning of effect. Equating effect with change tended to inhibit investigation of the massive historical and structural continuities between communications, the nature

and composition of message systems, and corresponding systems of social relations. What could be observed, and was indeed seized upon as something surprising and significant, was the complexity and difficulty of *changing* certain ideas and behavior patterns amidst generally unchanging social-cultural conditions . . .

An image (or behavior pattern) must be sustained to exist at all. Once a pattern is established and sustained, it affects messages and tactics as much as (or more than) the other way around. Specific attitude or behavior change may be the *least* significant indicator of effect unless it is part of a general transformation of the message-production and image-cultivation process and is, therefore, supported and reinforced by changing circumstances of life. . . . The history and dynamics of continuities, as well as of change, in the reciprocal relationships between social structures, message systems, and image structures *are* the "effects" of communication.

From that distinction between change as a measure of communications effect and the broad historic continuities that stable cultural currents cultivate came a recognition of television's unique characteristics in contemporary America. Twenty years of research on these characteristics led to the formulation, refinements, and extensions of cultivation analysis, as illustrated by the chapters in this book.

Publication of initial results, and debates concerning methodology, discussed in Chapter 1, resulted in both proliferation and confusion. Both have continued to the present day, prompting me to develop these cautionary notes. Perhaps somewhat dogmatically, but more to advance than to limit debate, I offer the points that follow. They suggest for the path of our "advances" six general considerations:

1. Television is a unique medium requiring a special approach to study.
2. Television messages form a coherent system, the mainstream of our culture.
3. Those message systems (content) provide clues to cultivation.
4. Cultivation analysis focuses on television's contributions over time to the thinking and actions of large and otherwise heterogenous social aggregates.
5. New technologies extend rather than deflect the reach of television's messages.
6. Cultivation analysis focuses on pervasive stabilizing and homogenizing consequences.

Television is a Unique Medium Requiring a Special Approach to Study

Television is the only medium that enters the home for over 7 hours a day and provides the environment of symbols into which children are born. Literacy, mobility, prior tastes, and predispositions are less relevant than they are for other media.

Other media are introduced when some values, tastes, and habits have already been acquired in the home, and after parents and other family members have played the role of principal storytellers about life and the world. However, with television the process is reversed. It is the child who is "inserted" at birth into a television environment. Television competes, usually successfully, with all other storytellers. The extent and depth of the child's immersion in the world of television depends on the style of life of the family much more than on persons or programs.

Viewers watch by the clock. Despite the proliferation of VCRs and increased cable penetration, they watch whatever is offered to them. The size of audiences available for broadcasters to sell to advertisers is determined by the time of the day, the week, the season. Programs compete for socially marginal (though financially crucial) advantage in relatively stable markets. Demographic shifts, industrial consolidation, and new advertising outlets may erode old market contours (e.g., the major networks) but those are also marginal changes of little or no consequence for content (as opposed to channel) selection. Selectivity is necessarily reduced, especially compared to other media. Our studies have shown that the mix of programs and the relative coherence of the television world, including cable and even most video cassettes, is such that the average to heavy viewer (about 3 consecutive prime-time hours or more per day) cannot escape repetitive exposure to the same thematic and dramatic program elements day after day. There has not been a medium or institution like this since preindustrial religion.

Before television, "predispositions" resulted from the learning of tastes and values in the home and school, and led to selective exposure to media. But early childhood exposure to television can influence, and continuous cultivation maintain, the formation of those predispositions. This makes the usual research considerations of selectivity, "before-and-after" exposure, "intervening variables," and predispositions themselves, along with all other factors influencing communication effects, less relevant than they are for other media.

Unlike other media, television is in the home and readily accessible when the child arrives; there is no before exposure condition. The theory of cultivation thus applies to television but not necessarily to other media that do not have television's unique characteristics of early and repetitive exposure, simultaneous and pervasive involvement of total communities (providing a common basis for communication and interaction), and the relatively nonselective exposure to thematically and dramatically coherent, stable, and widely shared message systems. Other media may present some similar and complementary messages, but if their systems of messages do not fit these criteria, they are unlikely to cultivate prevalent conceptions in the same universal way.

Television Messages Form a Coherent System, the Mainstream of Our Culture

Cultivation as a cultural process relates to coherent frameworks of knowledge and to underlying general concepts revealed in responses to certain questions, rather than to isolated facts or beliefs. These general perspectives are cultivated by exposure to the total and organically related world of television rather than exposure to individual programs and selections. Whatever ripple effects or confirming (or disconfirming) tendencies discrete programs and program "preferences" may have, it would be difficult to reliably attribute them to the programs and selections that presumably gave rise to them. Heavier viewers watch more of the general mix of programming than light viewers, regardless of their preferences. Except for rare and freakish viewing patterns, those who watch 3 or more hours of prime time (i.e, the majority of regular viewers) see much of the same mix of basic dramatic ingredients whether they say they prefer comedy, crime, or news. That is why a measure of total viewing rather than particular favorites or selections is the most efficient for purposes of cultivation analysis.

Even to the extent that viewers feel that they are being selective in favoring or avoiding certain types of programs, the thematic and dramatic elements making up different types and genres of programs are often quite similar. In cultivation analysis we should ignore plot configurations and formal variety as — while perhaps aesthetically and morally satisfying — concealing by their surface novelty the underlying uniformity of the basic "building blocks" of the television world: thematic structure, interaction patterns, social typing, and fate (success-failure, violence-victimization, etc.) meted out to the different social types. These over-arching elements expose large communities over long periods of time to a coherent structure of conceptions about life and the world. The investigation of this structure is the principal aim of cultivation analysis.

The coherence and stability of the symbolic structure of the television world is not due to the lack of creativity and talent producing it. It is an expression of the coherence and stability of the commercial and sociopolitical constraints on the industry. "Congress shall make no law respecting an establishment of religion . . . or abridging the freedom of speech, or of the press. . . ." states the First Amendment to the U.S. Constitution. But commercial broadcasting rests on laws making advertising a tax-deductible business expense, thus both establishing the functional equivalent of state religion and surrendering the press to the plutocracy of market concentrations.

The broadcasting-advertising industries depend on the profitable marketing of commodities and the existence of enabling and protective legislation. The only abridgment they fight is of their freedom of unrestricted marketing. Despite much lip-service about First Amendment rights, a proposal to tax advertising in a state brings threats of a blackout depriving its people of that sacred right. The need to sustain favorable and preempt or counter any other form of legislation and pressure, and to serve the largest markets at the least cost in a competitive environment, makes program production conform to exacting specifications underlying its surface novelty. Many of these specifications were embodied in the television codes. Many more are pragmatically derived. Our annual monitoring has found striking stability and similarity among networks and across genres in the dramatic "building blocks" of thematic and action structure, demographic characterizations, and the associations of different social types with different outcomes of power vs. vulnerability, and so on.

Steady repetitive exposure to these structural components tends to cultivate stable images of society and the self. Some of these images may be held in common and some may vary among subgroups of the viewing population. For example, the relative vulnerability of minority groups as portrayed on television, compared to the relatively powerful portrayal of the dominant groups, may cultivate greater insecurity and dependence among the former. Such socialization into a power structure is more likely to stem from the coherent and interrelated symbolic structure to which most viewers are constantly exposed than from any specific programs, idiosyncratic viewing, or selective habits. The existence of this coherent, mainstream system of messages is thus the basic "medium" of cultivation. It can best be measured by total amounts of exposure to the prevalent interrelated program mix rather than partial exposure to presumed preferences and selections.

Analysis of Television's Message Systems Provides Clues to Cultivation

Survey questions used in cultivation analysis should reflect the over-arching content configurations embedded in television's message systems presented to large groups of viewers over long periods of time, usually since infancy. Helter-skelter and exploratory questioning may be useful for a variety of theoretical and serendipitous purposes but do not test cultivation theory. The use of such data, or the comparison of responses of those who claim to prefer or view this and that type of programming, instead of measures of total viewing, is likely to yield confusing, contradictory, and misleading results.

Lines of questioning derived mainly from "real world" considerations, probing the cultivating characteristics of "informative" (i.e., realistic) styles, and interpreting content information fairly literally (sometimes called *first-order cultivation*) can lead to fruitful and interesting results. But I believe that equally important are the symbolic transformations (sometimes called *second-order cultivation* — a term that can be misleading) that exhibit the special power of symbolic life over and above verisimilitude. That is the special characteristic of terms of discourse to shift from specific cases to general classes and to be understood symbolically rather than literally. For example, in the television world, men outnumber women at least three to one. Taken literally, this would suggest that heavy viewers would underestimate the number or proportion of women in the world, which is not the case. Relative underrepresentation in the fairly rigidly structured symbolic world, however, is not only a question of numbers. It translates into differential "quotas" of life chances, ranges of activity, stereotyped portrayals, and levels of occupations. Questions dealing with these symbolic transformations of numerical deviations from statistical norms tap dimensions most relevant to cultivation.

Cultivation Analysis Focuses on Television's Contributions Over Time to the Thinking and Actions of Large and Otherwise Heterogeneous Social Aggregates

Cultivation is a process driven by the common symbolic ritual engaging large communities over long periods of time. Other media uses and life circumstances interact with that process but do not counter or cancel the major thrust of its independent role in cultivating frameworks of knowledge. For example, our research has found that heavy viewers from different subgroups tend to share the television mainstream conception of science as a somewhat odd, risky, and ambivalent occupation. Those who also read science magazines have a generally more positive view of science. But the heavy viewers among them still share the relatively hostile mainstream conception. (This "convergence" of heavy viewers toward the dominant television image is what we call *mainstreaming.*)

Cultivation is usually revealed in such comparisons and correlations between those who watch more or less television within otherwise relatively homogeneous and comparable groups. The comparisons are with respect to patterns of responses elicited by questions relating to the most frequent common symbolic configurations of the television world. Largely irrelevant or confounding are surveys based on partial viewing, specialized groups such as college students, degrees of attention or intensity of viewing, beliefs about the presumed "reality" of the portrayals, reports about likes and dislikes or program preferences, and other mostly speculative qualities of viewing. Symbolic functions do not typically conform to received notions about long-term aggregate consequences of exposure. Not keenly or even consciously attended to background information may be more easily assimilated than the foreground. Fantastic stories from fairy tales to cartoons clearly demonstrate how things work behind the facade of appearances. Macho adventures and family comedies of prime time also convey a sense of reality (or at least realism) despite implausible plots and may be projected onto real life as much as factual and literally believable accounts of what things actually are. The crucial role of drama and fiction in socialization (and thus cultivation) may largely depend on the unique ability of contrived accounts to illuminate the otherwise invisible dynamics of human and social relationships. Accounts limited to events and facts believed to be real, and not just realistic, may become intelligible only in light of a tacit understanding of fictional dynamics. That is why controversies about and censorship of fiction have been historically so prominent and important in social control by cultural means.

However, emphasis on symbolic functions for large and enduring social aggregates does not necessarily imply across-the-board uniformity of the cultivation process. Again, the amount of viewing is an integral part of the style of life of the home and family. Therefore, factors other than programming or personal preference typically determine the amount of television watched. These factors must be controlled in the analysis before the responses of light and heavy viewers can be compared and related to the message systems of television.

When other controllable factors are kept constant, and total amount of viewing compared within fairly homogeneous subgroups of large and representative population samples, the results often reveal complex patterns. Clearly, conceptions of life cultivated by television relate as much to the demographic and social characteristics of large subgroups of viewers as to the characteristics of the message systems to which they are all exposed. The same portrayals are likely to cultivate different but interrelated sets of responses among viewers differentially related to images of life, including their own lives, regularly presented on television.

Researchers finding "no significant difference" between total populations of light and heavy viewers, with or without multiple controls, have at times failed to examine subgroups within those populations. Such subgroups have been shown to have different and even contrasting responses to the television questions, with heavier viewers of the different subgroups sharing a greater commonality of meanings than light viewers (mainstreaming).

Conversely, substantial light-heavy viewer differences can be spurious if other social and life-style factors to which they may be attributed are not held constant. Other chapters in this volume detail the varieties of cultivation. Here I only want to stress the importance of aggregate and appropriate measures related to the symbolic functions of television message systems, uncluttered by extraneous probes and theories (possibly interesting for other purposes) as tests of *cultivation*.

New Technologies Extend Rather Than Deflect the Reach of Television's Messages

Cable systems, new independent stations, time shifting, and video through VCRs, give viewers more control over program delivery. They may displace magazine reading and movie going. There is no evidence that they substitute for, rather than simply add to, overall television exposure. On the contrary, the evidence indicates that although new technologies and channels present alternative ways of delivering programs, movies, and commercials, and thus may cut into network revenues, they do not substantially alter audience exposure to *network-type* programs. In fact, they may extend such exposure into time periods that had been devoted to more diverse activities.

The most popular cable and video programs are even more sharply targeted at the most exploitable appeals than television can be. Networks must present some balance; they cannot repeat the same programs too often. Cable, VCR, and videocassette users can and do watch their favorite programs as often as they wish, and that is more often than they get it from the networks. Installing fancy new boutiques in the same old cafeteria, repackaging the same food supplied by the same old wholesalers, does not change the substance of what is consumed. New delivery techniques, none of which produces much new or original fare, provide the appearance of greater and more attractive choices but in fact promote greater concentration on fewer "block-busters" and other "best-sellers."

Always touted as the dawning of new freedoms, new technologies typically penetrate new markets and eventually concentrate money, power, and choices. To that extent, they may intensify rather than dilute the central thrust of the cultivation process.

Cultivation Analysis Focuses on Pervasive Stabilizing and Homogenizing Consequences

Culture is the symbolic process that cultivates enduring conceptual and behavior patterns essential to human socialization. A central, cohesive, and pervasive cultural mainstream, which is what I believe television to be, is likely to cultivate relatively compact and cohesive conceptual and behavior patterns. That means that television's independent contribution to such patterns is most likely to be in the direction of homogeneity within otherwise different and diverse social groups, eroding traditional social and other distinctions. Again, this does not mean sudden change or bland uniformity. It means that large and otherwise comparable groups of regular television viewers from different walks of life share a stable commonality of meanings compared to the lighter viewers in the same groups, and the commonality reflects their exposure to the television mainstream, eroding other traditional group differences.

The patterns of exposure reflect the structure and constraints of a relatively stable society. Therefore, the building blocks of the symbolic world (rather than its shifting plots and surface novelties) are most likely to cultivate stable and lasting conceptions of social reality. These conceptions may well be more rigid than reality itself. The findings of cultivation analysis show not only a tendency toward homogeneity and conventionality but also the inclination to resist and reject such change as may be occurring in other aspects of life and culture.

I have characterized these dynamics as the 3B's: cultivation implies the *blurring* of traditional distinctions, the *blending* of conceptions into television's cultural mainstream, and the *bending* of the mainstream to the institutional interests of the medium and its sponsors. Blurring, blending, and bending into increasingly massive, global, and comprehensive total cultural arms of the transnational social order is what I see as television's fundamental challenge to democratic theory and practice.

The historical circumstances in which we find ourselves have taken the magic of human life — living in a universe erected by culture — out of the hands of families and small communities. What has been a richly diverse hand-crafted process has become — for better or worse, or both — a complex manufacturing and mass-distribution enterprise. This has abolished much of the provincialism and parochialism, as well as some of the elitism, of the pretelevision era. It has enriched parochial cultural horizons. It also gave increasingly massive industrial conglomerates the right to conjure up much of what we think about, know, and do in common.

The First Amendment to the Constitution has been used to protect practical monopoly control over that process. It now shields what is a virtual establishment of the functional equivalent of religion, forbidden by the same amendment. Better understanding of that process, its dynamics, and long-range social policy implications, will make it at least accessible to rational public discussion. Advances in cultivation analysis can help move us toward that goal.

Most other civilized countries have already addressed crucial issues of democratic culture in the television age and are experimenting with various responses to its paradoxes and dilemmas. Comparative study across cultures, our next task, and better understanding of the cultivation process under different sociocultural circumstances, will help liberate us from an unwitting acceptance of our present and largely invisible but binding set of controls.

References

Gerbner, G. (1958). On content analysis and critical research in mass communication. *Audiovisual Communication Review, 6*, 85-108.

Gerbner, G. (1966). On defining communication: Still another view. *Journal of Communication, 16*, 99-103.

Gerbner, G. (1973). Cultural indicators: The third voice. In G. Gerbner, L. Gross, & W. H. Melody (Eds.), *Communications technology and social policy* (555-573). New York: John Wiley.

About the Editors

NANCY SIGNORIELLI received her B.A. from Wilson College, Chambersburg, Pennsylvania, in 1965 and her Ph.D. from the University of Pennsylvania in 1975. She began work on the Cultural Indicators project in 1969 and continued as its Research Administrator until 1987. She is currently an Associate Professor and Director of Graduate Studies in the Department of Communication at the University of Delaware. Other research interests include mass media imagery, especially in relation to the portrayal of women and minorities on television, and children and television.

MICHAEL MORGAN received his B.A. from New College, Sarasota, Florida, in 1974 and his Ph.D. from the University of Pennsylvania in 1980. He began to work with the Cultural Indicators research team in 1976 and continued until 1983 as a research specialist. He is currently an Associate Professor in the Department of Communication at the University of Massachusetts. Other research interests include communication and democracy, media and the family, and new technologies.

About the Contributors

JEONGHWA CHOI is a doctoral candidate in the Department of Communication, Michigan State University, and will be joining the faculty of the Department of Communication Studies at San Jose State. His research interests include international and intercultural communication.

JULIA R. DOBROW is an Assistant Professor of Communication and Adjunct Assistant Professor of Anthropology at Boston University. Her research interests include intercultural communication and cultural aspects of new technology use.

GEORGE GERBNER is Professor of Communications and Dean Emeritus at The Annenberg School of Communications, University of Pennsylvania. His research and publications deal with mass media policy, content, and social consequences.

ROBERT P. HAWKINS is Professor of Journalism and Mass Communication at the University of Wisconsin, Madison. His research interests include social reality effects of television use, cognitive processes in communication effects, and the role of new computer technologies.

STEWART M. HOOVER is an Assistant Professor in the School of Communications at Temple University. His research interests include the relationship between communication technology and cultural formation in the United States and abroad.

ELIZABETH M. PERSE is an Assistant Professor in the Department of Communication, University of Delaware. Her research interests include uses and gratifications and parasocial communication.

SUZANNE PINGREE is Associate Professor of Agricultural Journalism at the University of Wisconsin, Madison. Her research interests include cognitive processing of mass communication, the nature and effects of soap operas, and new technologies.

ELIZABETH HALL PRESTON is a doctoral candidate in the Department of Communication, University of Massachusetts. Her research interests include the social construction of sexuality and the politics of AIDS.

BO REIMER is a Research Associate at the Unit of Mass Communication Research, University of Gothenburg, Sweden. His research interests include the cultivation of values by the media.

KARL ERIK ROSENGREN is Professor of Sociology at the University of Lund, Sweden. He is interested in the cultivation of values by the media and has written several books on culture and communication.

RON TAMBORINI is an Associate Professor in the Department of Communication, Michigan State University. His research interests include the cognitive and emotional responses to mediated communication.

DIANE ZIMMERMAN UMBLE is a doctoral candidate at The Annenberg School of Communications, University of Pennsylvania. Her research interests include the interaction between subcultural values and communication technology.

J. MALLORY WOBER is the Deputy Head of Research at the Independent Broadcast Authority in London, England. His research interests include children and the media as well as the economic and social factors involved in the assessment of television.

NOTES

NOTES

NOTES

NOTES

NOTES

NOTES